D0376794

PARIS WAS OURS

PARIS WAS OURS

THIRTY-TWO WRITERS REFLECT

ON THE CITY OF LIGHT

EDITED BY

Penelope Rowlands

ALGONQUIN BOOKS OF CHAPEL HILL   2011

Published by
Algonquin Books of Chapel Hill
Post Office Box 2225
Chapel Hill, North Carolina 27515-2225

a division of
Workman Publishing
225 Varick Street
New York, New York 10014

For permission to reprint some of the essays included
in this book, grateful acknowledgment is made to the holders of
copyright, publishers, and representatives named on pages 277–79,
which constitute an extension of the copyright page.

Library of Congress Cataloging-in-Publication Data
Paris was ours : thirty-two writers reflect on the city of light /
edited by Penelope Rowlands.
p. cm.
ISBN 978-1-56512-953-5
1. Paris (France) — Description and travel.   2. Paris (France) —
Social life and customs.   3. Visitors, Foreign — France — Paris —
Biography.   4. City life — France — Paris.   I. Rowlands, Penelope.
DC707.P256 2011
944'.36100922 — dc22   2010030560

10 9 8 7 6 5 4 3 2 1
First Edition

For Julian,
filius et lux

CONTENTS

L'Arrivée

I'M A PARISIAN of the recurrent, revolving-door kind. I first moved to the French capital in my early twenties with my then boyfriend, sailing grandly on the *Queen Elizabeth II,* which, thanks to a miraculous marketing gimmick known as Youth Fare, allowed us to take the six-day voyage to Cherbourg with all the luggage we could stash for the appealing sum of $125 each. It was late November — the last Atlantic crossing of the season — and the waves seemed as gray and menacing as sharks; the air, as we circumnavigated the upper deck each afternoon, felt embalming.

But we were past feeling. Finding ourselves in the middle of the ocean only reminded us that we'd taken a step that couldn't be undone. We were heading off to live in a city that we knew only glancingly but were sure that we would love, if only because of all the French movies that we had seen together at the hippie college we'd attended in upstate New York. We were major cinephiles, drawn, particularly, to the films of the director Jacques Rivette, whose spaced-out, chain-smoking young protagonists wore tight jeans and indulged in long nocturnal monologues. Just like us. One Rivette masterpiece, in particular, held us in its thrall: *Paris nous appartient,* which we translated, loosely, as *Paris Is Ours.* Soon, we knew, it would belong to us, too.

After we arrived at Cherbourg, we drove — inexplicably, it seems to me now — all through the night, through one dusky Norman village after another, with their narrow streets, looming, charcoal-colored houses, and apparent absence of life. Paris, at dawn, felt even grayer. The French postal system had been on strike for weeks; as a result, we'd set sail from New York without knowing the actual address of the apartment we'd rented, sight unseen. We parked the car in the first place we found, utterly lost, killing time until it was late enough to call the friend of a friend who'd found the apartment for us in the first place. I remember stumbling, exhausted, through the square Saint-Médard while Jamie — who spoke French, unlike me — asked a stranger if we were in the Latin Quarter. "You're in its suburbs," the man joked.

The apartment, when we found it, was even farther out than that — positively exurban, in an infinitely depressing *quartier populaire.* Still, we stayed there for the first half of that year, working at all manner of strange jobs, hating the city, resisting it, loving it, falling in with it. I learned the language, it seems, through sheer humiliation. I can still recall the needling: The waiter, for example, who refused to bring me a hard-boiled egg — that classic French worker's breakfast — in a café because I couldn't pronounce the malevolent short *u* that sits dead center in the word *dur,* meaning "hard." He was unabashedly gleeful as he made me repeat it, shrugging his shoulders, delightedly, in faux incomprehension each time. The more I stumbled, the happier he became. I settled for a croissant instead.

That same maddening vowel — the bane of many an English speaker — wedged itself between me and a prickly, middle-aged Frenchwoman (there seemed to be no end of these), my boss at one of the numerous peculiar jobs I held that year. My task, as I recall it, was to recite numbers from a long list — I can't imagine why — as this forbidding creature glowered at me from across her cluttered living room. It was late winter by then and the afternoons seemed cruelly short, the Parisian sky leaching of color, turning inky black far earlier than I thought it should.

"Au-dessus ou au-dessous?" *ma patronne* thundered at one point, with her pitiless regard, asking me to delineate exactly how one number stood in relation to another. Her question meant simply "Above or below?" but we both knew it was about much more than that. (The two words look alike, but their pronunciation, to the French ear, is not at all the same.) My foreignness — my pale English looks, my halting French — was, visibly, as irksome to her as it had been to the waiter; she'd seemed inclined to get rid of me since I'd first stepped through her porte cochere.

I knew the right answer, the one I needed to express, but it was the one with the evil *u* at its heart and therefore, as Madame herself knew all too well, hopeless. (It would be months before I could manage the short, breathy, almost whistling sound the vowel requires.) I plowed ahead anyway, but what came out, of course, meant "below," not "above." "Mademoiselle," she responded fiercely. There was nothing further to say. I left that afternoon knowing that I needn't bother to return. I remember walking by the river — her ground-floor apartment was just steps from the Seine — feeling entirely, thunkingly, lost.

And so it went, a year of highs and lows, mastering a language, scrambling for money, suffering the scorn of waiters and bus drivers, making friends. At one point we were so poor that we took the Métro to Fauchon, the luxury food shop off the place de la Madeleine, one of the few places that would accept the American Express card that Jamie's father had given us for emergencies. (Strange as it seems these days, credit cards were then rare.) We charged foie gras and fancy jams in quantity, then lived off them, unhealthily, for days.

We hated Paris and loved it all at once, and when we headed back to New York on the last transatlantic crossing the following winter, we did so reluctantly — and forever changed. I wore scarves — foulards, I called them — around my neck in a way that must have seemed ridiculous to my American friends, along with too-tight blouses more suited to (typically flat-chested) Frenchwomen than to me. Speaking English in public felt impossibly weird. I remember being astonished in Bloomingdale's, just after we returned, to find that I could speak to a salesperson in my native tongue and be understood. I knew what it was to think in another language by then, to tailor my thoughts to another world. Jamie and I even had a clutch of native friends. It was only later that I learned how rare this was: the French make few friends, as a rule, and keep them forever. (And so it has proved for me.)

From that point on, *la belle France* was a touchstone. Or perhaps it had always been. Born a dual national, I'd grown up between two cultures — England and the United States — and two cities, London and New York. My parents had separated, dramatically and transatlantically, when I was five. France became my middle ground. My Francophile father had taken me to Normandy from his home in London when I was sixteen. When, a few years later, I left his place to travel to Paris for the first time, he marked the occasion with a photograph of me wearing a trench coat, a green BOAC airline bag slung un-chicly over my shoulder. Below it, he'd captioned the image, touchingly, in ink: "Penelope on her first visit to Paris." I'd grown up with his stories of black-tie dinners on the *Liberté* and other French ocean liners; I'd been lulled to sleep to the sound of "Au clair de la lune." Is it any wonder that I'd come alive in the capital of France?

Almost twenty years after the morning when I arrived by car in Paris with my long-ago boyfriend, I moved back there again — that's where the revolving door comes in. This time I came from farther away. Jamie had died, abruptly and tragi-cally, in Manhattan six years after we'd returned from Europe; in the grim aftermath I'd fled to California to escape. When I next moved to Paris it was by plane from San Francisco, with a small child in tow. And although I circled back to America to live a few years afterward, I kept up with Parisian life by return-ing to France each summer to work. To this day, I still have a French cell phone and a checking account at the Banque Na-tionale de Paris, its contents tiny but its symbolism enormous. And I firmly believe that one day I'll spin through that entic-ing glass revolving door again, into the heart of Paris life.

Paris is the place where, more than anywhere else, I became who I am today. Although I've lived in a handful of other cities, this one left the deepest mark. Its effect on me, as on the other writers in this volume, was outsize: it's where we came into our-selves. As a group, we were typically young when we moved there, typically open, and the experience typically changed our lives. Which isn't to say that we were Francophiles then, or are to this day; at times the French capital, in all of its cold unyieldingness, felt like something to work against. But it impressed itself upon us with an almost mystical force.

Few places can draw in as many diverse souls, then mark them as profoundly, as this city — called "that siren, Paris" by the writer Francine du Plessix Gray — seems to do. Ask a casual tourist what brought him or her there in the first place and he or she is apt to mention style, beauty, *savoir vivre,* and the like. But for a long-term visitor the picture is, of course, more complex, the city's contradictory nature more clear. To actually live within the confines of the *périphérique* is to be brought face-to-face, on a daily basis, with the tough reality beneath the city's surface appeal.

Parisians of a certain milieu judge relentlessly, opine, weigh in. The words "Je crois que . . . " ("I believe that . . ."), delivered with flinty assurance, fill the air. This critical appraisal, of themselves and the world around them, is a constant. Parisian standards are high, even unforgiving. They're also double edged, explaining at once why the city's inhabitants look as good as they do, seem as cold as they can be, and have accomplished so much in art, music, literature, and more. There's a taut discipline beneath their seemingly effortless finesse, their knack for displaying almost anything — whether it's a plate of *moules,* a bouquet of wildflowers, or their own physical selves — to advantage.

For a foreigner living and working in Paris, the bar the city sets can feel impossibly high: to clear it is to feel as if you've conquered the world. The thirty-two writers in the following pages have done exactly that. They've entered a sophisticated, exacting, near-impenetrable society and been transformed by the experience. Some trajectories have been unlikely. Take Zoé Valdés, the omnitalented Cuban novelist, painter, and film-maker, whose spirited essay here documents her arrival from her impoverished native island — wearing a strange home-made coat that caused even the unflappable French to take notice — and her subsequent transformation on the Paris art scene.

Just as Indians under British colonial rule entered a new so-cial category after studying in the British Isles — becoming cat-egorized ever afterward as "England-returned" — Valdés and the rest of us who have spent time in Paris, succeeding there in spite of cultural differences we'd hardly known existed before, were deeply, permanently changed by the experience. We, the Paris-returned, *are* different, in ways large and small. We may have — mercifully! — stopped talking about foulards at some point, but we still knotted our scarves differently in the end. (And that's just the part of us that you can see . . .)

These gossamer bits of fabric trail through several of the es-says in the following pages, actually; a few (female) writers even allude to scarves as a kind of rite of passage, describing how women arriving in the city, finding themselves surrounded by *parisiennes* in artfully tied *carrés* or foulards, begin to emulate them (or at least try). As Diane Johnson puts it so memorably here, fashion consciousness, in the French capital, "steals in on you like fog."

Certain experiences are universal: The Métro runs, strangers are rude, the *minuterie* clicks the lights on and off. The great Samuel Beckett strolls through two of the essays, including one by an exuberant Iraqi novelist and editor, Samuel Shimon (here making his American debut). Even the bawdy cross-dressers of the Bois de Boulogne turn up, inspiring one writer, Stacy Schiff, to change her jogging route when her children are in tow. And Judith Thurman evokes another perennial fixture of Paris life, its ubiquitous lovers, as they entwine, eternally, on every bench, in every doorway.

In the following pages, some wondrously diverse writers parse their Paris moments, describing, in some cases, why they went there, in others what they found. All have spent serious time in the city or are living there still. Some are well known, others decidedly not. And one, a homeless French blogger named Julie Lacoste, hardly considers herself to be a writer at all, although hers is one of the more plaintive voices in the collection. Together, their words add up to one picture, a multi-faceted one that, in the way of a cubist painting, is all the more descriptive for the disparate elements it contains. It's an indelible portrait of an entrancing, at times exasperating, yet always fascinating place to live. The siren that is this city speaks to us insistently even after we've moved away. She belongs to us, truly, and to each in a different way. *Paris nous appartient.*

PARIS WAS OURS

L'Argent Is No Object

I INTERRUPTED HER: "Tell me again. Why exactly am I supposed to put money away?" Her jaw dropped. "Excuse me?" she asked. She had managed my portfolio for more than ten years, and not once had I expressed doubts about the need to plan for the future or unhappiness regarding her long-term investment strategy. "Why not spend my capital now, while I am still in good health?" I asked. She hesitated. Was I joking? Momentarily deranged? Exhibiting early signs of Alzheimer's? She tucked a strand of hair behind her ear. But I made no move to get her off the hook. She groped for an answer. Opened her mouth. Forced a smile. "You are kidding, of course," she said.

In retrospect, I remember this uncomfortable pause as the exact moment when I made up my mind to move back to Paris.

THE YEAR 2007 looked pretty good as my plane was banking over the countryside surrounding the Charles de Gaulle Airport. I had just sold my Brooklyn Heights apartment at the top of the market and was moving into a one-hundred-square-meter rental in the first arrondissement. How bad could that be? As we were approaching the runway, the snow-dusted landscape appeared fastidiously groomed, with its meticulously mapped fields, thick hedges, and regularly spaced apple trees. The well-tempered farmland of the Île-de-France was shockingly unlike the urban sprawl surrounding JFK. The silhouette of a small village huddled around its pointy church steeple echoed that of Paris — the profile of the Eiffel Tower poking out of the fog in the distance.

The insidious power of numbers had turned my life in the United States into a system of checks and balances. I woke up every morning wondering how I could be more productive. My freelance income was no longer what it used to be. My husband would lie awake at night worrying about his bonus. He agonized about meeting his sales projections. The most fun we had as a couple was comparing notes with friends about real estate values. The fear of health care bankruptcy was paralyzing us. Only the prospect of capital gain kept us going. Going where? Eventually we found out: a divorce and Paris.

Many of my French friends, who had fallen in love with New York decades ago and immigrated to the USA, as I had, could not afford to move back home because, paradoxically, they'd become too rich. The dreaded French Wealth Tax (ISF) would have taken too large a bite out of their life's savings. Mercifully, in spite of my portfolio manager's efforts, I didn't have this problem. But I could not have picked a worse time to convert my life from dollars to euros.

In Paris, no one talked about the looming international financial crisis. People read about it in the papers or heard about it on TV but somehow never discussed it. It was a presidential election year. Strikes, protest movements, and political rallies were aplenty, yet dinner table debates about how the dire state of the economy might affect one's pocketbook remained few and far between.

Apparently, public discontent was permissible, but not private disgruntlement.

With the Almighty Dollar in free fall, I would have loved to share my trepidations with someone, but details about my money worries were not deemed an appropriate topic of conversation. Parents, siblings, friends — no one would sit still when I tried to get their sympathy about my fiscal or financial situation. Each time I broached the subject, they would interrupt me, talk about something else, or find a pretext to leave the room. It was creepy. A couple of times I even wondered whether I was dead and only imagined that people could see me.

"You Americans talk about money all the time," my older sister eventually told me, as only an older sister would, her frosty tone resurrecting in me long-buried childhood terrors. In France, money is dirty. Very dirty. It was as if she had caught me playing with my *merde*. Seizing the moral high ground, she instructed me to call her accountant, an international expert who happened to be one of her former lovers. I traipsed to his fancy offices near the Champs-Élysées, where I was treated to a full-blown flip-board presentation, during which he feverishly scribbled a jumble of pie charts and diagrams. None of what he explained to me made any sense, but he was so tall and handsome, I didn't really mind.

As it turned out, he was the first of a string of expensive accountants I consulted subsequently, each one more attractive than the one before. My second attempt at elucidating my financial situation put me across the desk from a very busy yet utterly charming attorney who spoke at a breakneck speed and never stopped to listen to my questions. Finally, he advised me to waste no time and hire his own accountant, who lived in a project in a godforsaken suburb at the northern end of a subway line. I trudged there and found him eating a sandwich at his desk in an apartment whose front door was left open on a hallway resonating with the sounds of children crying, televisions playing, and vacuum cleaners running. He, too, was movie star material, which was a welcome treat, because by that time I had been rendered numb by the stress of trying to figure out my French fiscal status.

I HAD YET to meet someone who would listen to my story from the beginning. Even though private financial troubles are as widespread in France as they are everywhere else, they are not the stuff of narrative. For various reasons, mostly historical, tales of rags to riches are not part of the popular culture. The French bourgeoisie are notoriously tight lipped about their affairs, particularly in the provinces. Their love of secrecy is a legacy from prerevolutionary times, when tax inspectors snooped around the countryside, spying on everyone, listening to conversations, hoping to evaluate a person's fortune and figure out how much they could collect. For Parisians, mum's the word as well, but they deflect other people's curiosity about their money with more élan and panache than their country cousins. They'll wax poetic about the most modest objects in their possession but dismiss exorbitantly priced acquisitions as mere commodities.

Tourists are not expected to conform to this unspoken rule of silence. In Parisian restaurants, French patrons would never dream of discussing the credit crunch, promising stocks, or short-term loans, but they are remarkably forgiving of those "noisy guests" (translate "Americans") who are lamenting the cost of a six-day stay in intensive care or regaling their friends with their exploits in the stock market. In order not to be mistaken for one of those visiting Yankees (I have developed a slight American accent, and waiters still bring me the menu in English), I had to rid myself of certain habits I had picked up during my years abroad, such as pointing at merchandise and asking, "How much?" or blurting out "How's business?" when meeting an acquaintance.

When I tried to curb my money talk, though, I realized how much it dominated my thoughts. My dollar dependency was so ingrained, it tricked my brain. I'd confused not talking about money with talking about having no money. I'd assume that saying "I don't think that I can afford a three-hundred-thousand-dollar studio in Paris" was a show of restraint. I didn't understand why this comment only got me a glassy-eyed response from my French friends. They'd mark just a pause, but it was enough of a reprimand to fill me with shame. My blunders revealed to me how much I had been conditioned to rely on money as a universal system of reference. So I tried again, remarking in all earnestness that "I got the Epson Stylus printer because it was the cheapest option." Wrong again! Only after the fact was I able to figure out that I should not quote a price, bring up a cost, or mention an expense. How about, "It's either a small studio in Paris or three Cartier diamond necklaces. The Epson Stylus is neat, but no faster than a golf cart"?

"If you don't talk about money, what's left to talk about?" asked a Los Angeles friend who thinks that you'd have to be insane not to go crazy over the rising cost of everything.

What's left to talk about? The asparagus season, the Tour de France, Japanese art, the films of Jean-Luc Godard, photojournalism, Yoko Ono, how to silence creaky floorboards, women's sports, the wonders of foot surgery, Cartier-Bresson, revisionist history, great radio programs, the latest Grand Palais contemporary art exhibition, and, last but not least, best recipes for beef bourguignon.

Not talking about money is what cultural life in Paris is all about.

DURING MY FIRST year in Paris I didn't just learn not to mention the content of my wallet, my bank account, or my retirement investment portfolio; I also familiarized myself with the body language of monetary moderation. The new gestures associated with the distribution of funds were strangely exacting. Tipping waiters and cabdrivers demanded that I dole out small change with homeopathic precision. An overgenerous contribution to the cash economy could be construed as a criticism of people's hard-won, union-negotiated salaries. God help me if I tried to grab the check at the end of a meal with good friends. They felt insulted. I'd embarrassed my dinner companions whenever I waved my credit card in the direction of the waitress, to attract her attention and let her know that I wanted the check. When it came at long last, I was chastised for not studying it carefully to make sure that the amount was right. "Don't look like you are throwing your money around," I was told.

No one seems in a rush to make the cash register ring. To postpone as long as possible the moment when money will have to change hands, a lot of verbal reciprocity takes place across oak-veneered checkout counters or on either side of zinc-covered bar tops. In Paris, small talk with shopkeepers and waiters rates high as a health and longevity factor, as high as being happily married, exercising regularly, or eating at least three vegetables a day.

When finally it's time to close a deal, the transaction takes place on a downbeat, with merchants taking your cash or credit card almost reluctantly. Instructed to look away as customers type in their PIN, cashiers and waiters glance at the ceiling or examine their shoes to give you a moment of privacy. There is a hush, a strange stillness in the air, one that confers a delicious surreptitiousness to the act of spending.

PARISIANS APPROACH PARTING with money as they do foreplay: with plenty of time to spare. On more than one occasion I have stared in disbelief as French friends couldn't figure out whether to pay for their sandwich with a personal check or a credit card. Apparently, they enjoyed the suspense. Rushing the proceeding would have been crass. Standing by as they waffled, patiently waiting for them to make up their minds, was not unlike watching an excruciatingly slow sex scene in a foreign film.

In Paris, before possessing an object of desire, one tries to covet it for as long as one can. Yearning for something is believed to be more enjoyable than buying it. Monetary or amatory, preliminaries are savored leisurely. The same man who takes his sweet time deliberating over the best method of payment for an eight-euro tab will win you over by creating equally awkward *diversions d'amour* as he attempts to lead you from the bistro table to the bedroom. On the way, he will probably manage to get his car towed away, buy you flowers, ask you to tag along as he retrieves a package from the post office, and take you to visit his aunt in Neuilly. You are an emotional wreck by the time he decides to kiss you as you ride up in his creaky elevator. Alone with you at last, he might forget, in the heat of the action, to remove his black socks, step out of his trousers scrunched up around his ankles, or mention that he has a wife and two kids. He will most likely choose the moment when you are on all fours on his Oriental rug, looking for your lost earring, to declare that you are the most beautiful woman on earth.

With a man like this — a typical Parisian artist — the topic of money simply never comes up. At least not until you decide, as I did, to acquire one of his paintings. The occasion was an open-studio event, with all his friends milling around, munching on cheese and crackers and drinking champagne. A monumental canvas was beckoning me. I could not reasonably afford to squander rent money on such a frivolous purchase, but even in Paris, being broke is seldom an incentive to thrift. There was no price list, and so I could not evaluate what it would cost for me to buy this particularly handsome piece. However, trying to handle the situation like a pro was a challenge I could not resist.

"Would you part with it?" I asked him, motioning in the direction of the painting. He was surprised. "Is there a wall in your apartment large enough for it?"

Now, the sex had been pretty good, but this turned out to

be even better. I bought the painting from him without either of us ever having mentioned a price or negotiated an amount. The exercise presented itself as an equation in which not only was x an unknown, but so were all the other letters of the seduction alphabet. I finessed it by writing a series of random checks, which I mailed to him in envelopes containing other unrelated information regarding various art shows. When he called me, we talked over the phone about his recipe for rabbit stew. He e-mailed me pictures of his daughters taken that summer in Normandy. We made plans to go to New York to visit the Dia:Beacon museum. And then one day he rang my bell and showed up with the huge canvas wrapped in crisp paper the color of candied chestnuts. Our affair had been over long before, with no repeat performance scheduled anytime soon, but suddenly we were in love.

AT LONG LAST, I am getting the hang of it. Paris is becoming my personal tax haven, my Liechtenstein, my Gibraltar, my Aruba, my state of Delaware. Here I can evade greed, find respite from acquisitiveness, dodge my self-aggrandizing ambitions. I no longer feel the urge to rage against the hidden costs of banking operations, the abysmal exchange rates, or the extra charges on my phone bills. Give me a couple of months and I will stop fretting when the stock market takes yet another plunge. I may not even notice when it goes back up again. I can almost see the day when being broke will bother me about as much as breaking a fingernail.

Only last month I met a young Frenchwoman who had spent six years as a successful artists' representative in Los Angeles and had recently moved back to Paris, her hometown. Reentry was proving so grueling that she was exhibiting symptoms usually associated with road rage. She became incoherent as she tried to convey to me her vexation at being turned down by a local bank that had refused to let her open a checking account. I was not unsympathetic: that morning I had received a threatening letter from URSSAF, one of many organizations that levy heavy taxes on individuals to offset the cost of paying for the French government's generous social services. So I understood what she was going through — I understood, yet I refused to feel sorry for her. I knew that she would soon appreciate the irony of it all. Living in Paris is "priceless," but it will cost you. It ain't cheap, yet it is one of the greatest bargains on earth. In our day and age, there are only two ways to get free of money worries: either accumulate wealth, lots of it, or move to Paris.

DIANE JOHNSON

Learning French Ways

W HEN WE MOVED to Paris, fifteen years ago, I trusted that all I had heard about Frenchwomen — their perfect clothes, dedicated cookery, and elaborate wiles — would turn out on closer inspection to be untrue, and I would find they were just like the rest of us. Instead I learned that there's a lot to these stereotypes. I was sure of it with the first recipe I tried from the Sunday newspaper magazine, marked "Très facile": you began by removing the fish's backbone, rinsing the fish for twenty minutes, then boiling it for twenty minutes with leek, laurel, and thyme, then cooling, straining, and reducing the broth for twenty minutes — all this before you began cooking the fish. It was then that I knew there were some serious lessons ahead of me. Americans at their foodiest don't employ fourteen ingredients to make stuffed courgettes.

Much is expected of a French hostess, who presents an exquisite dinner — notice I don't say "cooks" it. When I gave my first Parisian dinner parties, I would buy *poulet masala* from Marks and Spencer (there was one here then), on the theory that no Frenchwoman would have heard of it, or none would use prepared food, but I was wrong about that, too. They are not *complexées* (their word) about making things from scratch, and whereas we might cheat but conceal it, they blatantly use frozen food and the microwave with no sense of transgression. Their object is, after all, a delicious *repas,* not competition. My game was up when, therefore, French hostesses also began to serve dishes from Marks and Spencer, to great enthusiasm.

As to that exquisitely turned-out look, Frenchwomen do shop carefully, buy two or three good things each year, and put them on to go to the store. They do indeed flirt with the butcher, which shocked me no end the first time I went marketing with my friend Charlotte: "Ooh, Monsieur Dupont, je sais que vous avez quelque chose de très, très bon pour moi," and so forth. Daunting as this resolute charm was, I told myself that perfection ought to be decipherable and imitable. Could I, a somewhat lazy and absentminded foreigner, learn French ways?

You can almost tell how long an American or English woman has been in Paris by whether she's wearing a scarf, only the most obvious sign that cultural reprogramming has begun. Every French person wears one, but Americans tend not to at first. Ditto the purse, a preoccupation that steals in on you like fog. You wake up one morning and find they are all wearing a sort of handbag you haven't ever thought of having in your wardrobe. Last week I noticed that every Frenchwoman was carrying a big, brown leather, rather rustic-looking handbag with wide straps and lots of buckles and studs. The ultimate version is from Bottega Veneta and costs two thousand euros, with Dior saddlebag-shaped ones not far behind. Lancel, Longchamp, Delsey, and every other saddler had them in leather; Monoprix had them in plastic.

The question for me was, how did *le tout Paris* know, at the same moment, to buy a bag like this? I read *Elle* and *Madame Figaro* like everyone else, but I hadn't noticed that my regular black leather bag was hopeless. When I go back to California for the summer, people will say "How French you look" for about two weeks, after which, I guess, I stop looking it. In France, I know I still stand out as a clueless American. At least, unlike us, they have cultural consensus. Perhaps this explains the strange predilection the French have for clothes and purses with the name or logo of the maker on them. We would never do that, or at least I wouldn't, and I've never seen T-shirts reading "Isabel Toledo" or "Marc Jacobs" on a San Francisco street, either.

The French do have a different attitude toward individuality and eccentricity. They keep personal idiosyncrasies hidden, if they exist, behind the comfortable uniform facade of fashion or, one could say, of timelessness. The Chanel suit, jeans, the trench coat, never go out of style, and such clothes form the core of everyone's wardrobe, no matter what age. At first I had a certain Anglo-Saxon scorn for this conformity, but I eventually came to see that for them it is liberating, like school uniforms. You put on your little suit, with its knee-length skirt and fitted jacket, scarf, and midheels, and that's the end of thinking about it.

In San Francisco, you can't but be struck, walking down, say, Union Street, by the number of shops that are clearly intended for the young, and no one over twenty would be caught dead in a miniskirt with rhinestones and so forth. In France, women seem not to have any idea of age appropriate clothes. French-women of all ages have the figures of their teenage daughters, and they all wear the same styles. There's a sartorial middle ground where girls wear ladylike clothes their mothers could wear, and their mothers wear the sleeveless dresses and short skirts we have been deeply programmed to avoid after a certain age. My English friend Hilary recently remarked that she had given up wearing jeans because one of her sons had commented, "Mutton dressed as lamb." Does this mean that jeans, in England, are only for the young, or for arty or delinquent people of any age? Anyhow, this irritating remark brought to mind still other national differences. I don't think many Frenchmen would feel that their mothers should dress like Whistler's mother, and I also think they would refrain from using that unfortunate figure of speech based on meat.

It almost seems that Frenchmen like women better than English or American men do. Frenchmen seem to admire what women do, and will participate in discussions about curtains and recipes. You see them looking at fashions in store windows and even reading women's magazines, whereas, as has often been remarked, Anglo-Saxon men seem to prefer the company of one another. It was fun to see *The Voysey Inheritance* at the National Theatre in London a few years back, but the status of the women in the big Voysey family of prosperous Victorians made clear a set of attitudes, condescending and protective, that may not have changed that much. All the important scenes take place with the mother and sisters out of the room.

My basic point is, Frenchmen are pretty uniformly gallant and approving of female appearance, and the result is more important than one might think. Since Frenchwomen are as capable as any of us, and maybe more capable, of getting themselves into misjudged outfits, it's necessary to look more deeply into the secrets of their chic, and looking more deeply one finds that the secret is confidence. Their men are cooperative and supportive. Tact, maybe even genuine goodwill, seems to prevail and give them the confidence never even to think they might look "wrong."

French compatibility between the sexes has even broader implications. An Englishman friend — a BBC filmmaker — whom I asked what he noticed that was different in French-women, said, "Well, they look right at you. English girls never do, they're so mousy and meek." Ah, I thought, that's because they don't want to be accused of being hussies or asking to be harassed. The concept of the "loose woman" doesn't seem to exist in France, though that of the femme fatale does and is altogether approved of. The higher status of women in France, including old women, becomes clear in French restaurants, where it's common to see an elderly woman in chic clothes dining by herself at a good table, with a good bottle of wine and the attention of waiters; elderly women in the United States or England are somewhat abject and tend to stay out of the way or stick together.

Because of confidence, a Frenchwoman wouldn't assume that a male colleague is harassing her when he says, "You look great today." Think of the recent case in Africa, where a house-guest was raped by a government minister who said he mis-read her signals because she crossed her legs. In some parts of America, it's unfortunately still true that a rape victim can be said to have been "asking for it" if she was wearing a low-cut dress or had ever had intercourse before.

Frenchwomen seem to have more confidence as mothers, bolstered by the approval of society if they work, helped out by the fine crèches and nursery schools — unlike in the United

States or England, where we are victims of the covertly Ger-
manic *Kinder, Kirche, Küche* ethic, however this attitude is
concealed, bolstered by hectoring, guilt-producing "experts"
who foster the idea that an Anglo-Saxon mother dare not leave
her child for ten seconds. The result: French children are civil,
equable, and pleasant to have around, no complexes.

Frenchwomen don't have a better take on everything, certainly not. There's the matter of the red hair, for instance.
Why do they dye their hair a red that has never been seen
in nature? (And certainly never seen in the English-speaking
world. I imagine there's an explanation obscured by the mists
of time — perhaps it was the admired hair color of a royal mis-
tress of the seventeenth century, or Edith Piaf or someone.)
It probably isn't the influence of a current movie star, for the
French seem relatively indifferent to celebrities (their most famous rock star, Johnny Hallyday, is now in his sixties), as if it
is easier to designate someone and just keep him, instead of
doing as we do: constantly dumping famous person A in favor
of the new person B, to be dumped in her turn. When I travel
to the United States or to England, I'm always baffled by the
change in celebrities: Who is Brangelina? Who is Katie? The
people in the headlines always seem new from a few weeks
before.

Anyhow, some generalizations are possible: The famous
English skin really is better (and in all ethnic groups), which
must be from the relative lack of sun; French women still
broil themselves on beaches and in tanning salons. (Nobody
seems to have told them cigarettes confer wrinkles.) Mostly,
French hair is short, much shorter than ours. In America, lots

of people don't dye their hair, and turn white early; in France, hardly anybody turns gray that you can see, and everyone over forty is a blond. Weight: Yes, the French aren't as fat, certainly not as fat as Americans, and not being fat affects everything else — for instance, wardrobe. When you have a girlish figure you can wear girlish clothes. My own theory is that the French diet has far fewer carbohydrates in it — but it also has smaller portions. The French walk more (but not more than in London, I wouldn't think), and they certainly don't eat between meals. But also, their attitude toward food is different from ours. It's not a reward; it's a subject of study and appreciation. Coming from a culture dedicated to keeping sweets away from children, I was horrified at the way some English mothers actually offer candy to their kids as bribes to be good. French children are given dessert because it's the proper conclusion to a meal. My little French grandson rebuked me once for mentioning a fish course out of order. "Pas de poisson avant l'entrée," he said.

The French seem to have overtaken us as gum chewers, though. The polite Americans I know in Paris would never chew gum or, for that matter, go to McDonald's. Why have the French begun doing this? If only we could save other nations from our cultural mistakes. (I would have forbidden the Chinese to get cars; they could have skipped that phase and gone right to some marvelous advanced form of public transport, but no — and now they have more pollution and congestion even than we.) I'd forbid the French to smoke, which they almost seem to do as an expression of anti-Americanism — on the street, now that they can't smoke in restaurants.

But mostly, in sum, I'd give them a thumbs-up for doing a lot of things right, and if they seem smug, which they certainly do, they've earned a right to it. Overall, I wish as Americans we would generally feel freer than we seem to be to adopt foreign customs that we admire or that work better than our native ones. Can't we have trains? Health care? Why not?

Becoming a Parisian

L IKE ANY FANTASY, it was supposed to be ephemeral. It was also supposed to be transcendent. But here I was, stuck in airport traffic, and the only question in my head on that dismal January morning was, "What have I gotten Patricia and me into?" The taxi was nudging its way into the bumper-locked queue of cars snaking toward Paris, snuffed or so it seemed by the smoky pea soup that often passes as wintertime air, and my abs and glutes knotted in involuntary acknowledgment that our gamble of moving to Paris could be a really bad bet.

A colleague who had also recently left the *Times* had spent months making his decision, with neat lists of pros and cons and extensive conversations with various newsroom counselors. Far less methodical than he — also younger, with no children and more blitheness of spirit — I had done none of that. My lists were all in my head and consisted mostly of people in New York I would miss and things in Paris I wouldn't have to miss anymore. My colleague was looking for a career opportunity, and my interest was mostly in a little adventure — a couple of years at the *International Herald Tribune*. My friend ended up staying away from the *Times* for about two years; then he went back. I never did.

Slumped in a battered taxi that was barely moving and blind in the fog, I had just begun learning Paris's best-kept secret: its gray, damp weather. January's short, sunless days are especially depressing. All Frenchmen who can afford it (and they save up so they can) seek a sunny antidote to winter's depths either on an Alpine ski slope or on some Club Med beach. Not me. I was headed in the other direction, swept along by what I counted on being adventure and what I now feared might just be naïveté.

Ironically, the fog reinforced one bit of clarity. I knew already that living in Paris would not be like visiting Paris, but I hadn't appreciated what that really meant. My previous trips to France had lasted days or weeks and had been marked by an epiphany at some museum or cathedral and a lot of feel-good time at sidewalk cafés or strolls in the long summer twilight. Vacation syndrome is dangerously seductive. You actually believe that this magical place you have come to allows you to be the contented, stress-free person you really are. There's a lot of vacation syndrome in Paris.

And now, fog or not, traffic jam or not, I was about to become a Parisian. And in two weeks, when Patricia had closed up the New York apartment, she would join me. The magic of that idea was powerful. Paris was the ultimate destination in my map of the universe. Even more than New York, Paris offered glamour and excitement as a place to be. And it was exotic. After eight years in New York — and still considering it my true home — I wanted an overseas adventure.

Exoticism aside, the immediate requirement, shelter, had been temporarily solved by Lydie and Wayne Marshall, New York friends who were generously lending us their apartment for several weeks in exchange for fitting some of their furniture into the small shipping container that Patricia had stayed behind to fill with clothes and other basic needs. We left everything else behind to be there when we returned. The Marshalls' little apartment, on the rue des Entrepreneurs in the fifteenth arrondissement, provided a place to sleep plus the experience of a quiet working-class neighborhood. When I had described the neighborhood to a colleague at the *Times,* I had called it "not very interesting." "There is no such thing as an uninteresting quartier in Paris," he corrected me. Maybe not, but it did seem remote from Paris's chic, mythic center.

And so did my next stop, the *Herald Tribune* offices. After the taxi finally crawled to the fifteenth and I dropped off my bags, I got onto the Métro and headed for Neuilly. The paper had moved several years earlier from rue de Berri off the Champs-Élysées. Its new offices, in a plush suburb on the western edge of Paris, are only four Métro stops beyond the Arc de Triomphe, so it wasn't geography that made it feel remote.

I had visited the *Trib* for the first time four months earlier and had left the job interview feeling very dubious about giving up my staff job at the *New York Times* for this. Patricia and I were also in love with the idea of being New Yorkers. When I was growing up in the Carolina Piedmont, television had just begun the great cultural leveling that over time washed away a lot of America's regionalism. The excitement and sophistication flowing down the coaxial cable all emanated from New York. I had wanted to be at the wellspring for a long time before I got there.

Another southerner, Willie Morris, wrote a book in those years called *North toward Home,* and the title described a path that had beaconed to me since third grade. Miss Frances Love, our teacher at the little school in McConnells, South Carolina, talked to her unwashed, barefoot charges about her trips to Manhattan. One day she got so excited as she talked of that place far, far from our Faulknerian hamlet that she turned to her blackboard and sketched the three most noteworthy skyscrapers of our day. Her chalk drawings did little credit to the Old World angles of the Flatiron Building, or the elegant symmetry of the Empire State Building, or the Chrysler Building's art deco froufrou. But the crude chalkboard images stuck in at least one young mind eager for impressions from the outside, and I recalled my early teacher's drawings when I moved to New York and began directly sharing her enthusiasm for the city.

Yet thoughts of working in Paris had grown, and I persuaded myself that it would be tantamount to a temporary reassignment, since the *Times* was one of the *Trib*'s owners. I also encouraged myself to believe that I would be moving from one legendary news operation to another. But the legends were made of different stuff — it was clear from the first instant that the *Trib*'s mythic reputation was much bigger than the tiny, impecunious reality.

So those were the pulls and the tugs as I had tried to reach my part of the decision about accepting the offer. Meanwhile, my *Times* bosses' principal strategy for trying to keep me was to make dismissive judgments about the *Trib*. You can *visit* Paris, said one, emphasizing the obvious. It's boutique journalism, said another. "Going to Paris is a lifestyle choice, but staying here is a career choice."

"I know," I replied, with far more callow smugness than smarts.

I was hardly on Abe Rosenthal's scope. The crusty executive editor had little time for production editors — he regarded us as necessary technicians, but not of the Brahmin class. But I felt a bizarre pride when he took enough notice to call me "shithead" in front of a large group of my peers. He told me that if I was considering leaving the *Times,* it probably meant that I should.

Meanwhile, from Paris there was little or nothing. The editor, Mort Rosenblum, himself new to the job, called from time to time to confirm the offer. But he could propose no moving expenses, nor money for a hotel or temporary apartment. One future colleague wrote a friend at the *Times:* "Whatever Wells thinks he has been offered, he should get it in writing. Promises don't mean very much around here."

It was in this atmosphere that Patricia and I had gone back and forth on the Paris offer. The gamble seemed greater for her — I would have a job, but she would be giving up a staff job for the uncertainty of freelance writing. Also, I had assurances that I could return to the *Times,* and whatever the shortcomings of the *Trib,* I could certainly take it for two years. And back at the *Times,* I would have "foreign experience" and experience managing a staff, not just deadlines.

But we had made the decision, and there I was, settling into the Marshalls' tiny apartment awaiting Patricia's arrival in mid-January.

When she got there and we unpacked, I was surprised to see that one of the items that the Marshalls had put in our Paris bound container was a new ironing board still bearing its $29.95 price tag. We had left our own behind in the West Side apartment for the renters who were subletting it. After settling in and looking for a Paris ironing board, we were shocked to find that the cheapest model cost 320 francs, or the equivalent then of eighty dollars. It was the kind of sticker shock we never got used to, especially not with the exchange rate of the period, which hovered around four francs to the dollar. We had given up two New York salaries for one in Paris, one that when multiplied by four sounded like a lot. But the dollar's exceptional weakness made the math very misleading. The apartment search drove home the point. Rent would cost us more than twice as much as our two-bedroom apartment in a doorman building on Central Park West.

One of our great Paris friends, Al Shapiro, told us more than once: "If you came to Paris to save money, you bought the wrong ticket." Like a lot of Al's observations, it was as funny as it was right-on.

The crispest memories of those early days involve prices. Besides the eighty-dollar ironing board, there was the radio that cost us both a week's walking-around money, one hundred dollars. It allowed us to listen to any of the stations then on the air, about a dozen of them, all blah-blah all the time. And most memorably, there was also the hundred dollars' worth of smoked salmon that I watched friends wolf down at a Sunday brunch.

But the best thing about that brunch was the bagels. Having rejected all that we had found as not up to New York standards, Patricia made a batch from scratch, and they were delicious.

There are also the memories attached to the details of settling in, all of them unfamiliar. We got to know the appliance stores to buy a refrigerator, a clothes washer, a stove powered both by electricity and by gas. Why? Well, the salesman explained, if ever the electricity goes out, or the gas fails. Then he added ominously, "If ever there's a war . . . ," revealing a frame of reference that was totally foreign. Subsequently, we became aware of the number of times that French acquaintances would say "pendant la guerre . . ."

There were frequent trips to various government offices and long waits once there. *Fiche d'état civil* was a new vocabulary expression, as were *carte de séjour* and *carte de travail.* We had to go for an interview at the neighborhood *commissariat de police,* where the interviewer talked to us about our new president, Ronald Reagan, "star de série B," and the old one, Carter, "un grand naïf." His eyes brightened when both of us said we had been divorced. "How many times?" he wanted to know, then seemed disappointed when we said only a humdrum once apiece.

Much of the early immigrant experience was often entertaining, but it was also hard. I could have cried the Friday night I got home — I was at the office until after the paper closed at midnight — and found Patricia on a stepladder painting yet another room. I felt guilty about what I had gotten her into, and I was also not happy at seeing how I was going to spend the weekend. And we both did cry the night I came home and found Patricia already in tears. I realized how lonely she was and remember saying to her, "This is the worst mistake I have ever made and it's the worst time of my life."

Whatever I had gotten us into, the fantasy was under way.

CAROLINE WEBER

Love without Reason

B Y ANY RATIONAL measure, I shouldn't like Frenchmen.
Allow me just a few generalities — albeit gross ones, as
generalities tend to be — and you'll see what I mean. I am tall;
Frenchmen are short. Most of the time, I am attractive, with
glossy hair, gym-toned muscles, and white, straight American
teeth (a Crest user's smile). Most of the time, they are funny
looking, with greasy hair, flaccid muscles, and yellow, crooked
European teeth (a Gitane smoker's smile). Whereas I approve of
feminism and even, to some extent, of capitalism, the Frenchmen I know class them disdainfully alongside those two other
dread American offenses: fatness and fake butter. And while
I don't think that the philosopher Louis Althusser was right
to kill his wife, nor that the film director Roman Polanski
should go unpunished for having raped a thirteen-year-old
girl, *mes français* celebrate both of these individuals as brave
nonconformists — Nietzschean superheroes unbound by the
shackles of moral convention.

None of this, then, would seem to add up to a history of love
connections between me and the Frenchmen whom — during
my first, fateful year as an American in Paris — I was quite
powerless to avoid. But in the immortal words of Blaise Pascal,

"Le coeur a ses raisons que la raison ne connaît point" ("The heart has its reasons, which reason does not know"). And just as Pascal's unfortunate humpback has had no bearing on my admiration for his work, so, too, have the Gallic male's dubious charms failed to deter me from dating him . . . in more than one incarnation. "I shouldn't like Frenchmen," declares reason. "Yet haven't I loved them?" asks the heart. The fact that "to like" and "to love" share the same verb in French (*aimer*) only highlights the conundrum that underpinned my earliest romantic choices in the City of Light. The conundrum according to which it is somehow possible to "love" people you don't even really like.

As it so happens, today's idiomatic French proposes a clear answer to this question, one that rivals even Pascal's famous quip for irrefutability and economy alike: *C'est comme ça.* More than its literal translation ("It's like that"), this phrase is best rendered as "That's just how it is" and refers to such varied Parisian phenomena as bureaucratic deadlocks (for example, a France Télécom employee informs you that you can't apply for phone service without having a bank account, after a Crédit Lyonnais functionary has told you that you can't open a bank account without having a phone) and perverse dining protocol (a favorite restaurant of mine serves its *amuse-bouche* course in a miniature shot glass, but with a soup spoon too wide to access the glass's contents; request a teaspoon or try to drink straight from the glass, and you receive the same scolding answer: "Cela ne se fait pas" — "That isn't done"). Wherever there is a mystery with no solution, this catchphrase is meant to pierce the fog of befuddlement, like the Eiffel Tower looming above the Champ-de-Mars on an overcast day.

That includes befuddlement of a romantic nature, for the confusion that attends most affairs of the heart is generally, in Paris, taken to be as inexplicable and incontrovertible as the weather. Indeed, it has always surprised me that the American TV series *Sex and the City* should enjoy such popularity among *parisiennes,* who are not given to the kind of anguished relationship dissection in which the show's lead female characters endlessly indulge. In real life, as in *Sex and the City,* a New Yorker asking "Why hasn't he called me?" or "How could he leave me?" is entitled to at least a few solid hours of thoughtful analysis (of the relationship's ups and downs), soothing compliments (for herself), and righteous indignation (against the man in question) from her girlfriend. In Paris, such a response is as hard to come by as, well, fat people or fake butter. There, a woman's interlocutor will merely offer her a blasé "C'est comme ça" — accompanied by a slight shrug that says, "In the face of such existential absurdity, *chérie,* calm acceptance is the only way. Now let's hit the *thalasso* spa and see what we can do about your cellulite."

But in Paris, whenever female confidences let you down, psychoanalysis can fortunately be counted upon to pick up the slack. The first time I moved there was in 1991, after graduating from Harvard with an undergraduate degree in French literature. Taken as I still was with the romance of that curriculum, I decided I could live nowhere but in Saint-Germain, among the ghosts (as I announced pretentiously to anyone who would listen) of Paris's most celebrated writers. Accordingly, I found a tiny apartment right on the border between the sixth and the seventh, around the corner from the erstwhile home of the late Jacques Lacan, aka "the father of French psychoanalysis." I still remember announcing the news to my senior thesis adviser on tissue-thin blue paper, marked PAR AVION in big red letters: "Dear Professor J——, Greetings from the Left Bank! Every morning I jog from my apartment on the rue des Saints-Pères (such a *formidable* location, *n'est-ce pas?*) to the Eiffel Tower and back . . . You'd be proud of me — my run takes me past Lacan's old house in the seventh, and whenever I pass it, I think about your lectures on his 'return to Freud'!" The earnest self-absorption of youth meets the brainy grandiosity of the Harvard kid, all for the price of an airmail postage stamp.

Still, I was telling the truth. The father of French psycho-analysis *was* on my mind a lot during my first year in Paris, and that preoccupation *did* have everything to do with his oft-invoked "return to Freud." This phrase, I had learned from Professor J——, alluded to Lacan's lifelong engagement with that most Freudian of concerns: the nature and workings of human desire. Which, when you're a sheltered American woman who has just moved from prudish Boston to racy Paris, and who is equal parts thrilled and terrified to live on her own in a big city for the first time ever, seems like a damn fine thing to know about. So I dutifully plunged into his col-lected writings, looking for insight into the behavior of the various Michels and Xaviers and Jean-Pauls who — as soon as I prevailed upon France Télécom to grant me a telephone number — began calling night and day. Surely, I told myself, with a little help from the master, I would graduate from the JV playing fields of gauche, inconsequential college dating into the major leagues of a grown-up *grand amour.*

The experiment met with mixed results. On the positive side, during that first year in Paris, I made more conquests than I ever, given the nunlike existence I had led in college, could have imagined. And despite my Parisian girlfriends' repeated insistence that "French people don't date," their male counterparts squired me around the city on a series of dizzying, dazzling adventures that consistently belied this claim. From all-day Godard film festivals in the Latin Quarter to all-night strolls along the Seine; from Berthillon ice cream cones on the rue des Deux Ponts to stolen kisses in the courtyards of the Musée Rodin, the Musée Picasso, and the Musée Carnavalet; from afternoons browsing through eighteenth-century tapestries at the Clignancourt flea market to evenings listening to Racine's hypnotic *alexandrins* at the Comédie-Française, my boyfriends took me on dates so romantic, so memorable, so seemingly, quintessentially *French* that in retrospect I'm convinced they were all drawn from some secret handbook, issued to every Parisian man upon completion of his military service, on How to Impress and Seduce an Ignorant *Étrangère*.

In fact, though, *ignorant* is the key term here, because notwithstanding the swath I had begun to cut through the City of Light, I hadn't made much progress with the Lacanian framework that I hoped would help me make sense of my experience. Indeed, the sad truth is that without Professor J——'s lucid and (I now realized) drastically simplified summaries, the father of French psychoanalysis proved almost impossible for me to understand. Granted, the man was notorious for his willfully obscure, intimidating prose: "Même plus difficile que Mallarmé!" warned my "philosopher" boyfriend Étienne, who suggested that I try someone less difficult: "Roland Barthes, par exemple!"

Defying what I wrongly took to be Étienne's unjust condescension, I declared a two-week moratorium on seeing him and everyone else. My next move was to select a "badge of courage": a single article of clothing that I would wear every day, both to motivate and to punish myself, until Operation Lacan was done. My choice? A black turtleneck — just perfect, I thought, for the venue I had chosen for my studies, Saint-Germain's legendarily literary Café de Flore. There, I avoided the hordes of tourists on the glassed-in terrace and the bustling crowds of regulars on the main floor, and holed up at a corner table upstairs, where my only regular company was a hatchet-faced, unsmiling waiter who did a double take at my daily reading material (Lacan's *Écrits,* volumes one and two) every time I called him over to order more hot chocolate. In Boston, I would have taken his stares as an invitation to small talk and asked him why my books had caught his attention. But in Paris, I knew better than to try to engage a waiter in conversation, so I kept my head down and my mind focused on the secrets of the human psyche.

After just nine of its fourteen prescribed days, however, Operation Lacan came to an abrupt and painful end. Although I had tried to take solace in one of the master's many enigmatic axioms — "one's unsuccessful acts are the most successful, and one's failure fulfills one's most secret wish" — the combination of his impenetrable prose, my own unwashed turtleneck, and my waiter's pointed stares was wearing me down. Finally, it was the waiter himself who pushed me over the edge: the edge being a humiliating breakdown that caused me to flee the café in tears and to avoid the place for the remainder of my Paris sojourn. This happened one afternoon when, looking pointedly at my furrowed brow, he leaned over my book and broke his silence to exclaim: "Ah, the 'mirror stage' essay? But that is his easiest one, mademoiselle!"

Maybe you agree with the waiter. But in my own defense, I humbly submit the following sentence, where Lacan describes the moment when an infant sees himself in a mirror for the first time and thus becomes aware of himself as an *I*:

> It is this moment that decisively causes human knowledge in its entirety to be mediated through the desire of the other; constitutes the human subject's love-objects in abstract equivalences through the other's cooperation; and transforms the 'I' into a sort of armature that is threatened by every 'blow' from an instinct, even though [such encounters between the 'I' and the instincts] should amount to a natural maturation — the very normalization of this maturation henceforth depending, in the human subject, on a process of cultural mediation that (in the case of the love-object) the Oedipus complex best exemplifies.

Um, *comment*?

Now I don't know how you — or my waiter at the Flore, for that matter — would have chosen to explain this line to a flustered twenty-one-year-old hopped up on *chocolat chaud*. Lacking any such guidance, I had had to content myself with underlining "the desire of the other" repeatedly in bright green ink and musing aloud that here, surely, Lacan was evoking Sartre's celebrated maxim, "L'enfer, c'est les autres." (Proud to be engaged in Deep Thought at Sartre's own favorite café, I tried to talk about existentialism there as often as possible; for lack of other company, though, I had to aim most of my remarks at the waiter, who of course refused to dignify them with a response.) This only partly accurate assumption, un-challenged by any further study of the *Écrits,* led me in turn to the (also only partly accurate) conclusion that for Lacan, a person's identity — her *I* — depends on her ability to elicit desire from someone else.

Perhaps, I mused, this was an *enfer* for some; but for me, whom an American expat friend had laughingly dubbed "the Left Bank kissing bandit," it sounded like great news. Cut loose though I was from all the moorings — linguistic, cul-tural, social — that had secured my identity at home, and ner-vous though I was to brave the daunting terrain of adult love affairs, I had found, in this faux-Lacanian insight, a source of reassurance. As long as I could elicit and maintain the *désir de l'autre* — the Parisian male still being, in my eyes, the ultimate *autre* — I would know who I was. Following Lacan's stated project of reworking, and revolutionizing, René Descartes, I coined the following motto: "I am loved, therefore I am."

With this in mind, I transformed myself into what an-other friend liked to call "a one-woman band of seduction," rapidly changing instruments and varying my performances depending on what my audience, at any given moment, seemed to most want to hear. To impress Pierre-Yves, a professor of international relations, I read five newspapers a day, keeping careful notes on all the obscure geopolitical conflicts that as an undergraduate I had — wholly absorbed in my thesis on French surrealist fiction — blithely ignored. With Étienne, who had poured his inherited wealth into a vanity publishing house for sleek, glossy philosophy tomes, I struck a more intel-lectual note. Perched on an uncomfortable minimalist sofa in his sprawling Marais apartment, I would "casually" interrogate him on subjects that I had determined in advance would get the conversational juices flowing. A sample question: "Do you think that radical evil, in Laclos' *Liaisons dangereuses* or in the novels of the Marquis de Sade, serves as a deliberate subversion of the Kantian categorical imperative?" Imagine my (artfully feigned) surprise when he answered with a broad grin that he had written an essay on *this very topic* and would be delighted to tell me *all about it*!

In my dealings with François, a haughty young count who saw ill breeding as the greatest sin, more superficial things became paramount. After a traumatic first visit to his mother's imposing *hôtel particulier* — "Ah bon," she said in mock innocence after scrutinizing me from head to toe, "Americans don't believe in having their clothes pressed?" — I worked assiduously to resemble a chic young woman of the *grand genre*. Naturally, my dry-cleaning expenses skyrocketed; so, too, did my expenditures at the secondhand designer-clothing shops of the eighth and the sixteenth, where the city's grandest dames would deposit the Chanel suits, Hermès scarves, and Lacroix party dresses they had abandoned after a season. This shopping strategy was not without its risks: I lived in fear that at one of the *fêtes mondaines* I attended on François's arm, a glamorous female guest would recognize my ensemble and cry: "*Mais tenez*! That looks *exactly* like the dress I just gave the maid to sell at Réciproque! In fact, I think it *is* the dress!" But luckily, this never came to pass, and François himself never seemed to wonder how my label of choice had come to change, almost overnight, from J.Crew to Chanel.

In retrospect, though, I'm reasonably sure that François

never even noticed; for as long as I was projecting back to him the image he expected to see, he didn't look too closely at me at all. Only when I deviated from the codes that, through him, I had learned to try to follow did he appear to recall that I was not what I was trying to be. In these moments, François did not treat me with kindness: he would viciously attack my "vulgarity," for instance, when I used such colloquialisms as "appart," "par contre," "mince alors!" and "bisous." (The first, in case you're wondering, should be replaced with the un-abbreviated "appartement"; the second, with "en revanche"; and the third, a mild swear word, with "flûte alors!" The fourth, a common sign-off in both speech and writing, should never be used at all.)

At the time, I tried to excuse his behavior by comparing my-self to the American newcomer to French high society whom Proust introduces in *Le temps retrouvé:* "Dinner parties and *fêtes mondaines* were, for the American girl, a sort of Berlitz language school. She heard [words] and repeated them with-out always knowing their value, their exact significance." But the comfort I found here was cold at best. Having embarked upon a mission to be loved, I realized from François's unalloyed disgust that whomever he had loved all along had not, in fact, been me.

As it turned out, the same held true for my other French boyfriends. Pierre-Yves never got over the fact that I hadn't, as I felt compelled to admit some months into our relation-ship, demonstrated against Operation Desert Storm back in the States. Étienne was shocked that *I* was shocked to learn — again, some months into our relationship — that he had a wife who lived in Brittany but visited him every other weekend in the Marais. Looking back at my calendar, I saw that those visits corresponded with Étienne's and my Saturday afternoon assignations in the Hôtel de Crillon: rendezvous that I had taken to be wildly sexy deviations from our usual stay-at-home routine, but that my lover had arranged for much tawdrier reasons. (Predictably enough, Étienne countered my chagrin with a philosophical argument: "But why does this bother you, *mon coeur*? Does Sade not remind us that Nature, which alone issues the laws that men are compelled to follow, abhors marriage and indeed all monogamy for the limits they place on Her transcendental *will to pleasure*?") Still another boyfriend, Charles, too often referred to me as an impersonal *quelqu'un,* as in, "It's nice to hold somebody in my arms like this," or in a raunchier vein, "I like it when somebody gives me a blow job." In both cases, it was clear that my place in his life was purely structural and could be filled by any old *quelqu'un* who came along.

When I was honest with myself, these incidents were more than demoralizing: they were devastating and left a permanent knot in the pit of my stomach. As a result, I more or less stopped eating, a development that all my lovers welcomed because it gave me the wiry, emaciated look of the archetypal *parisienne.* But of course, I wasn't a *parisienne,* archetypal or otherwise. Yet I had sought to win and retain my lovers' desire on that entirely fictitious basis: I had molded myself, time and again, into the woman I thought they wanted, and then was shocked to discover they had no interest in the woman I was. In that respect, the problem lay not with my boyfriends' Frenchness, but with my misguided "Lacanian" belief that *le désir de l'autre* would give shape, substance, and value to my still-unformed self.

Looking back, I see clearly how all the insecurity and self-doubt of the recent college grad were exacerbated, in my case, by immersion in a culture where my inexperience was thrown daily into fierce relief. However much I may have believed it — in my sad, masochistic heart of hearts — at the time, my paramours were not the villains in my ongoing Parisian soap opera. They were merely complicit in a game that I myself had recruited them to play: a mad chase through a fun-house hall of mirrors where, in all the refracted distortions, the pursuers never reach their target, because she is always already lost.

Translation from Jacques Lacan's *Écrits* by Caroline Weber

Keep Your Distance

K EEP YOUR DISTANCE from Arabs if you want to be successful in this city." I had heard this friendly advice from several Arab intellectuals I met when I first arrived in Paris; even the famous Arab poet Adonis told me when I met him for the first time: "You will get nothing from Arabs, only a headache, keep away from them — as much as you can." I remember Mustapha himself told me the same thing when he bade me farewell in Tunis: "I know Paris. I've been there several times and I've had difficult experiences with Arabs, believe me!"

But Mustapha contradicted himself, as did most Arab intellectuals in Paris. They give this "friendly advice," but you see them always together, everywhere together. Mustapha, for instance, whose knowledge of Paris and its streets and cafés is unmatched, gave me an appointment at Café de Cluny, although he knew very well that Café de Cluny was like a headquarters for Arab writers and journalists. Until then I had been there just three or four times and yet in those few times I had become acquainted with several Arab journalists, poets, artists — like Shamil, Abdelwahab, Nabil and Riadh, and Salem and others. But I agreed with Riadh that Café de Cluny was one of the best cafés in Paris. It was a large building situated at the point where the two great boulevards of Saint-Germain and Saint-Michel meet.

Once I went up to the first floor, and that day I had just bought my Erika typewriter from the Duriez shop nearby. I saw Riadh in the café working on a translation of poems by Saint-John Perse. He glanced up and said: "Look at that man!" I turned round to the man sitting at the window overlooking boulevard Saint-Germain. "Oh! It's Samuel Beckett," I exclaimed.

"Yes, and he always sits in the same place," said Riadh, adding, "You see, the customers on the second floor are better than those downstairs." It was clear that Riadh was alluding to the Arab journalists who usually gathered on the ground floor.

The moment Mustapha saw me, he laughed and shouted: "Come here, you Assyrian-escaped-from-the-museums!" And he hugged me.

"What are you doing in Paris?" I asked him quite spontaneously.

Mustapha looked at me for a moment and said with a smile: "This is an insult, not a question!"

"Why do you say that?"

"Because an Iraqi is not allowed to ask a Tunisian what he's doing in Paris. The right question is 'What is an Iraqi doing in Paris?' So, never ask a North African intellectual what he's doing in Paris!"

I answered him, joking: "Well, get me a visa to America and I will leave Paris to you, my friend."

Mustapha started scrutinizing me all over: "Look at you! In just a short time you've become healthy and handsome. When you were in Tunis you looked like someone with bilharzia."

"Did you summon me to Paris to mock me, Mustapha?"

"Not at all. I came from Tunis to arrange your life here."

"You came to arrange my life, Mustapha, or to destroy it?"

"I want to save you from your life of monotony and turn you into a legend!"

We came out of the Denfert-Rochereau Métro station and walked along boulevard Saint-Jacques. "First, I will show you Uncle Salih's bar. It's a very small, popular place. You will love it," said Mustapha, and as we turned into rue de la Tombe Issoire, where the bar is, he continued: "Uncle Salih is a very kindhearted Algerian. He came to work in Paris before your mother expelled you into this world to disturb us with your hallucinations about the movies."

We laughed.

I loved Uncle Salih from the first moment, and Mustapha also introduced me to his girlfriend, Martine, using such flattering words: "This is my friend the Assyrian god who escaped from the hell of Mesopotamia and the Arab Peninsula and wants to become a cowboy!"

We all laughed.

Martine said: "Mustapha has told me a lot about you."

And I told her: "He told me a lot about you, too, when I met him in Nicosia years ago."

Martine looked at Mustapha: "Have we known each other all that time?" And they laughed and kissed each other. Mustapha started reading poetry in French, and Martine put her head on his chest as he idly ran his fingers through her hair.

"Don't worry, you'll learn French very soon and discover how alluring this language is," he said, looking at me, before getting up to bring us another carafe of red wine.

Mustapha was in love with Martine. I remember, when I was visiting him at his home in Tunis, that he said: "I can't sleep alone anymore. I think of her all the time." When I asked him, "Why don't you try to settle in Paris?" Mustapha had given me an ironic smile and answered: "I am an independent man, and in love with a student!" He explained: "The Arab intellectual can only live in Paris for two reasons: asking for political asylum like you, or working for one of the Arab magazines based in Paris or London — you know, those magazines belonging to Saudi Arabia and Gaddafi and Saddam Hussein. And I, as I told you, am merely a poor and independent poet, I don't want to fall into the trap of producing propaganda for these dictatorial regimes."

He concluded, joking: "Is it not enough that I fell in love with a beautiful Frenchwoman?"

Mustapha poured the wine, then clinked glasses with Martine and kissed her. Because he loves to play the clown, he started telling funny tales about the things he and I used to do, and suddenly turned and looked me straight in the eyes: "What did your mother tell you when she looked into your eyes?"

"I don't remember, I don't know what you're talking about," I answered, embarrassed in front of Martine.

"Oh, you've become a shy guy suddenly, huh?" said Mustapha, cackling with laughter. He put his arm round Martine: "He told me once his mother looked into his eyes when he was a little kid and told him, 'You have beautiful eyes, like the eyes of prostitutes.'" We all laughed. And Mustapha didn't stop until two in the morning, when he fell asleep in Martine's lap. And we all went to the university campus in rue Dareau, a few meters' walk from Uncle Salih's bar, to Martine's room.

The next day, Mustapha told me he had an appointment with some friends and suggested meeting at four o'clock. We were in place du Châtelet. "Do you know how you can spend the time until then?"

I answered: "I will find me a nice bar."

Mustapha looked at me: "I told you I came to arrange your life. I don't want to hear about bars every time I meet you. I suggest you go and spend a few hours in Centre Pompidou."

"What is that?"

We walked five minutes and Mustapha pointed to a huge, modern building. "This is the Centre Pompidou, I'm sure you'll like it."

When Mustapha left me, he didn't know that he was giving me the most valuable present of my whole life. Centre Pompidou was an incredible mine from which I extracted all that I had been deprived of during my twenty-eight years. That afternoon I became captivated as I walked between the shelves in the library, with books of literature, of movies, music, and art, dictionaries, even cookery books grabbing my attention.

"I would love to be jailed here," I said to myself as I sat on the floor leafing through several books at a time about making movies, writing scripts, about the lives and memoirs of actors, directors, and filmmakers.

Translated from the Arabic by Christina Phillips

Friends of My Youth

I T WAS STILL possible to live on five dollars a day when I was a student in Paris, but only if you took your main meal every day at the university restaurant. Five dollars worked out to roughly twenty-five francs back in 1972, ten of which went to pay for my vest-pocket room in a charming pension right around the corner from the Duroc Métro station, where the boulevard des Invalides discreetly disappeared into the boulevard Montparnasse. Other friends lived in cheaper lodgings in crummy neighborhoods on the outskirts of Paris, but I had already spent my childhood in crummy lodgings back home in Philadelphia and saw no reason to repeat that experience here. Living in such a central location meant that I rarely had to waste money on public transportation, as I could easily walk home from the Comédie-Française or the Théâtre des Champs-Élysées or the Cinémathèque or the Latin Quarter at any hour of the day or night, while other friends had to watch the clock and make sure they grabbed the last Métro before the subway system closed down, around one in the morning. Otherwise, they'd be walking forever.

The remainder of my budget was disbursed in three equal parts: five francs a day were set aside for alcohol and tobacco;

five francs were earmarked for entertainment; and the remaining five francs paid for food. For thirty-five francs a week, thanks to dirt cheap student ticket prices, I could go to the opera, attend two or three piano recitals, and take in a couple of plays. Five francs a day would also cover a baguette, a couple of oranges and bananas, the occasional liter of milk, and a once-a-day trip to the student restaurant. By economizing — say, by skipping a Maurizio Pollini or Alexandre LaGoya concert or a Genet play at the Odéon — I could slip in a weekly dinner at the Alliance française on the boulevard Raspail, where the food was both plentiful and good. This would set me back five francs, but if I cut my sliver of camembert into sufficiently tiny portions and matched each tranche with a massive slice of bread, I could consume enough to go without eating the entire next day. A meal at the student restaurant, by contrast, cost just one franc sixty centimes, roughly thirty cents. But even at that rate, it was overpriced.

There was a theory bandied about at the time that the French government had never forgiven students for bringing the nation to the brink of civil war four years earlier and that the food served in the university restaurants was designed along explicitly punitive lines. Soggy, revolting eggs, noodles that seemed to be vaguely animate, bread with the texture of macadam, and an assortment of grotesque entrées that seemed to have been lifted from the Jean Valjean Cookbook were the standard nightly fare concocted by the despised Pompidou administration. It was awful food, demoralizing food, and the fact that it was food served in a country renowned for its cuisine was an irony that was not lost on us. But it kept us alive, so we ate it.

Not all of my friends dined in the student restaurants. Some shared flats with friends and had kitchens of their own. Some lived with families as au pairs or tutors. And some simply earmarked a larger portion of their daily budget for food and ate in inexpensive restaurants. But those of us who had little money, or who wanted to stockpile as much cash as possible for concerts, plays, books, and alcohol, always ate in the student restaurants.

In Paris, I had many friends, some of whom remained close friends for the next forty years. Others I never saw again once my *Wanderjahr* was over. But I always tried to keep my disparate groups of friends segregated from one another, as their passions did not dovetail and I am sure some of them would have hated others. One group consisted of drinkers and carousers. A second group was made up of intellectuals, including a brilliant young composer who would later found the Tibetan Singing Bowl Ensemble and a German American in an impudent fedora who was always devising Ten Best lists but could never complete the one ranking the great composers because after according the obvious titans — Bach, Mozart, Beethoven, Brahms, Verdi, and Wagner — the top slots, he could never decide which of the remaining colossi — Schubert, Liszt, Chopin, Stravinsky, Berlioz, Schumann, Haydn, Debussy, Mahler — most deserved the remaining positions. So the next day, he would switch to novelists. Or painters. But the result was always the same. Where did you put Botticelli? How could you leave out George Eliot?

A third group consisted of American medical students I met at the reviled student restaurant that bordered the jardins du Luxembourg. They would go to school for a year, flunk out, and come back the next year to do their first year all over again, once they had learned a bit more French. Some of them had already done the same thing in Cairo or Guadalajara. The French didn't mind them coming back again and again, as long as the students themselves didn't mind getting flunked. By doing each year twice, these desperate, indomitable young men hoped to eventually be admitted to some third-tier American medical school. They were splendid fellows, but I am not sure how many of them ever became doctors.

A fourth group consisted of people who had roughly the same eyeglass prescription as me. Shortly after I arrived in Paris, I set out for Pigalle with three Canadian friends who also lived in the charming little boardinghouse on the rue Mayet. Right down the street from the *funiculaire* that carries overweight tourists up to Sacré-Coeur, we were set upon by a group of Algerian revelers while exiting a restaurant. No harm was done, though a fair few punches were exchanged, but I lost my eyeglasses and my passport during the melee. The passport resurfaced a few days later, thanks to a Good Samaritan who dropped it off at the American Embassy, but the eyeglasses were gone forever. When I found out that replacing them would set me back several hundred francs — about two weeks' living expenses — I decided to do without them until I returned to the States a year later.

This worked out well enough at concerts and movies, where I could sit close to the screen, but up in the rafters of the Comédie-Française, which I would visit perhaps twice a week to take in *L'avare* or *Le médecin malgré lui* or *Oedipus rex,* it was hard for me to make out the actors' facial expressions at such a great distance. And so I got into the habit of trying on complete strangers' glasses whenever my paths crossed those of the obviously bespectacled. Mostly, they were young women. Initially, when I explained my predicament and asked if I could try on their glasses, they might have thought this was some sort of ingenious come-on, but they soon learned that I was quite sincere, as I would usually stop conversing with them as soon as I had established that our prescriptions did not match. This was true even if they were phenomenally cute. My interest in them was purely ophthalmological.

The girl whose prescription most closely matched mine was a plump, vivacious girl from Finland named Una. We met at the Alliance française, where I first bumped into so many of my friends, because Beck's beer cost just one franc forty, and shortly thereafter she agreed to lend me her eyeglasses on nights she herself would not be needing them. We became friends of a sort — I once visited her at the house where she worked as an au pair in Versailles, where she made me lunch and rowed me around the Grande Jatte — but my interest in her was never romantic. I was only in it for the eyeglasses.

The principal members of my carousing group were an Australian surfer who could hold his liquor and a breathtakingly handsome young boy from Boston who could not. I became friends with Mick, my friend from Sidney, after I met his French girlfriend, Claudine, in a Monoprix on the rue de Rennes. There, after determining that I was American, she informed me that her boyfriend — who spoke little French — did not actually like French people and would be very happy to meet an American. We soon became the best of friends. Looking at the periphery of that group was a feisty bohemian type from California named Annie and a girl from Seattle named Terry, who had a friend named Cammy from Long Island, who talked me into accompanying her to Morocco, where she could buy colorful Goulimine beads to be sold in America to raise enough money to bring a French girl named Josiane to the States. On the way back from Morocco, while we were crossing a bridge outside Pamplona, a white horse suddenly appeared on the far side of the river. It seemed terribly symbolic, though I never figured out of what. But I think about that horse every day, and when I do, I think of my African adventure with Cammy. Finally, there was a lanky sophisticate from Saint Louis who was destined from birth to desert the Show Me State and move to New York City. When I visited Jay in Saint Louis two years later, his house was filled to overflowing with *New Yorkers*, the magazine that has long served as an intellectual and psychological lifeline to so many sophisticated provincials who dream of a magically urbane life in the Big City, yet are presently stranded in the prosaic hinterland. The whole time I knew Jay I understood that it would be impossible for him to live in Saint Louis after spending a year in Paris. Impossible.

At the edge of that group was Rob, the aforementioned Adonis, whose parents were college professors and who had more money than the rest of us combined. One of his forbears had built the Panama Canal. Mine had not. Rob drank more, and more often, and with more determination and abandon, than anyone I ever met. And he didn't mind spreading his money around. Rob and I would regularly find our way into weird subterranean nightclubs, where we would have the time of our lives and get completely blasted, and then never be able to find our way back to them again. Rob insisted that we once met Herbie Hancock fooling around on the piano in one of these gin mills, but I have no recollection of this event. We would get so drunk that I started keeping a notebook in my trench coat pocket in which I would ask our co-revelers to write down anything dramatic that had happened to us during the night that they felt we really ought to know about. Also, any relevant phone numbers.

One Thursday afternoon, after getting thrown out of his flat for excessive imbibing, Rob checked his bags into the Hôtel Parnasse, around the corner from my boardinghouse, then disappeared for the weekend. None of us knew where he had gone. That Sunday night I spotted him outside our favorite watering hole in the Latin Quarter. He was standing atop a dinky little Deux Chevaux, blind drunk, flailing his hands, madly inveighing against the myriad injustices of modern life. A meat wagon filled with cops drove up, slowed down, and pulled up alongside. A mutton-faced cop stuck his head out the window and told him to cease and desist and get the fuck down. The cop had a submachine gun in his lap, so Rob complied with the request. Rob, I soon discovered, had flown home to Boston for the weekend to shake down his parents for some more cash.

Such an escapade was an unforgivable transgression against the unspoken rules of the *Wanderjahr,* where our only contact with our native lands while we were away in France was supposed to be postcards or letters and maybe a phone call if someone was dying. Going home during the year away from home violated the very spirit of the enterprise. The *Wanderjahr* was supposed to be time out of time, the period when all ties with our homelands were sundered. The rest of us understood this, but Rob did not. It was perhaps why Una and the others never had much time for him. The rest of us had to fend for ourselves. The rest of us had to make ends meet. The rest of us had to eat in student restaurants.

I loved each and every one of these people, even though none of the non-Finns had the same prescription as me. Inside our group, affections flourished but bore no fruit. Jay had a crush on Annie, Annie had a crush on Rob, Terry was quite taken by Jay, and I was altogether smitten by Terry. Rob had no more than a passing interest in any of them, and Mick and Claudine had each other. Nothing ever came of our flirtations because we all had crushes on the wrong person. I also had a French girlfriend and a Czech girlfriend and a Japanese girl-friend, all of whom I met in a little storefront around the cor-ner from the Alliance française where foreign students could practice their French with natives, including a diplomat who had once served in Yemen. The little shop was operated by the Catholic Church. I never found out why, as religion was rarely mentioned.

None of these liaisons lasted long. The women were taking me off the lot for a trial spin around the block, and I was doing the same with them. It was like going out with a cracker or a redhead or a Mennonite just to say you had done it. This was the only reason I went to Morocco: to get the statutory visit to the third world out of the way early in life so I wouldn't have to do it again. I did have a very nice day at the Louvre with the statuesque Czech, who was a few years older than me, and asked if she would like to do it again. But then I met her husband, not a Louvre-going type at all. And that was the end of that.

Rob and Mick and I would regularly convene at a dive on the rue Saint-Jacques called Qui Êtes-Vous, Polly Maggoo?

Often, some of the others would join us. The bar was a Lilliputian, malodorous hole-in-the-wall jam-packed with hundreds of young people who were more than happy to pay twice the going rate for a beer in Paris merely to be jam-packed into a tiny sliver of a room jam-packed with young people who were also willing to pay twice the going rate for a beer in Paris just to be in that room. The youthful clientele was supplemented by several mysterious adults, including a North Carolina war vet named Cat, who had reputedly been involved in black ops in Vietnam in the early sixties, and a suspiciously unworldly "sea captain" who had perhaps sailed one or two seas, but certainly not all seven of them. There was also a fierce Dutch woman with a wandering eye who is the only person I ever met who told me that she disliked me purely because I was American. None of these people were especially interesting, yet we went to Polly Maggoo's three or four nights a week and always ended up spending time with them. To this day I have no idea why. It was like fulfilling a lifelong dream that you have never actually had.

One night I turned up at Polly Maggoo's after seeing the cadaverous Arthur Rubenstein play Chopin at the Théâtre des Champs-Élysées, where the premiere of Stravinsky's *Rite of Spring* had caused a riot sixty years earlier. That night I met a thirtyish Peruvian with a punched-in face who looked like the last Incan night watchman. He worked as a chef in the student restaurant system, a job he did not like. He had been around the block a time or two and seen a few things. I had not.

"If you are in China and you eat in a Chinese restaurant and you order duck, you will get dog," he told me. People were always telling me things like that. They found me callow, untested, a babe in the woods, a tabula rasa. It may have been because I was from Philadelphia. "If you order chicken, you will get cat. If you order beef, you will get rat."

"What will you get if you order duck in a Peruvian restaurant?" I asked.

He did not answer.

Later that night I advanced my theory that the fare in student restaurants was deliberately intended to keep students undernourished and ill and despondent so that they could no longer raise the red flag of insurrection.

"Only some restaurants," he informed me. "The students at the law school and the medical school are always holding demonstrations, so the food in those restaurants is terrible. But the language students and the art students never protest anything. If you go to their restaurants, the meals will be outstanding."

The next week he gave me a mimeographed copy of the menus from several student restaurants. The restaurant up the street from the Luxembourg Gardens was serving the same old pig swill. But the language school over on the Right Bank near the Petit Palais was offering chicken and rice and fresh bread and even some kind of rudimentary pastry as dessert. It was a bit of a hike from where I lived, but I dutifully hoofed across the river one night, and sure enough, the food was superb. From that point onward, I never ate in the student restaurant near the Latin Quarter.

Late in my stay in Paris, I inherited a tiny sixth-story maid's room from one of the American medical students, who had gone back to Staten Island for the summer. By this point, the dollar had come crashing down — after Nixon conceded that the war in Vietnam was lost — and I was strapped for cash. I had given up my room in the boardinghouse, which was costing me three hundred francs a month, and moved into the maid's room for less than half the price. My neighbor was a good-natured lady of the night named — what else? — Chantal, who had a boyfriend who was an out-of-work Elvis impersonator. His name was Ringo. He was a splendid chap, though thick as two planks, and he was always ready to share his cigarettes. He told me that his dream was to fly to Las Vegas and meet Elvis. Her dream was to meet a sugar daddy at the place Saint-Michel and ditch Ringo. Around that time, I got a job working in an outdoor fruit market, courtesy of the French girl on whose behalf I had trekked all the way to Tangier. Her father, a black marketeer during the war, had his own fruit and vegetable business, which set up shop twice a week in Malakoff, a working-class district just to the south of the Porte d'Orléans. It wasn't far from where Samuel Beckett lived, and several times I saw him in the street.

The men who ran the market insisted that I eat tripe and drink calvados at five o'clock in the morning, just to watch my face turn green. They also made me holler out things like, "Regardez mes belles pêches, mesdames et messieurs! Cent cinquante la botte!" It was the only rite of passage I ever actually enjoyed. Our customers thought I was kind of cute. So did my co-workers. I could barely understand anything they said to me, though one afternoon they personally thanked me for the Allied landing at Normandy. "Lafayette, nous voilà," I responded, channeling Black Jack Pershing arriving in France in 1917. I had waited my whole life to say something like that, though I suspect the allusion was lost on them.

Eventually I developed terrible problems with my teeth,

and my money started to run out, and I decided it was time to go back to the United States and put away the things of a child and start my career as a writer. Mick and Claudine had headed south by this point, to a drab town on the Atlantic coast where the beaches were lined with German pillboxes and all the streets were named after Lenin and Stalin. Rob had long since gone home to Boston. Terry had flown back to the West Coast, Cammy had returned to Long Island, my Canadian friends had headed back to Montreal and Halifax.

Just before I left Paris, I joined Una and Terry and Josiane and Jay and a French teacher named Elizabeth and a few other people in a Montmartre fondue joint where the owner sang and danced and gallivanted around and drew the blinds and locked the door to any new customers as soon as the place was full. We ate a lot and drank a lot and sang a lot. Then Una unexpectedly burst into tears.

"Why are you crying?" I asked her.

"Because we'll never see each other again after tonight," she exclaimed. "We'll never all be in the same room together again."

"Yes, we will," we consoled her, but we were wrong. Some of us stayed in touch, some of us crossed paths again. But most of them I never saw again, not Terry, not Josiane, not Elizabeth, not Una. We were all saying good-bye to the best year of our lives that night, and only Una was smart enough to realize it.

Thirty years later, on one of many return trips to Paris, I was walking through the Luxembourg Gardens when I spotted Jay standing in the middle of the path, perhaps twenty yards ahead. He was positioned not far from that horrendous student restaurant that had kept me alive so many nights when my bankroll was getting thin. He seemed lost in thought. I was now at the point in my life when I was nostalgic for the city of my youth. When I first came here at age twenty-one, Paris was old and I was young. But now Paris seemed young and I felt old. Maybe Jay, whom I was seeing for the first time in twenty-five years, even though we had both lived in New York the whole time, was thinking the same thing.

"What are you doing here, Jay?" I asked.

He looked up, not at all surprised to see me, as if we had just seen each other the night before at Polly Maggoo's, as if the last quarter century had not somehow vanished without our noticing.

"I could never get this place out of my head," he said, smiling. He might have been talking about the jardins du Luxembourg, or that particular spot in the jardins du Luxembourg, but I knew he was talking about Paris. No, none of us could ever get Paris out of our heads. None of us ever could. Wherever you are, Una, thank you for the eyeglasses.

Fledgling Days

THERE IS AN old photograph of my mother standing in
front of the Paris Opéra in 1955. Wearing a plaid suit, a
pair of brown gloves dangling from her ringless left hand, she
is holding on to her hat with her right hand and smiling into
the wind. It is a picture of independence, and like everything
about her life before my father, the photograph was a source
of endless allure. Bold, dramatic, fascinating, my mother's adventures as a single woman seemed to be part of a trajectory of
pure freedom.

My mother was twenty-three years old when she moved to
Paris. She had lived in New York for a while by then, and felt
ready for a change, but had no desire to return to the confines
of the Jewish community in small-town Antwerp, Belgium,
that she had so eagerly escaped at the age of nineteen. It was
a time when ladies still wore gloves, gentlemen wore hats, and
the little sparrow known as Edith Piaf held sway over all of
Paris. For a little more than a year, my mother stayed with her
distant cousin M. and his wife, R., in the sixteenth arrondissement, in a large, rambling, antique-filled apartment whose
prize possession was a birdcage that had once belonged to
Marie Antoinette.

The truth is, it wasn't an especially happy period for my mother. She didn't have a gang to run around with as she had had in New York, nor did she have anyone in her life romantically. Paris is a good place to be young and melancholy, she used to tell me. After she got started talking about those days — this usually involved her playing some of her Piaf records and telling me how truly those songs about love and loss had moved her — she ended by asking me to swear I'd be married by the time I was twenty-five. I always refused. I got mad at her for trying to boss me around about something so important, something over which she theoretically shouldn't have any say. Besides, she herself hadn't gotten married so young. Reminding me that she didn't want me to go through the difficulties she had experienced, the loneliness and doubt that had tormented her until she finally married my American father at the age of thirty-four, long after her family had given her up as a lost cause, she always finished with one of her favorite child-rearing maxims: "Do as I *say,* Valerie, not as I *do.*"

I didn't really believe my mother when she said it had been hard to be alone. In Paris she worked for Air France. Because of her gift for languages, she was given a job behind the check-in desk at the airport, and I would imagine her, fetching in her uniform, having conversations with a long line of handsome travelers, each en route to another mysterious destination. My mother tried to tell me that it hadn't been that exciting. But then there must have been other times, I countered, of going out in Paris, of being young and beautiful and unattached. My mother explained that beneath the glamour of being single there had been a lot of sorrow and anxiety, even a few mishaps. During that year, for instance, a friend of hers called her up and asked her if she wanted to be in the Audrey Hepburn–Fred Astaire movie being filmed around town. The day my mother arrived on the set it was pouring, and as an extra in the train station scene, she was soon completely drenched. She couldn't help noticing that Miss Hepburn, as the star of the movie, got whatever she desired — a cup of hot chocolate, a fresh pair of shoes. My mother, however, got nothing, other than pneumonia, which meant that her last three months in Paris were spent in an extremely unglamorous fashion — sniffling in bed.

For the rest of her life, my mother loved Paris. Everything about it inspired her — the city's rich past, its magnificent buildings, its vibrant intellectual scene. She appreciated the French dedication to life's refinements, and spent hours truffling through the city, unearthing the best handbag maker, the bakery where you could get the most delectable coffee éclairs. Whether on a trip with my father, my sister, and me or, if we couldn't join her, on one of her regular solo jaunts, she would pack her days with lunches and dinners and teas, interspersed with visits to museums, galleries, and all kinds of specialty boutiques. Some of the women she knew there would refuse to go out to dinner with her unless a few men were invited, too, not wanting to be seen in public unescorted, but my mother had no compunction about navigating Paris on her own. (Why would she? She had my father, that sturdy anchor, waiting for her back at home.) Bursting with presents and stories and energy, my mother would come home to our Manhattan apartment with beautiful new clothes for me and my sister, a handsome homburg for my father, and, invariably, another batch of funny, self-deprecating tales.

The few times we went, just the two of us, my mother insisted on only one rule: there was no being tired. There were too many plays and exhibits to see, haunts to revisit, places to discover. Typically, we'd arrive at the hotel, drop off our bags, and then head out on the town, walking and shopping and stopping for lunch at someplace like the Bar des Théâtres, a lively bistro on the avenue Montaigne. I loved going there with her. On one such trip — I was seventeen, my mother was fifty-two, just having recovered from a round of chemotherapy for the breast cancer that had struck her, and by extension our family, out of nowhere — she and I found ourselves seated in the front room next to a table of older men, who leered boisterously at every young girl who walked by, only to turn back to their own conversation, which consisted mainly of listing their aches and pains and complaining, each one more insistently than the last, about their various doctors. As we observed that combination of braggadocio and old-man resignation, my mother and I, without saying a word to each other, started laughing. We couldn't stop. When we left the restaurant a few minutes later, she explained to me, wiping a few tears from her eyes with a tissue, that if people spoke loudly in a restaurant, it wasn't eavesdropping — they *wanted* you to hear them.

After briefly going back to the hotel to change for the evening, we went to see Tina Turner in concert. Afterward, proudly toting our oversize programs, we went to La Coupole, feeling "branchées," as the French say for "hip," as we walked through the rows of bustling, well-lit tables to our own. We were so high on the thrill of being in Paris, of spending time together, of doing all the things we loved to do, that it was no problem for either of us to stay up so late. Of course the fact that I was seventeen probably had something to do with it in my case. For my mother, I think it was the sheer excitement of being alive.

It wasn't such a huge leap, then, for me to decide that I, too, should go to Paris at the age of twenty-three. My mother had been gone for a little more than three years by then. I had graduated from college and had a year on my own in Washington, D.C. (a place I was drawn to because it had no connection to her in my mind), and, I, too, was ready for a change. Most of all I didn't want to be at home in New York without her.

I arrived in September and stayed in a cavalcade of apartments, finally moving to the rue Saint-Sulpice just as the rainy season was ending and it was beginning to get cold. My studio, which I discovered through a friend of a friend, was small, but I found it charming, with slanted wooden eaves and recessed windows covered by brown velvet curtains. Each piece of furniture had its own sense of humor: an uneven little table, two chairs whose legs splayed at odd angles, an armoire whose door wouldn't close.

I wanted a job, a life, a circle of friends. But most of all, I was on a mission to find my mother, to try to relate to her as a young woman. For some reason, during that year in Paris, the search to rediscover my mother, to know her in all her aspects — both as she was when I knew her and as she must have been long before I was born — took a geographical bent. In pursuit of my mother's memory, I stopped before the odd, silvery green of the city's art nouveau Métro signs that she had admired so, went back to museum rooms to spend time with paintings we had seen together, sat for long spells at her favorite people-watching cafés, wandered down the little shopping streets in the sixth arrondissement where she had loved to go, all in an attempt to feel her effervescence once again coursing through me. Sometimes, if I was in the wrong mood, the beauty of a place would turn cold on me. I could see in the site of some former or imagined happiness only my mother's absence, and I felt even more alone. Then Paris became for me like a vault to which I had no key. Instead of repositories of treasure, I had access only to a series of chill, blank exteriors.

Other times it worked, and I felt an urge to laugh, her spirit a gorgeous secret known only to me. Standing before a butcher's window to watch the care with which he placed a row of frilly paper flowers on the tiny bone stalks of a prized rack of lamb, I appreciated his delicacy and patience all the more for being certain they would have delighted her.

When I started looking for a job in Paris, I sent my résumé to someone my mother had known socially, a woman in her fifties, and arranged for an interview. She was curt on the phone, but quite engaging in person. She looked at me intently with her clear blue eyes, and I saw warmth and interest. She asked me about my mother, and when I told her she had died, she stood up and kissed me in the French way, on both cheeks. I told her I would work very hard for her. She said, "We'll try each other out for one month. If you're happy, and I'm happy, we'll take it from there." I knew that she was in public relations, that she represented the best chefs and restaurants and hotels in France, and that she was friends with the likes of Polanski and Paloma and Isabelle. Her office was in her apartment, and there were photographs everywhere of her hanging out with celebrities.

I was impatient to start. My new boss seemed plugged in to every interesting cultural event and personality in the city. It would be glamorous and exciting, everything I secretly wanted for my year in Paris. I was flying high, barely able to downplay my excitement to friends who asked what I would be doing.

When I arrived for work at the beginning of September, she was away, so I met the two other girls with whom I would be working. One had been there for six months and wisely kept calm in the face of our ignorant enthusiasm. The other girl and I spent a lot of that first week smoking (even though we had been told it was absolutely forbidden) and discussing our near, bright future, what happenings we would be attending, whom we would meet there.

Walking through the place on the first day my boss was back, I noticed the atmosphere was charged, electric. For one thing, the apartment was full. She had brought back her eighty-two-year-old mother, an ill, complaining woman whose one solace in life — aside from her daughter's great success — was her parrot, Coco, whom she had had for forty years. As I walked in, I saw my boss on the phone. Her eyes flashed at me. She was wearing three watches and a dozen chain necklaces around her neck, and I immediately knew that the nature of the job — along with my dreams of it — had changed.

Gone was the charm of our interview. With her staccato commands and short hair, she was a drill sergeant and school-mistress rolled into one. On her orders, she addressed us informally as "tu," and we responded formally, with "vous." I had never known the word *minable* before, but I learned it quickly. It means "of a pitiable mediocrity." She used it anytime we asked a question, or if she caught us using anything but her signature brown ink. There was brown ink in the copy machine, the fax machine, the printer. We even took messages with brown pens. I went home in a stupor.

Every day brought new horrors. I heard her say, after hanging up on the best florist in Paris because she couldn't get her way with him, "I will destroy that man." I would go into her bedroom in the morning to tell her she had a call, and she would look up at me with fifty needles in her face from the acupuncturist. I lost weight. I woke up in the middle of one night in a panic, realizing I had forgotten to take out the mail. It didn't matter that I had left after dark, long past the last pickup. The next morning it was without much joy that I pressed the downstairs buzzer — marked, ironically, by a giant red heart — that rang up to the apartment. The minute I got to the top floor, I was castigated for my stupidity by the maid, the mother, and finally the boss herself.

I tried to comfort myself by thinking of one of my mother's sayings for not letting things get to you — "Let it glide over the back of your indifference" — but it didn't work. It got to the point where I talked of nothing else with my friends, as if nothing existed but my boss and her insane behavior. It finally made sense to me that she had had sixty assistants in less than six months. If old assistants called, to try to ask for moneys owed them, she would say, "Only if you come in person," which usually settled the matter. One assistant did come back, and even brought a man with her for protection. I had stayed late and got to experience the tumult from another room. I overheard my boss screaming that she would ruin the girl's chances in all of Paris. Luckily, as far as I know, none of these threats were actually carried out.

Although I wasn't happy about the idea of leaving before the month was up — I thought of myself as a good girl, after all, someone who didn't quit — after about two weeks I had had it. This was not at all how I had envisioned my year in Paris. I went into work in the morning and asked if I could speak with her. "When I have a minute," she replied. It was eight o'clock at night before she turned to me and asked what I wanted. In the meantime, I had gone out to lunch and had a steak and a glass of red wine to fortify myself.

I planned to tell her I would be leaving. I looked her in the eyes and began to speak. I said, in a very calm voice, that I was not stupid, and that I was willing to work very hard for her, but that I thought the way she treated us sometimes was just not acceptable. She replied, zinging my words back at me, that she thought the things we *did* sometimes were not acceptable, and not only that, but she thought that my mother would think she was right, and I was wrong, and that she would be ashamed of me. I felt as though I had just been hit by a truck. I managed to stammer, "Maybe I should just leave." She replied, "No, no maybes. Do you want to *stay,* or do you want to *go*? Because if you *don't* want to stay, I would rather just close the office for the next couple of days and have *no one* here." She was leaving on a trip to Texas the following morning, so that her mother could visit a heart specialist recommended by Jerry Lewis. Before I even knew what I was doing, I stood up and said, "I'll stay." We shook hands across the desk.

What followed was utterly bizarre, like a scene out of an army movie. She led me around the office, calling things out to me and waiting for my reply. She stood next to the bulletin board and yelled, "Now what happens when a journalist calls for the such and such hotel?" I yelled back the correct procedure. We did this for a while, until we ended up in the copy room at extremely close quarters. She started waving her hands around, pointing to the many files stacked up on the wire shelves. "I did all of this, this is all me. I came from nothing. If you do things the way I say to do them, you will be doing them right. I had no fancy education, I had no parents spoiling me. Everything I have I built myself." We were so close I could see her facial muscles straining. I felt a new regard for her. I felt that I could handle the challenge she was offering me, that maybe she wasn't so bad after all, just some kind of crazy perfectionist. If I could only follow her system to the letter, I would be OK. When I left that night, it was as if we had reached a new understanding. "Je compte sur toi" — "I count on you" — she said as we shook hands again by the door.

I lasted two more weeks, and although things improved, and I felt she treated me with a kind of gruff respect, ultimately it wasn't where I wanted to be. The purported glamour wasn't worth the price. A few days before my month was up, I told her my plans would be changing. She said, without flinching, "You won't have it as easy anywhere else. It's not everyone in Paris who will give you your Jewish holiday." (I had taken the day off for Yom Kippur.) I pretended not to hear her. I left that apartment for the last time on a rainy night. I'd had an appointment in the Saint-Germain area, but by the time she let me go I had missed it. The soft rain coated my face, soaked through my clothes. I was shivering a bit when I got to the friend's house where I was having dinner. She gave me a glass of brandy, the way you do with someone who has just experienced a shock. I had made it out alive, but my confidence that I could make the right choices in my mother's absence, take as good care of myself as she had always taken of me, had been badly wounded.

Soon after, I accepted an invitation from my mother's close

friend Julia and her husband to go hunting. We would be going to Touraine, and the weekend would be dedicated to ducks. I was a little nervous, never having gone hunting before, but I reasoned that it would be an interesting experience, and that since I was very fond of eating duck, I could not raise any moral objections.

Every weekend, a different family was assigned the responsibility of organizing the meals; the weekend in question, it was Julia and her husband's turn. We would be about thirty people for lunch, including the gamekeeper and the head of the hunt, the various husbands and wives and their assorted children. I was the only American there. We went into the kitchen and started our preparations: unwrapping cheese and washing fruits and vegetables. There were some local women helping us. At one point, amid the slicing and washing and chopping and boiling, I noticed a large salad bowl filled with slivered endives. Without giving it a thought, I reached out my hand and popped one of the vinaigrette-coated leaves in my mouth. Suddenly I froze. I heard a nightmarish voice in my ears, berating me for taking a piece of salad. *How unsanitary! The salad was for everyone — what have you been thinking?* I turned around, but I was alone in the kitchen. I had only imagined my boss was still castigating me.

That Saturday in Touraine, after lunch and a walk in the woods to pick *cèpes* — fat wild mushrooms that we would sauté in garlic — the families all disbanded to different houses. I remember feeling incredibly sleepy, lulled by the fire and the adult conversation and a glass of heavy red wine.

The next morning we woke up and dressed while the room was still dark. We got in the car and drove back to the lodge.

There were about twenty of us. Some of the women — in olive green from head to toe — were extraordinarily well dressed, with bright feathers in their small, jaunty hats. I knew my mother would have admired their sporty elegance. From the lodge, we walked on a muddy path to a nearby lake. The head of the hunt, a white-haired man with a great red nose and a shining brass hunter's horn attached to his suspenders, broke us up into groups of four.

Each group went to a point around the lake, where there were docks made of old, pale gray wood. I followed my group as we walked low, almost crouching, to the end of our dock. I could see the other groups scattered along the border and the white, cloudy sky reflected in the water between us. The ducks, hundreds of them, were in the center of the lake, quietly nosing one another and diving for food. All at once I heard the silvery notes of the horn, announcing our presence in the unfettered light. There was a great flapping and squawking as the ducks lifted themselves into the sky. They rose in a swarm, like a reverse whirlpool, and flew out in all directions. As the two men in my group shot again and again, my ears rang and my mouth filled with a metallic dust. Then there was quiet. Before I knew what was happening, the dogs we had brought with us plunged into the water. They swam in a straight line for the dead, and one by one brought them back and laid them at our feet. The ducks were long and plump, their capes of dark feathers molded wetly to their bodies. Amid the barking of the dogs and the cries of congratulations and bonhomie, I felt a secret joy for the ones that had escaped.

It was the ducks that had flown straight up in the air that had gotten shot, I realized, whereas the ones that had stayed low, parallel to the water, had made it into the woods. It was a flight pattern to live by. With this job, this year in Paris, I had been too eager, too confident that I had found the answer. I cringed when I thought about how high my hopes had been. Life had humbled me once again. It occurred to me that perhaps my mother had been right after all, that Paris was a good place to be young and melancholy, a city in which, despite your best lofty intentions, you ended up being thrown back upon yourself. The ducks had been like a drove of young girls, like me and my friends — like my mother, all those years ago — as we set out in life. From now on, I would try to lie low, not get swept up in undue excitement. For the rest of my time in Paris, and long after I moved back to New York to face my future there without her, I called it the flying-duck theory, a reminder not to let myself get carried away.

In the afternoon, the bounty was placed in a circle on the ground. The hunters lifted each darling by its feet and bagged it. I was handed a bag with two ducks in it. It was the first time I understood the word *deadweight*. I gave them to Julia, and once we got back to Paris, they were put in the freezer. Months later, we ate them, roasted to a tender crisp. I am sad to say that, like the bruised dreams of the young, they were delicious.

The Tapeworm Is In

N O GREAT COLLECTOR of music, I started off my life in Paris by listening to American books on tape. I'd never been a big fan of the medium but welcomed them as an opportunity to bone up on my English. Often these were books I would never have sat down and read. Still, though, even when they were dull I enjoyed the disconcerting combination of French life and English narration. Here was Paris, wrongly dubbed for my listening pleasure. The grand department store felt significantly less intimidating when listening to *Dolly: My Life and Other Unfinished Business,* a memoir in which the busty author describes a childhood spent picking ticks out of her grandmother's scalp. Sitting by the playground in the Luxembourg Gardens, I listened to *Lolita,* abridged with James Mason and unabridged with Jeremy Irons. There were, I noticed, half a dozen other pasty, middle-aged men who liked to gather around the monkey bars, and together we formed a small but decidedly creepy community.

Merle Haggard's *My House of Memories,* the diaries of Alan Bennett, *Treasure Island.* if a person who constantly reads is labeled a bookworm, then I was quickly becoming what might be called a tapeworm. The trouble was that I'd moved to Paris completely unprepared for my new pastime. The few tapes I owned had all been given to me at one point or another and thrown into my suitcase at the last minute. There are only so many times a grown man can listen to *The Wind in the Willows,* so I was eventually forced to consider the many French tapes given as subtle hints by our neighbors back in Normandy.

I tried listening to *The Misanthrope* and Fontaine's *Fables,* but they were just too dense for me. I'm much too lazy to make that sort of effort. Besides, if I wanted to hear people speaking wall-to-wall French, all I had to do was remove my headphones and participate in what is known as "real life," a concept as uninviting as a shampoo cocktail.

Desperate for material, I was on the verge of buying a series of Learn to Speak English tapes when my sister Amy sent a package containing several cans of clams, a sack of grits, an audio walking tour of Paris, and my very own copy of *Pocket Medical French,* a palm-size phrase book and corresponding cassette designed for doctors and nurses unfamiliar with the language. The walking tour guides one through the city's various landmarks, reciting bits of information the listener might find enlightening. I learned, for example, that in the late fifteen hundreds my little neighborhood square was a popular spot for burning people alive. Now lined with a row of small shops, the tradition continues, though in a figurative rather than literal sense.

I followed my walking tour to Notre-Dame, where, bored with a lecture on the history of the flying buttress, I switched tapes and came to see Paris through the jaundiced eyes of the pocket medical guide. Spoken in English and then repeated, slowly and without emotion, in French, the phrases are short enough that I was quickly able to learn such sparkling conversational icebreakers as "Remove your dentures and all of your jewelry" and "You now need to deliver the afterbirth." Though I have yet to use any of my new commands and questions, I find that, in learning them, I am finally able to imagine myself Walkman-free and plunging headfirst into an active and rewarding social life. That's me at the glittering party, refilling my champagne glass and turning to ask my host if he's noticed any unusual discharge. "We need to start an IV," I'll say to the countess while boarding her yacht. "But first could I trouble you for a stool sample?"

With practice I will eventually realize my goal; in the meantime, come to Paris and you will find me, headphones plugged tight in my external audio meatus, walking the quays and whispering, "Has anything else been inserted into your anus? Has anything else been inserted into your anus?"

My Bookstore High

IT HAD BEEN an interesting afternoon, I said, though some of the guests were rather . . .

"Strange?" she said, finishing for me. "There are some unusual ones, aren't there? I think George likes them that way."

"George?"

Eve stopped her stirring and peered at me.

"You mean you don't know who George is?"

She beckoned me deeper into the apartment. We entered what appeared to be the master bedroom, which contained a king-size bed, more books, and a collection of photographs lining three walls. Some of the pictures featured Hemingway, Miller, Joyce, and such, while in the rest, another man figured prominently. Depending on the year the picture was taken, he sported either a curling goatee and a wild skew of brown hair or tufts of short gray hair and rumpled suits.

"That's George." Eve was pointing to one picture where the man was leaning over a table covered with books, a broad smile on his face. "He runs Shakespeare and Company."

She said this as if it explained everything, but it still didn't make sense. Nothing made any sense: the tourists out front, the man at the wishing well, the men making soup . . . and the beds! There were beds everywhere.

"But what exactly goes on here?" I was gripping her arm a tad tightly.

Eve smiled like a teacher smiles at her student and gently unfurled my fingers. "The bookstore is like a shelter. George lets people live here for free."

She left me alone in that back room, gazing at the picture, marveling at fate . . .

AFTER THE TEA party, I felt so exhilarated that I climbed the six flights of stairs to my hotel room effortlessly. For hours, I leaned out the narrow window of my room and watched smoke curl from the clay chimneys on the surrounding roofs. It was long past midnight when I finally tried to sleep, but even then I could only lie awake with the restlessness of a child before Christmas.

From what Eve had told me, George welcomed lost souls and poor writers. I qualified on both counts. Considering the precious little money in my pocket and the scarcity of options before me, it didn't take long to decide that fate had brought me to Shakespeare and Company that rainy Sunday afternoon. For the first time since the threatening phone call, I began imagining a future. I would write a brilliant novel at the bookstore, I would be acclaimed a genius, I would bask in untold fame and fortune. It was absurd, of course, but I reveled in this sudden ecstasy of optimism after so many bleak days. I felt the adrenaline of a gambler who watches the roulette wheel spin with his last chips on the table. Outside the window, the sky was molting from night black to morning gray before I finally fell asleep.

The next afternoon, I washed thoroughly in the bathroom down the hallway from my room and even hung my best shirt outside the shower to smooth its wrinkles. Standing before the cracked mirror, I practiced my smiles and rehearsed my introduction. Nothing seemed good enough. By the time I was ready to leave, I was so nervous that even though the line 4 Métro cut almost directly from the hotel to the bookstore, I decided to walk so as to better measure the mission before me.

With each step toward the bookstore, I became more apprehensive, my stomach a sour mix of a thousand first dates and job interviews. Who was I to go live in a bookstore? Would I even be accepted? And that constant nagging worry: What exactly was I doing with my life?

I walked by the African groceries and call shops of boulevard Ornano, then under the iron beams of the elevated Métro at Barbès, where men offered gold chains from their coat pockets. Past the Gare de Nord, then the Gare de l'Est, a voice inside wondering if maybe I shouldn't just hop a train and try my luck in another city. Three times, my resolution faltered and I started back toward the hotel. But I always turned and continued on to Shakespeare and Company. There was really no other choice . . .

SHAKESPEARE AND COMPANY sits on the very left edge of the Left Bank. The store is close enough to the Seine that when one is standing in the front doorway, a well-thrown apple core will easily reach river water. From this same doorway, there is an inspired view of the Île de la Cité, and one can contemplate the cathedral of Notre-Dame, the Hôtel-Dieu hospital, and the imposing block of the main police *préfecture.*

The bookstore's actual address is 37, rue de la Bûcherie. It's an odd cobbled street that begins at rue Saint-Jacques, runs for one block, hits the public park of Saint-Julien-le-Pauvre, then continues on for another two blocks before ending at the square Restif de la Bretonne. The bookstore is on the part of rue de la Bûcherie close to rue Saint-Jacques, where, thanks to a quirk of city planning, there are only buildings on the south side of the street, which is what gives the bookstore its splendid view.

This end of the street is reserved for pedestrians, but this is only part of the reason it retains a certain calm. There is also a tiny city garden that separates the bookstore from the racing traffic of quai de Montebello and then the sidewalk widens in front of 37, rue de la Bûcherie to create an almost private esplanade for Shakespeare and Company. For the coup de grâce, there are two young cherry trees on this esplanade and a green Wallace drinking fountain sitting majestically to the side. All this gives the bookstore an air of tranquillity that is shocking in the midst of the frenzy and noise of downtown Paris.

As for the bookstore itself, there are actually two entrances. As you face the shop, the main part of the store with the narrow green door I entered on the day of the tea party is on the right. It is here that one finds the famous yellow and green wooden Shakespeare and Company sign and the broad picture window. To the left of the main store, there is a second, smaller storefront. This is the antiquarian room. Along with the shelves of centuries-old books, the antiquarian room has a desk, a lovely stuffed armchair, and, of course, a creaky but thoroughly sleepable bed.

WHEN I ARRIVED after my coffee with Fernanda, it was nearing dark and the streetlights were flickering to life around me. The window of the main shop glowed a soft yellow against the early night, and at the desk there was an elderly man with a rumpled suit and a faraway look in his eyes. From the photographs I'd seen the day before, I knew this man to be George. Taking one last breath for courage, I stepped inside.

The door creaked to announce me, but George kept gazing out the window, deep in private thought. In the store's irregular light, I could see his uneven tussle of fine white hair and the thin wrinkles that lined his face. After long moments, he shook his head as if awaking from a dream and turned to look at me. His eyes were an impossibly pale blue.

"What do you want?" he demanded.

His voice was so gruff that I took a step backward. My rehearsed lines disappeared, and stammering, I mumbled something about being a writer with no place else to go.

"I wouldn't stay for long," I finished. "Just enough time to catch my feet. I've hit a bit of a rough patch."

He stood there, appraising me with those pale eyes, stopping time.

"You've written books?"

I nodded.

"Are they self-published?"

Using a vanity press is akin to buying sex, but more shameful in a way. Visiting a prostitute is at least a private act, while paying to publish one's book is a very public display of creative desperation. Despite my nervousness, I took affront to the question. Though the crime books I'd written were hardly works of great literature, I was proud of what I'd accomplished.

"No, not at all," I replied, trying to keep the anger from my voice. "I'm not saying they're the best books ever written, but I had a real publisher."

George waved the back of his hand at me as if I were speaking nonsense, but a smile crept across his face.

"A real writer wouldn't have asked; he would have just come in and taken a bed. You, you can stay. But you'll sleep downstairs with the rest of the riffraff."

And like that, things changed forever . . .

DURING THE WEEKS of living cheaply at the hotel, I'd devised a series of maneuvers to eat at little or no expense in Paris. There was a restaurant on rue de Clignancourt that served limitless plates of free couscous and vegetables on Friday nights so long as you ordered a half glass of beer. The large American Church in the seventh arrondissement had an almost free all-you-can-eat pizza night with a minimum of sermonizing. Then there was the constant delight of the four-franc baguette and the endless cheeses that could be had so inexpensively at the city's supermarkets.

A particularly sublime discovery came from a teacher at the French school I'd attended. Anne was a graceful woman who took the job as language teacher after her husband died She thrilled in introducing neophytes to the enchantments of Paris and by chance took an interest in polishing my rather rough crime reporter self. Anne suggested operas to see, offered books to read, and, most wondrously, introduced me to the nutritious world of the Paris vernissage.

Vernissage is a derivative of the French word for varnish. In reference to the last shining coat that artists layered on their paintings the night before their shows, opening parties became known by this name. In an art-rich city like Paris, there was always some gallery launching some artist and they lured visitors with bottles of wine and plates of hors d'oeuvres. Though these pleasures were intended for the journalists and potential patrons, if one dressed correctly and knew how to behave, these events made for delicious meals.

Anne knew the best of the Left Bank vernissage scene, and while she toured these venues in search of new artists and old friends, I somewhat crassly focused on the food. The protocol was simple: browse the art with an attentive eye, compliment the artist, then hover by the food table for long enough to gorge on a day's worth of calories. There was one night when a gallery on the Left Bank served hundreds of miniature spinach and salmon quiches; another time, it was sushi and rice wine on a boat moored in the Seine; my favorite was an event for a painter of Lebanese descent that featured hummus, tabbouleh, kafta, and a divine array of falafels.

LEAVING SHAKESPEARE AND COMPANY that night, Kurt and the rest dismissed my schemes as the work of an amateur. With everyone nearly broke and no proper cooking facilities in the lower part of the bookstore, the residents had become expert scavengers. They swore they would initiate me in their ways, and the lessons were to begin that very night. We turned left out of the bookstore, crossed rue Saint-Jacques, and took rue de la Huchette. The narrow street had once been among the filthiest in Paris and home to a young Napoleon Bonaparte when he first arrived in the city. Now it was a garish tourist ghetto, filled with Greek restaurants that competed for customers with displays of skewered seafood and the scent of burning fat. Touts stood in the restaurant doorways, playing merry with the crowds and shattering cheap porcelain plates at the feet of the more promising herds.

Shakespeare and Company residents clearly weren't worth wasting plates over, so we negotiated the street with ease. Emerging at place Saint-Michel, we cut past the spouting stone lions, along the flower shops and trendy bars of rue Saint-André des Arts, then down boulevard Saint-Germain until we arrived at a dismal gray building on rue Mabillon. Two guards stood slouched at the front door, but Kurt told me to walk straight in as if I belonged. We climbed two flights of stairs and came to an enormous *cafétéria* with row after row of benches and a long, snaking line at the food counter.

This was a student restaurant, one of more than a dozen in Paris. Subsidized by the government, a full meal cost fifteen francs here, just two American dollars. Technically, one needed a student identification card, but the line was full of other impostors like us: a family with three small children, a couple with shaved heads and scalp studs, a drunken man with a variety of stains across his shirtfront and down his pant leg.

In exchange for a colorful meal ticket, one received two bread rolls, a thick bowl of vegetable soup, a generous slice of brie, half a boiled egg with a squib of dijon mayonnaise as garnish, a main plate of grilled lamb, sautéed potatoes, and green beans, a strawberry yogurt, and even a slice of honey sponge cake with sliced almonds for dessert. With each morsel of food added to my tray, the more inclined I was to agree with my companions: this was the zenith of the cheap Paris meal.

We sat at one of the long benches, and while we ate, Kurt acted as spotter. Whenever a fellow diner left behind a tray with an untouched piece of cheese or a fair-size chunk of bread, Kurt raced out of his seat to grab the bounty. The objective was to collect enough abandoned food to furnish late-night snacks for the entire bookstore family.

"Watch him well," the Gaucho advised. "Next time, it's your job."

Throughout this strange meal, Ablimit asked questions about my work at the newspaper and freedom of the press in Canada. As the dictionary I saw him with that first day suggested, he was in fact from China, but not Chinese, he stressed. He was Uighur, an ethnic minority from the northwest of the country. For more than half a decade, he'd worked as a television reporter and documentary producer, but he became frustrated by the censorship and pressure to put a positive spin on the news. Two years before, shortly after his thirtieth birthday, he'd managed to get a visa and then headed west, stopping first at a kibbutz in Israel, then moving up to Paris and Shakespeare and Company.

"People just find themselves here," said Ablimit, shrugging.

As I ate, I felt bliss. Part of it was the simple pleasure of a full belly. I had always been thin of frame, consistently weighing 170 pounds for my six feet and one inch in height. But during that scant month in Paris, I'd nearly starved myself trying to conserve money, eating one meal a day instead of three, fasting entirely when I knew there was a promising vernissage that night. The week before, I'd passed a pharmacy that offered the free use of a scale and I'd availed myself of the service. The digital display read seventy-four kilograms, so the shock didn't come until I scratched out the conversion in my notebook. It translated to just under 163 pounds. Between the forced diet and the long hours of walking, I'd lost seven pounds I could ill afford to lose. Now, thanks to the combination of George's pepper soup and this plentiful *cafétéria* dinner, my body rejoiced in the sudden rush of salts and fats.

I was also coasting along on my bookstore high. It was nearly miraculous that I'd found such an exotic solution to my predicament, and I felt giddy that the fear of homelessness — or worse, being forced to beg for a loan from my parents — had been lifted. Of course, if I'd rationally analyzed my situation, I would have realized it was barely better than before: I still had no money, no job, no plans for the future, and the bed in the bookstore certainly wasn't the height of stability. But the day you move into an infamous old bookstore certainly isn't the day for rational thought. I was eating with three intriguing and gregarious men from three very different corners of the world; we were sharing stories and laughing like friends. It was all good.

Chantal's Gift

To be a writer," Chantal insisted, "you must come back to Paris."

"But I just gave up my room at l'Hôtel des Rats!" I exclaimed.

"You don't need a room. I have one. You can stay with me."

Two days after Chantal left for Paris, I packed up my bags and took the train back into town. Chantal was always taking in stray dogs of one kind or another, so asking me to stay over in her apartment was nothing out of the ordinary. But as her flat was located on the edge of the city, she thought it best if we met near the publishing house where she worked, at a café on the rue de Buci.

"BONSOIR," A VOICE behind me said. "I have made you a gift. But it is at home. Shall we go? It is only a small walk."

Tourist that I still was, I had no choice but to follow her on a one-hour forced march across half of Paris. On that particular night it was hot as hell, and still being very much of a New Yorker, I twice insisted on taking a cab. To this rather normal request, however, Chantal answered me with every Parisian's favorite word: "NO!" So, we kept on walking.

"Are we there yet?" I asked, after crossing all of these very charming Parisian intersections, where one false step can result in a very long hospital stay, or worse. But Chantal just remained silent and we kept on walking. Then, finally, after an hour had elapsed, she looked up into the sky and said: "There it is."

It was a small, plain-looking apartment on the seventh floor of a 1930s building, with one extraordinary feature: a gargantuan terrace with an unobstructed view of what I still thought would be a jumping-off point for me, the Eiffel Tower. There were three other apartments on the floor: two were converted maid's rooms and one was larger — the size of a walk-in closet. All three shared a common toilet located down the hall. Only two had running water.

Chantal's apartment was the largest one on the floor, with complete bathroom facilities, and it was about as clean and organized as any immaculate French home can be, or at least it was until I moved in. It would have felt airy and spacious, save for one omnipresent structure. I called it the Never-Ending Bookcase. Like all of her friends, Chantal was trying to squeeze the lost Library of Alexandria into a couple of very tiny rooms. Not so much impressive as they were enchanting, the endless rows of books came in all varieties of shapes and languages, including, as hard as it was for me to believe, English. There were newly minted children's books, collector comic books, atlases, history books, and at least a thousand novels, all commingled with more than a few cigarette-pack-size volumes so old and fragile, they seemed as if they would crumble if you just thought of taking their covers in your hands.

"Dust mite heaven," I murmured under my breath.

"What was that?"

"Jesus Christ," I replied. "When you said that books meant something to you, I thought you were just shitting me!"

"Do you always use curse words?"

"What?" I asked, confused. "I cursed? That wasn't cursing." She would eventually see the veracity of that statement, as the years went by.

"And you've read all of these books?"

"Of course not," she said. "They're all here because they are important."

I plucked one particular volume from a shelf and read from its jacket cover: *The Story of a Swiss Yodeler's Life with the Nomadic Tribes of Yemen.*

"This is an important book?" I asked.

"A book does not have to sell fourteen million copies to be important," she snapped back. Then she gave me one of those Frenchwoman looks. Chantal has radar that would make NORAD jealous. And in this case, it cut through me like an MRI, cross-sectioning my brain for instant analysis.

"That is what is stopping you, is it not?" she asked. "You think you need to impose great wealth upon yourself, or writing is a waste of time." Her English was still a little sketchy back then, but I got her meaning. "You write for the money and not for the beauty of the words, do you not?"

"I don't come from the same culture as you do," I replied, flustered by her ability to read my mind.

She then pointed to a couch, completely surrounded by bookshelves.

"That is your bed," she said simply. "It opens up."

"Thanks," I answered. "How long can I stay?"

THE POOR THING, if she had only known the consequences of not answering that question correctly, she would probably have said, Leave right now! But instead she simply replied, "That depends on how well you do your job."

So that's it? I thought to myself.

"I did not mean it that way," she said suddenly. Her radar was obviously turned up full blast.

"Then what job are you talking about?" I asked. "You want me to do a little work around the house? Like clean the terrace, maybe?"

"You will see," she replied. "Would you like some food from my mother for dinner?"

"Sure? What's on the menu?"

"A whole pigeon in a jar with mushrooms picked between the trees."

"Minus the feathers and feet and the lethal fungal poisons, I assume?" I was trying to be funny. It did not work.

"But before I go inside and heat it up," Chantal continued, "I want to show you something."

She pulled a disheveled bundle of papers out of nowhere and summarily thrust them into my hands. It looked like the rough draft of a children's book, with a whole bunch of English and French words, scribbled and then scratched out, both typed and handwritten.

"Welcome to France," she said simply.

"What is this?"

"A manuscript!" That Frenchwoman look again.

"But what am I supposed to do with it?"

"You speak English, do you not?" she asked.

"Not really," I replied. "I come from the Bronx."

She ignored my bad joke.

"And you are a writer, no?"

"Also in doubt."

"Then, stop doubting," she said. It was the first time — but not the last — that I heard that distinctive snap in her voice.

"This is one of the French children's books we are trying to present to an English publisher for distribution."

"You don't have translators at work?"

"The person we normally use is on vacation."

Big surprise! I thought to myself.

"But I have no experience," I said. "No credentials."

"Do you want to be a writer or not?"

I looked down at the layouts. I'd seen bigger messes while working as a copywriter on Madison Avenue, I can tell you that.

"It may take me some time."

"Then take it."

"So, let me get this straight. I can live here for a while and not worry about doing anything but write?"

"You may start right now," she said. "I will call you when the pigeon flesh is heated."

I STARED DOWN at the manuscript and then in the direction of the kitchen. Chantal was cooking some potatoes to go with the jarred pigeon and they smelled truly divine. Above the crackling sound of the potatoes frying, I also heard the pop of a cork being pulled out of a bottle of wine.

"Go out on the terrace and work out there, if you like,"

Chantal yelled from the kitchen. "And send your eyes toward the Eiffel Tower! It is about to illuminate itself."

It was still light outside for being so late at night, so I walked out onto the terrace and saw it: the tower's brown metal beams blanketed in a soft yellow hue. I spread the rough drafts on the same table on which I am writing this story today — and I shook my head in despair.

"This is hopeless!" I yelled.

"No, it is not," she yelled back from the kitchen. "After dinner, we will sit down and I will instruction you on what we need done."

AFTER DINNER, CHANTAL proceeded to give me my first "instructions" on how to bring her manuscript up to snuff. Schmuck that I was, despite being given this once-in-a-lifetime opportunity to be a writer in a land where I could not even spell out the words *Go to hell,* I looked down at all of those scribbles and drawings and . . . had absolutely no desire to work as a ghostwriter on some second-rate children's book. Of course, I feigned interest, occasionally assuming a pensive look, playing out the charade, as Chantal talked and I listened. Then she talked a little more and I listened even less. The phone rang, and after she was finished, she kept talking. She made some tea, we drank it, and she still kept talking. The night birds started chirping, and she still kept talking. In fact, not unlike people attending a French dinner party on a work night, I am sure that she would have kept on talking until the first light of dawn, had I not intervened.

I finally interrupted her monologue. "Chantal," I said.

"Sorry about all this, but I must kindly, politely, sympathetically, and graciously decline your generous offer."

I might as well have made a lot of whistling sounds through my nose or crossed my eyes a dozen times, because guess what? There was simply no way I was not going to do this. I was going to finish this manuscript and there would be not one more word about it. I would work hard. Never give up. And if it didn't work this first time, then there'd always be another. The subject was hereby closed. Chantal was right. She was always right. And more important, she definitely knew what was right for me. Then. Five years ago. Now. And for God knows how long? We had one more small disagreement over the subject (the first in a series of thousands over the next thirteen years), and as usual, I lost.

It was day seven of my new life in France. And writer or not, I was on my way.

My Day with Mr. D.

M Y DAY WITH Mr. D. in Paris was the best thing that happened to me when I was fifteen. I left my mother back in the Latin Quarter with the Vanderveers. I crossed to the Right Bank in a cab. The lobby of the Ritz Hotel where he stayed was drenched in a golden light. Mr. and Mrs. D. greeted me in the living room of a vast suite, Mrs. D. in a tapestry bergère, Mr. D. on his feet, Michelin Green Guide in hand. Mr. D. asked me to telephone the lobby for a phone number. The concierge on the other end of the phone dictated a long number to me, and I got the number right, realizing that the French have a different word for seventy than the Swiss. Mr. D. said, "I asked you to call because your French is better than mine." I lived off that idea for a long time, the idea that my French was better than Mr. D.'s and that I could be useful to him because of it.

Mr. D. and I said good-bye to Mrs. D. for the day and walked to the nearest Métro. Mr. D. bought a booklet of first-class tickets. It was my first time in the Métro and I hadn't known there were first- and second-class tickets. First class was empty. I was sure we were the only people in Paris who were riding first-class that day.

We saw a day student from the Collège du Léman at the Tomb of the Unknown Soldier. "He's with his parents," I thought, "and I'm with Mr. D." I looked at his parents with him, I looked at Mr. D. with me. There were so many tourists, I couldn't see the tomb. I didn't care about the tomb. We crossed the river to the Sainte-Chapelle. We stood still in its center. The stained glass windows turned the air around us a saintly blue. On the Left Bank of the river, we went to the art gallery whose phone number I had gotten for Mr. D. The owner greeted him enthusiastically in English. Mr. D. informed her that he was with me, a whiz in French. She was to speak to us only in French. After we had seen the painting he was considering adding to his collection, we crossed the street to a boutique favored by Louise and Mrs. D. Mr. D. said I could have whatever I wanted. I knew it was rude to want anything extravagant, so I chose a scarf. It was a *carré* (a small square), rather than a longer foulard, in gold and blue. We bounded toward the Jeu de Paume next, where the impressionist paintings used to be kept before they redid the Gare d'Orsay. Mr. D. was an indefatigable walker; he loved to walk in the woods and he loved to walk in cities even better. I could barely keep up with him, as he would walk and point and talk, like a guide. There was nothing he liked better than to show Paris to a young person for the first time.

We stood in front of Manet's *Olympia* in the Jeu de Paume.

"Look at that painting, what do you see?"

I saw a naked woman lying on a couch with her black maid standing behind her.

"A woman lying on her side with no clothes on and another woman in back of her, a maid, holding flowers."

"Now, look at the colors. What color is the couch?"

"White."

"Is it just one white?"

The painting had a zillion different kinds of white in it, beige, gray, snow, ivory. As soon as I began looking for all the different whites, the painting changed utterly. The picture itself dissolved, but the paint came alive and I could see the brushstrokes, see that a person had been there, working, to make the illusion.

Seeing the painting change like that before my eyes made me feel sharp-sighted; I felt I was getting to the substance of my vision, to the meaning of it. I attributed my new eyes to Mr. D. and also to the city of Paris, which seemed to be organized for looking. I had never been in a place where there was so much to observe: the benches, the wrought-iron balconies, the long cars that looked like bugs, the policemen with their huge caps, the food sold outdoors, bookstalls outside along the river. Everywhere I went, there was a new tableau to take in.

Mr. D. and his wife took me and my mother to dinner that night. He ordered a special soufflé for dessert that came out high in the waiter's hand; when I put my spoon in it, all the whites from the Manet painting came staring up at me, and I ate the truth and light of impressionism in my soufflé.

Parenting, French-Style

A NEW ZEALAND FRIEND, a mother of three, recently texted me: "I am in the park and just saw a French mother kick her son hard, then go on talking to her friends while he cried. What is wrong with these people?"

A few days before that, sitting in a café near the Luxembourg Gardens in Paris, which is unabashed baby central, with my (French) husband, I saw something even scarier. A tiny child, just walking, was trying to catch up with his chic and slender mother, who was furiously pushing the buggy deliberately too fast for the baby to get close to her.

The child was crying frantically, red in the face and holding up his tiny arms begging her to carry him. There was no way he could catch her. And she knew it. "Non, non, non," she screeched in a high-pitched voice. She strolled ahead faster, leaving the baby in the dust.

"Don't say it," my husband warned seconds before I nearly said, "What is wrong with these people?" Instead I muttered, "Well, that kid will be in therapy for the rest of his life."

I joke about these things, but it's not altogether funny. One of the toughest things I have had to get used to in an otherwise idyllic Paris is the huge gap between Anglo-Saxon (or Italian American in my case) parenting and parenting French-style. The French are certainly stricter. They shout more. They slap more. And they enforce manners.

But as a result, you find beautifully brought-up children, and many of my French friends who are parents will argue endlessly that instilling discipline and setting boundaries is the way to show the utmost love.

Dr. Caroline Thompson, a French child psychologist and family therapist who was educated in America until the age of eight and had a British father, agrees to some extent that children should not be completely indulged.

Although Thompson favors the early educational system in America, which is more loving than in France — where children start strict, all-day school at the age of three — she recently wrote a book entitled *La violence de l'amour* (the Violence of Love), about how dangerous it can be to make children the center of the universe.

She points out that in Anglo-Saxon cultures, certainly in American culture, children are generally thought of as being the center of the world, whereas in France, they are most certainly not.

It all starts from the cradle. In Britain, new mothers read the gentle and loving Penelope Leach; in America, they read the classic Dr. Spock. But in France, mothers read one of the gurus of French child development, Françoise Dolto. Dolto was an authoritarian who believed that children should be separate from their parents and live their own lives.

"Dr. Spock would be too lovey-dovey for a French parent,"

Thompson says with a laugh, adding that this all filters down to the educational system. "In France, it is not about blossoming. It's about the transmission of knowledge."

Which is not altogether a bad thing if you have spent time in America and observed the phenomenon of spoiled-rotten American children. I will never forget my husband's horror when some visiting Upper West Siders I barely knew arrived at one of our dinner parties with their uninvited nine-year-old son.

That would have been fine, except that Seth was one of these precocious Manhattan kids who had to sit at the table with the adults. He completely took over the evening, interrupting adults' conversations, and — to the delight of his besotted parents — performed a ten-minute hip-hop routine between courses.

In France, that would simply never have happened. The child would have been paraded out to say *bonsoir* and peck cheeks and then would have scurried back to his or her room to read or study.

"Children in France are seen but not heard," says one American friend, Katherine, who is a mother of two. "Except on the playground, where the parents don't get involved and then it becomes *Lord of the Flies*."

Because I am accosted with a version of French parenting every day — I live in front of the Luxembourg Gardens and see the endless parade of mommies — I do an informal survey of my Anglo girlfriends in Paris on their view of French parenting. The response is staggering.

One friend writes, "What do I think of French mothers? Mean, mean, mean." She tells of a mother of two whose youngest child was in the hospital for a week. When he was released, the family immediately left on a beach holiday, along with a nanny the baby had not met before.

The mother wanted to go to the beach and instructed the nanny to feed him. When he would not eat with the stranger, the mother sent him to bed hungry and screaming. He ate when he woke up, ravenous, and this time, he let the nanny feed him. "That will teach him," the mother said proudly. The boy was seventeen months old at the time. "This is a true story," my friend writes.

Another American, Mary, also the mother of two, blames it on the French educational system, which does not encourage creative interpretation. She also believes that child rearing has not progressed beyond the 1950s.

"What has always puzzled me is why generation after generation of Frenchwomen raise French girls to become Frenchwomen — bitchy, competitive, antifraternal, unsmiling, the preternatural *froide*-ness."

An English friend, Sophie, wrote of seeing a French child eating sand in the park. When she politely informed the mother, the woman — who was deep in a book — retorted, "Maybe she will get sick and it will be good for her. She will learn her lesson."

Sophie's explanation is that France has one of the highest percentages of working mothers in Europe. "I am amazed at how fast they dash back to work, leaving three-month-old babies in the crèche," she adds.

But other friends rushed to the French mother's defense. One Englishwoman, a mother of three who has lived in France for twenty years, said the hardest thing she had to get used to was how schools and hospitals shut out parents. "You leave your children there, and voilà!" she says. "You don't see them again."

But she explains that it is purely a cultural difference. "You see, they firmly believe in institutions. So if you take your kid to school or the hospital, you have no say in the matter. It's up to the teachers and doctors to decide what's best, not you.

"That is why you see children alone in the hospital all the time. The mothers aren't mean. They are just conditioned. It would do their heads in completely if they had to think out of the box."

An American friend, Susan, who grew up in Paris and is the mother of three boys, explained: "It's always shocking for Anglo-Saxons to hear the shrill 'Ça suffit!' that is the refrain of all French mothers. They speak with a sharpness that is alarming to the uninitiated."

However, Susan does not see their behavior as mean. "They think they are doing their children a favor, which is to civilize them. Teaching your children proper behavior from the earliest age is of almost moral importance."

She recalls taking her five-year-old son to the park and telling him repeatedly not to do something. An elderly woman was eavesdropping and suddenly reached over and pinched the boy's ear until he squealed. "Listen to your mother!" she said sternly, in French.

Susan was not offended. "I know she, and every other French grandmother, would think that is for the good of the child. Anglo-Saxons tend to see children as charmingly thick savages who can be taught manners in a superficial way. The French grasp the deeper meaning of civilized behavior as soon as they can speak, and drill it into them."

My son's godmother, who is French, also believes in discipline (though she is a highly loving and supportive mother and godmother). She says, "There is something called *l'heure de l'adulte*. That is when they go away and leave us alone." Children, she says, have to learn boundaries. "The big difference is that the French believe strongly in creating those divisions. And it works. Look how well behaved French children are, compared to American children."

I have to say, she has a point. When I see my six little French nieces and nephew, lined up neatly with braids, scrubbed freckled faces and pinafores, parroting, "Bonjour, tante Janine," and "Merci, tante Janine," and going off to their violin and piano lessons, I know she has a valid point.

But the hippie earth mother part of me still wonders about originality, creativity, and freethinking. (There is no such thing as an earth mother here; it is simply not chic.) I worry that all this repression and enforced manners will kill any creative drive.

But then I think about Seth, the kid from the Upper West Side who invaded my living room and destroyed my dinner party. On that note, I am very happy to live in France and follow the French model. Slightly.

Deal With It

THERE ARE NO tryouts in Paris kitchens. That American ritual of trailing another cook during the service just to see how things are done doesn't exist. It doesn't matter what your place is in the hierarchy of cooks, the process is the same. You're thrown in. Deal with it. A late delivery, bunched-up orders, a cook's cut hand — pretty much anything can slow a kitchen's pace and lead to an apoplectic, screaming *maître d'hôtel*. When you're a kitchen minion in Paris, you get used to going from calmly nursing an espresso at a nearby café to French bedlam with little if any transition. If you pull through it as a young person, you're a cook. If you pull through it as a foreigner, you're also a Parisian.

When I came to the role, there was a lot to simplify: child of expatriates, born in Spain, my childhood a messy jumble of countries. I grew up in a postromantic expatriate world where everyone had gotten over the idea of being Zelda Fitzgerald or Hemingway's Jake Barnes but had decided to stay on in Europe anyway. I have pictures of my parents hamming it up on the quays of the Île Saint-Louis under a gun gray Parisian sky in what I realize now was an attempt at reconciliation. Years later, Paris for me became the Gare d'Austerlitz, where I, like the

Moroccan workers heading home, started journeys in crowded trains that went down through France and then Spain. My father lived in Spain; my mother, in Ireland. As a teenager I often felt that this crowded station represented my own strange version of the innocuous transfer points where divorced parents pass a child between them. When I returned to Paris at nineteen after dropping out of Trinity College, Dublin, I was ready to stop.

The phrase "learning to cook in Paris" is so vague — I write it down without quite knowing what it means. Are you learning to cook when you buy your first knives at Dehillerin? Have you learned to cook when you're trusted to send out a dish? To me the decisive moment is not culinary at all; it's when the cooks accept you, with a quick *salut* and a handshake, as one among them. Kitchen crews everywhere develop unit cohesion, but in Paris they're battling not just the nightly onslaught but the demands of the city itself. Cooks live like outsiders in many of the arrondissements where they work. They cannot afford the seventh, eighth, sixteenth, or seventeenth, and they'll soon be priced out of the ninth and the fifteenth — even in the hinterlands behind Montparnasse. Thus the cooks of Paris start their days waiting not at Métro stations but at the platforms of RER stations, the train system that links the City of Light to its not so glamorous suburbs. In outlying towns like Créteil, people say they work *sur* Paris, "on" but not "in" Paris. The language chosen, hinting at distaste, describes their fraught relationship with the city. Meanwhile, to the inhabitants of the leafy seventh, sixteenth, and seventeenth arrondissements, towns like Créteil and Antony sound like the punch line to a joke.

Within the kitchen itself, the learning of cooking in Paris has a simple trajectory: you go from the cold stations to the hot ones. The arc may not be concluded in any one restaurant; in fact, it probably won't. Speed is important to them all, as is delicacy of movement: ladling too much vinaigrette can ruin a salad as quickly as burning shallots in a hot pan during a quick deglazing. But heat does add to the tension, increasing the opportunities for matters to head quickly south and for a young cook's nascent self-confidence to be wiped out by a torrent of invective. There are any number of people in a kitchen who can let you have it. The chef, of course, for whom it's a seigneurial right, but also the old-timer who has perfected the movements of his station and for whom you — a note-taking, flop-sweating mass — are an annoyance. Then there's the culinary up-and-comer who will be damned if you make him look bad in front of the chef, on whom he depends for a good word to get his next position.

The atmosphere is always conflicted. On the one hand, if you don't put out your food with dispatch, you'll be screamed at; on the other hand, you are one of them, you are included in the round of handshakes that all cooks must perform when they enter the kitchen. You learn to separate the worlds. Just because you received a "bordel de merde" rant for your abject failures at lunch doesn't mean you won't find yourself with that very person, playing pinball at the local café in the drawn-out hours between lunch and dinner — interminable hours in a Paris winter — when the city is heading home and you must gather energy from somewhere deep in your being to face a manic second shift.

I see them now with the affection that one has for those with whom one has gone through hard times. It was a camaraderie of the constantly exhausted. There was the Breton chef who, bellowing from the garde-manger station, ran the subterranean kitchen near Invalides and kept me close by his side, supervising my every move. That he was my superior was never in doubt (among my duties was splashing just enough white wine into his cup while preparing large trays of *maquereau au vin blanc*). And yet each evening we said good night at the Invalides RER station — where he started the journey toward his distant suburb — with the clipped "Salut" of equals.

I see Gaetan, the *commis* at the Michelin one-star in the sixteenth whose promotion depended on my not screwing up while under his supervision. We'd commiserate over staff meals such as roast rabbit heads (I kid you not) and a yogurt. This just before launching into preparing *suprême de volaille aux truffes*. One day, a crippling flu (which is pretty much what it would take) made him unable to come to work. I was thrown into the breach. When he returned, the chef told him that I'd managed to get out of my own way enough not to have the entire restaurant come to a logjam at the vegetable station, and Gaetan ribbed me for the next few days by calling me "chef."

For me the decision to leave Paris was certainly gradual, so gradual I wasn't even aware of it. If anything I was getting further and further into Paris. I was taking catering jobs in distant restaurants. I was the fill-in guy a chef could call. I had made the transition from being one of the many who are constantly descending on the city to being someone who could, in a pinch, handle a station and whom you could contact. The twist — it is the expatriate twist itself — is that you have to reach this level of familiarity with a place before you understand that it is not part of the future that awaits you.

After four years of cooking at various restaurants, I had finally reached *commis* at the meat station of one of them. I was not *chef de partie,* the person directly responsible, but it was still a huge responsibility. The dish we specialized in was a *salmis de pigeon,* and if French cooking is a story of great stocks, this dish defined it. The term *salmis* was borrowed, since classically it is a stewed pheasant preparation requiring a long cooking time. We instead took the pigeons from the oven, delicately lifted the breast meat off the carcass, and made an instant *salmis* sauce, hitting the bones with an intense brown chicken stock and giving it an additional gaminess with a ladle of hare stock. The sauce reduced on a high flame, received the requisite knob of butter and pinch of herbs, and was ready to be spooned over the plate.

We must have made that preparation forty times a night. I still think the chef was right to do it the time-consuming way he did. Preparing the sauce at the last minute allowed it to remain a bouillon, a good broth, one that was capable of evoking, if only distantly, simmered country roots. A finished sauce, heated to order or kept warm throughout the service, might have been more practical, but it would have sucked the lyricism out of the dish. So it was worth it. Not that I thought that as I waited for a train at the Argentine Métro station on the avenue de la Grande Armée, nor when, exhausted, my head bobbed against the glass window all the way to Bastille. I'd drag my legs up to the maid's room where I lived, tucked under the eaves of the building. In summer I'd crawl out the window and sunbathe on the slope of slate. Now it was winter. The vegetable oil above my camping stove was often solid from the cold. I guess it was on one of those spent nights when I took out the American passport I'd always kept and said to myself, "Why not?" It was as easy as that. An exhausted cook saying to himself, "It can't be harder than this over there."

During the next few weeks it was difficult. I was still shaking hands dutifully at the start and end of each day, but something had changed. I had made a decision to leave. I saw dishwashers who'd quickly cleared pans with food I'd burned before it was seen, and I realized just how they had saved me. I saw the young cooks with whom I'd worked in a new light. We were wiping down the kitchen after the week's last meal, and I understood that I owed them everything. They'd taken me in when they had no reason to; they'd allowed me into a world, to develop professionally, to figure things out with few questions asked. More than anything, I understood that to them this was not a phase; wherever I might be going after learning to cook in Paris, they would still be here.

I caught the train down to Spain to tell my father of my decision. He agreed it was the right one — he who had sailed out of Hoboken, New Jersey, in 1952 in a camel hair coat with enough money guaranteed by the GI Bill to see him through. Though I had an American passport, I didn't feel American. Nor did I feel Irish, Spanish, or French. I did feel like a cook, though. I was someone who was wrapping a pairing knife bought at Dehillerin in an apron and placing it in my suitcase. But more than that, I felt like a Parisian cook. Surviving in the crucible of the city's kitchens gave me the confidence to face whatever awaited me. I knew how to break down a recipe to an efficient series of movements, just as I knew that it was not my role to escalate an argument. In the years to come, it would serve me well to remember that a professional "Oui, chef" was the only acceptable reply to a chef's cries of "Bordel de merde!"

Two Paris Poems

On the Métro

On the métro, I have to ask a young woman to move the packages beside
     her to make room for me;
she's reading, her foot propped on the seat in front of her, and barely
     looks up as she pulls them to her.
I sit, take out my own book — Cioran, *The Temptation to Exist* — and no-
     tice her glancing up from hers
to take in the title of mine, and then, as Gombrowicz puts it, she "affirms
     herself physically," that is,
she's *present* in a way she hadn't been before; though she hasn't moved
     an inch, she's allowed herself
to come more sharply into focus, be more accessible to my sensual per-
     ception, so I can't help but remark
her strong figure and very tan skin — (how literally golden young women
     can look at the end of summer).
She leans back now, and as the train rocks and her arm brushes mine she
     doesn't pull it away;
she seems to be allowing our surfaces to unite: the fine hairs on both our
     forearms, sensitive, alive,
achingly alive, bring news of someone touched, someone sensed, and
     thus acknowledged, *known*.

I understand that in no way is she offering more than this, and in truth I
    have no desire for more,
but it's still enough for me to be taken by a surge, first of warmth then of
    something like its opposite:
a memory — a lovely girl I'd mooned for from afar, across the table from
    me in the library in school,
our feet I thought touching, touching even again, and then, with all I
    craved that touch to mean,
my having to realize it wasn't her flesh my flesh for that gleaming time
    had pressed, but a table leg.
The young woman today removes her arm now, stands, swaying against
    the lurch of the slowing train,
and crossing before me brushes my knee and does that thing again, as-
    serts her bodily being again,
(Gombrowicz again), then quickly moves to the door of the car and de-
    scends, not once looking back,
(to my relief not looking back), and I allow myself the thought that
    though I must be to her again
as senseless as that table of my youth, as wooden, as unfeeling, perhaps
    there was a moment I was not.

Racists

Vas en Afrique! Back to Africa! the butcher we used to patronize in the
    Rue Cadet market,
beside himself, shrieked at a black man in an argument the rest of the
    import of which I missed
but that made me anyway for three years walk an extra street to a shop of
    definitely lower quality

until I convinced myself that probably I'd misunderstood that other thing
and could come back.
Today another black man stopped, asking something that again I didn't
catch, and the butcher,
who at the moment was unloading his rotisserie, slipping the chickens
off their heavy spit,
as he answered — how get this right? — casually but accurately *brandished*
the still-hot metal,
so the other, whatever he was there for, had subtly to lean away a little, so
as not to flinch.

Understanding Chic

PARIS WAS MY first taste of a Latin country. I was thirteen and went with my godmother, Marigold Johnson, and her three teenage children. We traveled by car. I cannot remember crossing the channel — we were coming from England — but I do recall a noisy traffic jam caused by a motor bike accident. It was a hazy afternoon, our car windows were rolled down, and I was struck by the smell of baked baguettes wafting along the street, the feisty honking of cars, and a toddler with a blunt fringe catching my eye and slowly sucking on her lollipop. The Parisians were different, I quickly registered.

A FEW HOURS later, I poured water and shook sugar into my first *citron pressé*. The next morning, I found myself admiring the clipped lawns of the jardins du Luxembourg. Topping everything off was the discovery of school notebooks packed with cubed pages as opposed to lined ones. I remember gliding my hand down their brightly colored covers and liking the rainbowlike array they formed in my suitcase.

Ten days later, I returned to my family and became a Paris Bore. Every conversation became an occasion to slip in tales

from my Parisian adventure. Someone adult pointed out that
I had been to Paris in August and that "no one chic ever stays
there then." I refused to give the woman's remark much cre-
dence. Besides, what on earth was "chic"? Undaunted, I bounced
along in my enthusiasm. Paris was hard to fault. Unlike London of the mid-1970s, it basked in the beauty of tradition —
the ritual and order were an indication of that — and there was
a respect for vegetables. In shop windows, polished tomatoes
were lined up like jewels. French civic pride.

Visiting the château de Versailles, I briefly stepped on the
cordoned-off lawn, an easy enough mistake that had a shocking consequence. A Frenchman — not a guard — came forward and slapped me full in the face. Whatever prompted him
to *gifler* (slap) an ungainly teenager was his problem — but it
became briefly mine. I burst into quick, embarrassed tears.
My godmother quickly admonished him, as did the rest of
the family, a brave brood when tangled with. Apparently, we
all hugged afterward. I write "apparently" because I mentally
zapped this drama from start to finish, only to be reminded
of it thirty-three years later. (No doubt I did this because the
horrible man and his offending *gifle* did not fit into my perfect,
picture-postcard memories.)

In retrospect, I doubt whether the experience would have
put me off. Still, it might have prepared me for how tricky
the French can be. Am I suggesting that behind every French
person lies an unexpected slap? That would be unfair. But my
experience with the Parisians is that, mentally, there is a slap
instinct — mild in some, more fervent in others. Defensive, they
tend to attack. The briefest grasp of their city's history offers

reason for this: being besieged several times leaves its mark. Yet that very "slap instinct" is both the Parisians' strength and their weakness.

It also explains why Paris remains the fashion capital. Fashion, when exciting, is all about the shock of the new — the equivalent of a swift slap. And being chic can be viewed as a visual slap enforced by the wearer's character, taste, eye. It's being au courant and yet daring to be different.

When I announced my decision to move to Paris in 1989 — I was then living in New York — my acquaintances were surprisingly negative. Indeed, apart from my mother and my then boss Shelley Wanger, there was underlined outrage and a hint of resentment. It showed in a sequence of questions: Did I speak French? Where would I live? What would I do? I was well armed for all three. I had been taking lessons at the Alliance française, I had found an apartment in the Marais, and thanks to *Vogue*'s Anna Wintour, I had letters of introduction to all the top couture houses. Surely, this should have satisfied, but the mention of fashion led to their trump card. "Oh my God, but aren't you terrified?" I can still hear the feline malevolence to certain voices. "No, why should I be terrified?" I asked, already geared up by the energy of the upcoming move. "Because the women running those places are both terrifying and terrifyingly chic," was the gist of their answers.

I was too rebellious to be terrified. Besides, I knew about chic. Well, I could recognize it even if I could not yet personally express it, clotheswise. Antonia Fraser, my mother, helped matters. In the public eye and much photographed, she had a clear image of herself. Her cupboards were spare. "Endless choice confuses" was her style philosophy. She wore only dresses by

Jean Muir but was zany with jewelery, sporting prominent rings and necklaces, often made of lapis lazuli or coral. She believed in being different. Two of her girlfriends — Diana Phipps and Grace, Lady Dudley — also had strong, individualistic taste. Both were tall, both wore Saint Laurent, and although their styles were incomparable, whether they were wearing wool crepe, taffeta, or velvet, it always looked effortless. My mother and her two friends understood their bodies, were womanly, and brave: three essential ingredients in achieving chic. Yet it was from attending a convent school that I really learned the most.

I thought then, and continue to think, that nothing is as elegant as a nun's habit. On a daily level, the sacred sisters instilled the importance of discipline, from learning to make beds with hospital corners to collecting that week's laundry in designated hours — or facing the consequences. The nuns were tough and unforgiving about sloppy behavior. So are Parisians. The sacred sisters' rules and regulations were perfect preparation for braving the City of Light.

I also possessed personal pluck. After I moved here, a famous director, a playboy ex-boyfriend, and an heiress girlfriend all separately decided to fly in and treat me to expensive restaurants in order to give his or her version of the following advice: "You're penniless and will never survive in Paris." I went from being surprised to being hurt to gratefully remembering something my late father used to say: "An adventurous spirit tends to irk others."

Fortunately, Parisians find an adventurous spirit intriguing. In general, they are too canny or conventional to be fearless themselves, but they do notice courage. Just as they dismiss someone who apologizes too often as being victimlike, they are quietly amused by someone with character who doubts their rules and dares to do otherwise. Not that they are big at handing out bravos — power animals, they recognize the need to withhold — but when dealing with foreigners, they respect authenticity. They will admire someone more for being authentic than for playing at being Parisian.

STILL, THEY ARE deeply unwelcoming. Or politely put, they are born cynics who lack an Anglo-Saxon's curiosity about strangers. On that level, I was not remotely prepared for moving to the City of Light. I had jumped from London to Los Angeles with great ease and, obviously, with even greater ease when leaving the West Coast for the East. But Paris, it paralyzed. The daily humiliations I encountered until I realized that the accepted protocol is to bite back! How the endless *non*s morph into a honeyed *oui* when you stand your ground! And learning to accept the acerbic humor even if it stings! Imagine asking a middle-aged man for directions — it was my very first day — and being served with, "Mademoiselle, do I look like a map?"

Although accustomed to licking my wounds in private, I never felt compelled to pack it all in and leave. Instead, it made me determined to dig in my heels further. To win over the chic savages was impossible, I reckoned. But to find a comfortable even ground remained a goal.

OF COURSE, I had been warned — "Paris is great apart from the people" and other tired sayings. I was determined to see otherwise. Why be negative about a race when you are attempting to live alongside it? Besides, I had held a good opinion of the French since primary school. Traumatized by being the only nonacademic sibling in a family of high achievers, I was wary of all my teachers apart from two women — both French and called mademoiselle. One, who taught me from the age of five, cast me as the huntsman in a school production of *Snow White* because I had "such a kind heart" (said with an affectionate ruffle of my mousy brown hair).

The second entered my life when I was eleven. She had almond-shaped eyes, a broad smile, and in the warmer months favored a pair of thick gold slave bracelets pushed up high on her toned arms. Considering she taught in a convent, she had quite a racy reputation. The *on-dit* was that she had slept with a woman. Or was it a threesome? The details were irrelevant. Mademoiselle was above reproach in both the nuns' and pupils' eyes — appreciated for her excellence in the classroom and her personal charm and flair in the school's drafty corridors. Whether she was wearing a skirt or a dress, there was an appealing urgency to her presence; her firm limbs seemed to dance with each step.

Were her clothes chic? I recall earth tones and the occasional imperial purple or royal blue. They made less of an impression than the nuns' habits, which were a case of holy couture, a lesson in precision. There was the immaculate fit of the starched white wimple, the flowing black veil firmly pinned on either side, the short, capelike bib covering the chest, the creaseless waistband, the flawless pleats, the large button at the back that allowed the nun to hook up her skirt when major movement was required.

The nuns' appearance trained my eye to the fall of fabric, to the many shades of black, and to the elegance of a crisp white cotton collar and cuff set against a somber shade.

When I worked in the Chanel studio — it was my first professional job in Paris — I had little idea that Gabrielle "Coco" Chanel, the fashion house's founder, had been convent trained. Thinking back, it makes perfect sense and explains why the color palette and air of devotion at work in this couture house felt dimly familiar. In the studio, during sessions with Karl Lagerfeld, my fellow assistants, and the seamstresses from the ateliers, I gleaned endless tips about fit and accessories, both key tools behind gaining chic. Yet in spite of this, and unlike a heroine from a Nancy Mitford or Diane Johnson novel, I did not leave transformed.

There were many reasons, but the main one had to do with lacking attitude and forgetting that chic lies within. I also did what no self-respecting Parisian does: I focused on my shortcomings and suffered from an "If only I lost x pounds" syndrome. Desperately, I aimed to please. I sought out the opinions of people who knew the contours of my body less well than I. My style lacked fluidity. Dressing for me was a potluck scramble. I had a mild case of style schizophrenia: there were accomplished hits, there were dowdy misses, but nothing quite gelled or clicked. It was only when I was commissioned by the British version of the fashion magazine *Marie Claire* to write a meat-and-potatoes-type article on how chic Parisians were buying middle-range labels that I had my chic watershed and found the right key for my particular lock.

Suddenly, I could see the forest for the trees. It had only taken me nineteen years! For the first time, I observed how elegant Parisians *d'un certain âge* shopped. It was equivalent to watching a military operation in action, with the women playing sergeant major and casting the racks of clothes as soldiers on parade. They tried on T-shirts as seriously as jackets. Sour disapproval appeared on their faces when a skirt did not fit; they were always convinced that it was the fault of the design as opposed to their bodies.

They refused to get lost in the fuzz of fashion. Ignoring the advice of shop assistants, they stared long and hard in the mirror. The concentration and considerable time they took, I realized, was not about vanity. It was an essential part of a complicated process in which they worked out if they needed an item, if it did them justice, and more. Often a good half hour would go by before they simply handed the garment back. Such behavior might be deemed thoughtless but, actually, these women were only interested in being thoughtful to themselves. Feet squarely placed in the present, they bought what they would wear immediately. Flights of fashion fantasy were clipped midair as opposed to being purchased, cast aside, and eventually given away.

In short, the "slap" was there in full force — particularly in their ability to resist the gushing compliments of the shop assistants. I could not help admiring how directed they were. Their decisions seemed to be guided by an inner chic compass — the Parisian's secret weapon! They never lost sight of themselves, were curious about clothes, yet remained liberated from their constraints. And they never indulged in victim behavior. They were happy to move forward with a different designer or label — but only if it showed them to maximum advantage.

My favorite discovery from all my hours of changing-room Nosey Parker behavior was in recognizing how much chic is personality based. Since chic forgives flaws and favors the positive, size turns out to be irrelevant. The secret to acquiring chic, I learned, is to correct negative thinking. The overall message? All is possible with strength of character and a little practice. Chic demands, above all, patience and discipline. I have learned from living in Paris not to count on miracles but to depend on both those elements to make things work.

JULIE LACOSTE

It's My Home, That's All

Sunday, November 23, 2008

When I began this blog last September, it was just to describe what the three of us were living from one day to the next. I originally planned to send a letter each week to Daniel Vaillant [mayor of Paris's eighteenth arrondissement] to describe to him in concrete terms what it's like to be homeless, because I had the impression that, at the mayor's office, they simply had no idea. And then I told myself that this exchange of letters . . . would end up in a pile of files. I thought that [by sending them in quantity] I would be more likely to receive an answer from the mayor's office . . . It was my brother who suggested that I write a blog about my situation. I hesitated, I wasn't sure that I wanted everyone to read my life . . . And I couldn't at all see how people would even come across it . . . I was far from imagining the scope it would assume!

I have to say that I've felt really beside myself in these last days. I needed to step back a bit. I received so many messages of support, suggestions, offers of help, advice, encouragement! People have offered temporary shelter, help with moving, little tips to make the children feel good, gifts of clothing. People have even offered to take care of the children! People have written to me from all over the world, men and women from every social class, parents or nonparents, former homeless people, grandfathers and grandmothers, students, even adolescents who have said, "I'm only twelve years old but I find it revolting [that you can't find affordable housing]." I would really like to be able to thank all of you. It's incredible that so many people are touched by our circumstances. You can't imagine how comforting it is to know that we are not all alone!

I also received a lot of other offers from the press, radio, and television. For now, I'd prefer not to follow up. My priority right now is to find a place to live and to take care of my children. I began this blog with that urgent goal and I'm going to continue, but I don't have time to do more than that, and I don't want to expose us [to the public eye] any further. Some people wanted to make me into a kind of oracle for the homeless. But I don't see myself in this role. I don't have the soul of a spokesperson, that's not me at all. Of course, I would like what's going on now to be useful to those who, like us, need a roof. But everything I can do, I'm doing through this blog. A few publishers have even suggested that I write a book! That really made me laugh — it's a bit much.

On the other hand, I did agree to meet a journalist from a show called *Arrêt sur images*, which airs on the Internet, but it was for a written article that appeared on their site. Their approach is different. The article talks of the solidarity that was created by the "blogging mothers" and attempts to trace how that movement was formed. I swear I was interested in understanding it myself! What was funny was that the journalist found the first person to link my blog to hers (called *La mare enchantée*), and it turns out that I know her very well, but she hadn't let me know what she was up to. If this turns out to be true, then everything has happened because of her . . .

I also saw that there has been some debate on that blog and apparently elsewhere. I suspect that this is inevitable when one is the subject of an article that's at once personal and public. I don't need to respond to this often badly informed criticism, but I do want to clarify two or three things that might have been ambiguous in the article about us in *Le Monde.*

First of all, the article leads you to believe that I had a "job" in Bordeaux that I had left to come to Paris. In reality, I was training at a stable, and we had one week of school for every two weeks of internship. I worked like this in the stables for four years without being paid. When I left Bordeaux, ten years ago now, it was at the end of my training and I had no work. When I arrived in Paris, I began to earn a living doing part-time jobs.

In addition, when it comes to Madiop, the father of my children, I don't want people to think that he's absent, negligent, or irresponsible. We are separated but we remain close and we respect each other a lot. He's not able to help us financially at the moment, but whenever he can, he's there for the children. I sometimes leave work late, and he's the one who goes to pick up Jules at school and Orphée at preschool, and he cares for them regularly in the evening.

Finally, I want to answer the many people who advise me to leave Paris for the suburbs or the provinces. If I don't do it, it's not out of stubbornness. It's that it's out of the question: My whole life is here. My work is here, the father of my children is here, my brother is here, my friends are here, Jules's school is here, all of his friends are here, Orphée's preschool is here . . .

If I leave Paris, I'll have nothing left. I want to stay in Paris because now it's my home, that's all. I don't want it to be a luxury reserved for rich people. I think that everyone should be free to live where they want, no matter what their income might be.

I see that Mr. Vaillant left a comment on my blog on Thursday evening! I thank him a lot for this answer, which I read attentively. I have no doubt that he and his team are doing their best to solve the problem of housing in the eighteenth arrondissement. I want to assure him that I never thought that all this publicity would bring me subsidized housing right away. It would be too easy if you had only to be in a newspaper for everything to fall into place!

I'm not asking for favored treatment. I'm very conscious of how many urgent problems the mayor's office must have, but there is a real problem here and I'm part of it.

If I can give my opinion, I find it depressing that politicians always answer with, "We can't do any more . . ." I don't know what politicians would have to do to solve the housing problem, but it's up to them to know, not me! If they agree that it's not right that dozens of families live in the street, if they agree that cases like ours aren't isolated ones but add up to a real social problem, then it's their job to find solutions, no?

Mr. Vaillant, you're certainly right to remember that rules are rules and that they're the same for everyone. I very much agree. But don't forget that you're the one who makes the rules! It's your responsibility to decide to build more subsidized housing, to decide if it's better to give it to the poorest people or to the middle class, to decide if people whose incomes are above the set limits should still be allowed to live in housing projects or if there should be more movement . . . I understand it when my social worker tells me he can't do anything more, because I know that his ability to act is limited by choices that have been made by elected officials. But you, you should not be able to say such a thing because, as a politician, it's your job to find solutions to problems, no? It's difficult, I'm sure, but it's your job and you've chosen it.

My own job, at my low level, is to explain the situation to you so that you can better understand how homeless people live and you can better respond to their problems. That's why I began this blog. Others react differently, they agitate or demonstrate; I do what I can with this blog. Even if it changes the politics of housing slightly, it won't have served for nothing.

As for emergency accommodations, such as hotels, it's true that I didn't accept this help from social services. Mr. Kossi, to whom I was assigned, also insisted on this, but hotels are very expensive, even with financial assistance. You can't live in one from day to day the way you can in an apartment (you can't cook, the toilets are often in the hallway . . .). And I know so many families that have been in them for years . . .

For the moment, I've had no news about project housing, and life is continuing as it was.

On Monday, I finally found a free moment to go to the basement storage area where Jules's outgrown clothes, which I'd like to use for Orphée, are stored. I was totally happy when I got there. I overcame my phobia of the dark to find the light at the end of the basement, then opened the door that I'd last closed several months before. I'd never been back since and didn't remember how we had arranged things inside. It was a veritable Tetris in 3-D! Everything was piled up from floor to ceiling—I hadn't imagined when I stored these things that I might need to take just a few at once — with the result that I didn't find anything. I closed the door, turned out the light, and left with some bitterness. That evening, when I told Emmanuelle of my disappointment, she immediately got up, went to a closet, and took out lots of clothes that had belonged to her daughters, were now too small, and could also work well for boys!

We didn't have to move last weekend and, suddenly, we could enjoy our days. We went to the park to meet friends, and since our children are the same age, and since they're little guys, they played soccer. It may seem boring, but these are just moments of joy.

We're leaving Emmanuelle's apartment in several days. I'm very grateful to her, not just for her welcoming attitude, but because we really got to know each other well. She and her daughters didn't go away on vacation, finally. Léah was very sick and in no condition to travel. As a result, we spent a lot of time together. The advantage of living through difficult times is that it makes you stronger and you meet amazing people.

This time, I'm going to sublet an apartment for a month. We're going to stay in the neighborhood one more time, between the jardin d'Éole and rue Marx Dormoy. I hope that this will be the last, that afterward we'll have an apartment of our own.

Translated from the French by Penelope Rowlands

Just Another American

IN FRANCE, I was liberated from the Vassar girl/project girl conflict. No one judged me on specifics, and I had nothing to prove. The French saw me as just another American, though I didn't see myself that way at all. I viewed Americans as white patriots in "Love It or Leave It" T-shirts, with a flag on their lawns, who didn't want me in school with their children. I was black, period. The French drew no such distinctions, which meant I no longer had to worry about making *African Americans* look good. Or bad. Whatever I did was attributed to Americanness, not blackness. What a switch — a black person with the power to make white people look bad. Given how negatively the American media routinely portrayed us, I was tempted. School began in October. I took language classes with foreigners at the Alliance française and literature courses with the French at the Sorbonne. The French system of instruction seemed rigid and formal after the fluidity of Vassar. At the Sorbonne, a professor lectured at a podium while students feverishly took notes. No first names, no class participation, no give-and-take. The weekly discussion groups held in smaller classrooms were slightly more relaxed, but I found the Gauloises-laden air toxic.

I enjoyed moving about in a big city, and the bustle and energy of Paris reminded me of Manhattan. The similarity stopped there. The beauty of the City of Light's gently curved wrought-iron balconies and sculpture-studded gardens far surpassed New York's glass-and-steel chaos. Over time, I began feeling more comfortable exploring my own and nearby arrondissements but didn't dare venture much farther for fear of encounters of the French kind. Such as the newspaper vendor who flew into a rage when I politely asked directions. All I understood from the stream of invective he spewed my way was: "They come here and can't even speak the language." Or the charming *pâtissière* who tried to sell me seven croissants when I'd only asked for one. She wrapped one as I was pulling out my francs. Then she wrapped another, and then another. "Non, non! Un! Un suh!!" She sneered, "Vous avez dit sept, mademoiselle!" then mumbled to herself, "Ah, mais ça, alors . . . ça, c'est chiant." Exuding contempt as only the French can, she shoved one croissant across the counter and overcharged me.

Rather than interact with the French, I preferred wandering the wide, shaded walkways of the Luxembourg Gardens, following the narrow streets of the Latin Quarter, and climbing the stone steps inside Notre-Dame to take in, alongside ancient gargoyles, the low aerial view of Paris.

After classes, we did the French thing and hung out in cafés over cups of *chocolat chaud* and *croque-monsieur* sandwiches. Before departing New York, the program director lectured us about our status as "honorary ambassadors of goodwill for the United States." She had the wrong diplomats. Our gang was always true to stereotype: haughty Americans with appalling accents and boisterous behavior. Outlandish in purple plastic sunglasses and her grandmother's fake fur, Nikki was a scourge on the French, and the rest of us loved her for it. "Garçon! Garçon!" she commanded, waving impatiently. "Doo chocolaz, see voo pleeze." Her French accent usually evoked a look of incomprehension in the garçon ranks. "The French are so backward — they don't even understand their own language! *Doo, misshur, doo. Comprende? Un, doo, twa? Doo.*" Exasperated, she'd hold up two fingers. She forbade tipping. "Don't leave that bastard anything. Look how long it took us to get service. He sees niggers sitting at a table and walks the other way. Tip, my ass!"

Travel was rarely without incident. If Nikki was sitting in their special designated area, the elderly, disabled, and war veterans would just have to stand. "My ancestors already made the necessary sacrifices," she said. She was fearless, daring even to tangle with that most daunting class of Parisians: old Frenchwomen. One elderly madame made the mistake of snarling when Nikki refused to give up her seat on a crowded bus. Hunched under a black shawl, the woman let loose a flood of French insults. Nikki was nonplussed.

"Do you be-*lieve* this shit! She's gonna *make* me get up and give her my seat. *Madame,* you need to take your *derrière* elsewhere, and *vite!*" They stared each other down, Nikki seated, Madame standing, until our stop arrived. The cantankerous old Frenchwoman was a sacrificial lamb made to pay for all the daily slights and insults inflicted on American students. Our friends cheered Nikki's American diplomacy. As for school, Nikki was notorious, a wild woman among hardworking drones. Despite cutting classes whenever she wanted and taking off a month to spend with her boyfriend, she aced her

"Sciences-Po" exams, graduated from Yale, earned a master's at Johns Hopkins, and became a banker.

I also met Francesca, the daughter of an Egyptian father and an Italian mother, who had been raised in upper-class London. Francesca resembled a light-skinned black American and was tormented by her yearning to have blond hair and blue eyes. "All the boys I liked in boarding school preferred the blond girls," Francesca complained in her very English accent. "I wish they could see that inside I *am* a blue-eyed blond." I knew few mixed-race people and was moved by her candor and obvious suffering. My sympathetic words failed to console, however, and Francesca agonized all year about her "cruel fate."

She was much more helpful to me than I was to her. Her father had come to Paris on business and wanted to take Francesca and a couple of her friends to dinner. I panicked when she invited me. The only "restaurants" I'd been in up to that point were pizza shops and Chinese fast-food places. A wealthy businessman, Mr. Rahkla had made reservations in a fancy seventh arrondissement restaurant. "Suppose I mess up," I asked, "or use the wrong silverware?" "Just do everything I do," she said. At dinner, I concentrated on Francesca's every move as she worked her way from the outside in, through a row of shiny cutlery. Intimidated by everything, from the way the garçon leaned toward me to take my order to the enormous cloth napkin bunched up on my lap, I participated little in the conversation. But other than momentarily forgetting myself and asking in English, "Do you have soda?" I did all right that evening, although I barely remember the food. Francesca's simple lesson would serve me well years later as I made the rounds, as a Paris resident, of innumerable French restaurants, fancy and otherwise.

Winter brought gray clouds and wrapped the city in cold. It took that long for me to learn, after being scolded in first class by a Métro agent glaring at my second-class ticket, that there were two classes in the Paris subway cars. And that, no matter how hard you stared, the car door would not open automatically. Language progress was just as slow. I had made some improvement, but my questionable grammar, child's vocabulary, and ringing American accent still caused the natives to flinch. My American friends were fun, but they weren't going to help me learn to speak French. Only the French could do that, but the French girls in the *foyer* limited conversation to a polite "Bonjour" as they rushed down the corridor. I had the impression that we *américaines* were considered vaguely corrupt and certainly corrupting, a little too independent and tomboyish by French standards of femininity. Or maybe they avoided us because struggling through the awful noise of our butchered French was simply too painful. For whatever reason, by the end of the year not one of the four Americans living in the residence had developed a friendship with a French European. Francophones who were not European were much more open.

At dinner one evening, I glimpsed the top of a tall Afro leaving the refectory. I didn't know there were any other black people in the residence and was intrigued by the dark-skinned young woman retreating with a tray of food. The next time I saw her slipping out with her dinner, I said, "Bonsoir." Her friendliness surprised me; she invited me to drop by her room anytime. Her name was packed with syllables — Myrianne Montlouis-Calixte — and she was from Martinique, a place I hadn't heard of, and was in Paris studying math. She spoke almost no English and my French was in its infancy, but we managed to communicate. Appearances notwithstanding, Myrianne wasn't antisocial, just anti-French. She found Parisians as cold and gray as the city, and missed her island home.

Through my new friend, I discovered an entire community of *antillaises* from the West Indian bourgeoisie tucked away in the residence and was invited to some of their social gatherings outside the *foyer*. These girls from Guadeloupe and Martinique ate alone or in each other's rooms. They were elated to meet an African American and bombarded me with questions about racism, Harlem, black entertainers, and anything that touched upon the lives of black people in "America." They giggled at my French and laughed outright when I attempted to explain that I was black, not American. *"Mais,* Jeannette, you are so ver-ry *américaine,"* said Marie, who spoke a little English. She said I looked American, dressed American, and walked like an American.

I was curious about their hostile attitude toward the Paris-born *antillaise,* who took her meals with French friends and described herself as *française*. They said the French didn't accept them as equals; therefore, French West Indians should refuse to claim a French identity. Even more annoying to them was Binta, a twenty-year-old Senegalese married to a much older French businessman. The relationship incensed the West Indians, and the framed photo of her husband that Binta kept on a bedside nightstand did little to improve her standing. Binta certainly was a special case. Just before my return to the United States, she begged me to send her some American skin-lightening cream. "I want to be light-skinned and beautiful like Diana Ross and Donna Summer." These and other cross-cultural friendships were eye-opening: while African

Americans continued to reel from the destructive legacy of slavery and racism, people of color worldwide struggled with their own forms of racial turmoil. I realized that the social and psychological effects of racism transcended national borders. Other friends I made that year were equally fascinating. Much of my time was spent with Linda and Ernie, Indonesian twins who were classically trained pianists. The three of us had long conversations in each other's rooms and were sometimes joined by Ike, also Indonesian. Ike's father had named her after his hero, President Eisenhower. I was also very close to Wisdom, a gorgeous African from Togo whose dream in life was to move to Colorado and "live like an American." His father had given Wisdom's four brothers names that were just as remarkable: Peace, Light, Love, and Might. There were times in Paris when I felt as if my brain could barely process the wealth of new impressions, surprising names, and puzzling accents.

During spring break I traveled to the walled town of Saint-Malo in Brittany. I explored the ramparts, cruised around on a rented Mobylette pretending to be a member of Hell's Angels, and, at low tide, ventured out by foot to Grand Bé Island to visit the tomb of Chateaubriand. By year's end, I had visited Martinique, fallen in love with French literature, and read everything available on the experiences of African Americans in Paris; no one claimed France was perfect, but many African Americans saw it as a haven from racism. My greatest accomplishment, however, was that I had learned to speak good French, which couldn't be said of the American students who had continued through the year to huddle together in cafés

Senior year, I returned to Vassar with a stack of French records and an obsession with Paris. I'd also fallen head over heels for a teenager from Martinique, but the long-distance relationship didn't survive the voyage across the Atlantic. I kept French as my major, and the year passed in a flurry of term papers, thesis research, and preparations for graduation. Unable to come up with a feasible plan for my future, I applied to graduate school in French literature as well as to law school, in the hope that fate would make the decision I couldn't. No such luck. I was admitted to both. Unable to decide one way or the other, I enrolled in an NYU master's degree program in France and deferred admission to Cornell Law School until the following September. All I wanted was more of Paris; real life, with its dreary careerism, could wait a year.

Graduation day sparkled with flashbulbs and grins. The French department gave me an achievement award. Ernest had also successfully completed four years — in prison — and had been paroled; we posed for photos and called ourselves "The Graduates." I was a project girl *and* a Vassar girl now, and glad to be both. A bright sun slowly crossed campus, pulling with it light and shadow, just as I had done.

Toward a Politics of Quality of Life

THERE WAS A book that I wanted to write, during the nearly six years that I spent in France, called *The Tyranny of Seduction*.

I had become convinced that Frenchwomen were on the Wrong Track — obsessed with their looks, preoccupied by their men, mired in a perpetual game of kittenish femininity. They were willing participants, it seemed to me, in a culture that made a fetish of sexual difference, with women's part of *différence* being a constellation of outdated ideas that sapped their brains and spirits and ultimately made them incapable of (indeed, unfit for) equality.

My sense of this was confirmed in large part by the French media. For that was an era of aggressive chest beating in France about men being men and women being women, all irresistibly attracted to one another. And in so being, they guaranteed a degree of social harmony that, the pundits said, was utterly lacking in the United States, where a virulent strain of feminism had turned women into wannabe men, effectively ruining relations between the sexes.

Even French feminists shared this view. "We want to keep the freedom to be seduced — and to seduce," wrote the feminist

philosopher (and wife of the French prime minister) Sylviane
Agacinski, as she argued against the "politically correct" Amer-
ican model of gender relations in her 1998 book, *Sexual Politics*.
"There will never be a war of the sexes in France."

It seemed to Agacinski, as to many other European feminists,
that by embracing a public image of gender-neutral egalitarian-
ism, American women had cut themselves off from the perks
of being female — good maternity leave, for example. And even
from the little, politically incorrect joys of life — doors being
held, a chance to be treated, in private life, at least, with a pleasant, noncompetitive gallantry.

In other words, American women were living dogs' lives.

While I lived in Paris, I persisted in thinking otherwise.
Sure, I discovered, when I had my first baby there, life with a
child was easy. The social protections were fantastic, even for
a foreigner. A five-day hospital stay, tax breaks to help pay for
a nanny, wonderful part-time preschool starting at age sixteen
months, all underwritten by government funds. Some of my
French friends, who were fully covered by the system, had even
better perks: six-month paid maternity leaves, government sub-
sidies, the right to work a four-day week.

But as a reporter for *Newsweek* specializing in women's issues, I also saw a dark side to these special privileges: a workplace culture with pervasive sexual harassment — after all, if
men were men and women were women, you couldn't stop the
"attraction" between them; and near-institutional sex discrimi-
nation, as employers seized upon the costs and constraints of
the country's protective laws to avoid hiring women of child-
bearing age. And how, I reasoned, could it be otherwise? If
women wore their sexuality like a banner, in public as well

as in private, it was only natural that they would bring upon themselves all the reactions that their sexuality generates: age-old prejudices, intolerance, hostility. By playing the femininity card, Frenchwomen had mired themselves in the confines of traditional sexism.

I was particularly convinced of this in 2000, when the French passed a new "parity" law intended to encourage a fifty-fifty split of elected posts between men and women. This was promoted partly on the grounds that women, being more concrete in their thinking, more honest, cooperative, and down-to-earth than men, would change the way France is governed. This initiative, which was put to the test for the first time in municipal elections in 2001, brought voters candidate lists that were 50 percent female. It also brought an onslaught of Minnie Mouse candidates — unschooled, unprepared, unable in any real way to govern. Like Sabine Fettu, a conservative candidate for city council in the Paris suburb of Courbevoie and a self-described schmoozer, who campaigned in a fur coat urging other women candidates to dress appealingly and went around spouting, "We're all products. We'll do anything to make a sale."

This was not what I had associated with women's equality. As an American girl of the 1970s, as a feminist coming of age in the 1980s, I was a devotee of the girls-can-do-anything school — a socialization that rested on the idea that, not only was biology not destiny, it was largely irrelevant. And I truly believed, as I gazed back at my country from France, that American feminists had managed to secure for American women a sex-free public space in which they could operate with dignity as people first and women second.

And so, when a French phone salesman tried to sell me a junky, light blue "feminine" cell phone, or when a French source suggested that I'd get better interviews if I were less direct and more "feminine" in my approach, I felt a shiver of superiority. "I am an American," I told the phone salesman, as though this meant that as a woman, I had risen to a higher sphere of personhood. It was the closest thing to nationalism that I felt in those years abroad.

It's very easy, when you're an expatriate, to idealize your homeland and project onto it all the virtues lacking in your host country. Especially when your thoughts of home are supplied by CNN and the movies you see on the Champs-Élysées. My years in France coincided with the era of Janet Reno and Hillary Rodham Clinton and Ruth Bader Ginsburg. Of Madeleine Albright and Christiane Amanpour. Of *G.I. Jane* and a kickboxing Ashley Judd and a black-belt René Russo playing a character who can break heads while pregnant, and a whole slew of new female action heroes looking fabulous as they ran around with walkie-talkies and guns.

I would watch these American Amazons and thrill to the virile virtues they projected. I would leave the theater and see the Frenchwomen lighting their cigarettes, tugging on their male companions' arms, and pouting their way into the night, and I'd think: God bless America. We're doing something right.

And then I moved back to the United States.

My family and I settled in Washington and I started casting about for work. I met with an older woman who worked for a female politician. I casually asked if there might be any kind of writing I could do on the Hill. "That's not for you," she said. "That's for a young person, without children."

I made some interested noises about working for a magazine. "You wouldn't want to," I was told. "None of us have children."

I had moved to France as a childless twenty-nine-year-old. I came back to America a mother of two. And this was an eye-opener.

American women, I found, weren't more evolved than Frenchwomen. If anything, they were caught in sex roles more traditional than those I had seen in France. Suddenly, the horizon seemed lower, for me and my peers — who, quite honestly, really did seem to be leading dogs' lives.

THE STAY-AT-HOME MOMS had no time of their own. They were on an infernal treadmill: school and play dates and soccer and violin and gymnastics and ballet and tutoring. Mommy and Me and volunteering, with do-gooder meetings running into the night. And topping it all off, a mental chorus of admonition, running in their minds like the drone of NPR in their minivans: Did anyone realize how hard they were working? Did anyone realize they still had a brain? Did anyone appreciate the time they were giving? Did anyone care about what they had to say?

This übermomming represented a level of selflessness that would have been considered downright neurotic in France. No woman with a family life, the thinking would have run (once the laughter subsided), no woman who wanted to preserve her family life (which, after all, was anchored around her husband), would be out doing children's activities all day, let alone at night.

As for the working mothers I got to know in America: They looked tired and harried. And adding to their stress was their own background noise, the media-fed dirge of guilt: Were they doing the right thing with their lives? Had they made the right choices? Were their children well taken care of? Should they be working less, differently, not at all? Were they really good enough mothers?

This level of guilt was something I had never come across in France, where I had worked since my first child was four months old. Indeed, I had never, in the many work-family conversations I had had with French friends or in interviews, even heard the word "guilt." It wasn't in the air. Had I expressed it, it would have sounded, once again, like sheer neurosis. Work was seen as an essential component of modern motherhood, a component of good motherhood, in fact, because it was something that helped women feel happy and whole.

Particularly odd was how readily my American peers accepted all their stress and guilt as a natural consequence of motherhood. It didn't seem to dawn on anyone that there could be another way.

I almost felt as if I had stepped into a time warp. It was as though we were still caught in a 1970s-era discussion about women's lib, still living in a time when women felt the need to debate whether or not they should work. Still ignoring utterly the facts that the bad, old-fashioned French so heartily embraced: that the vast majority of women do work, that work is actually a good thing for them and their families, and that it is something that need not be experienced as unduly stressful or guilt-provoking or a sacrifice.

It seems to me that the French, where mothers are concerned, have wedded their society's belief in *différence* to a realistic and humane view of modern women's lives. We Americans, on the other hand, have wedded an abstract belief in equal opportunity to punitive notions of women's "choice" and women's "compromises." The result is that once children come into the picture, women retain the right to compete in the marketplace but lose the right to any kind of decent quality of life. Or as Sophie L'Hélias, a French businesswoman who lived and worked in America for the better part of a decade, once put it to me: "It's much more difficult to have a balanced life here. The equation is more complicated. There are more choices to be made."

French labor laws help encourage "balance." Mothers have long had the right to work a reduced week, and long vacations go a long way toward resolving the problem of what to do with children in the summer months. Yet a government-mandated restructuring of the workplace, of any sort, is unlikely to happen in America anytime soon. And at any rate, it isn't government directives that dictate behavior, even in a dirigiste country like France. If things are better for women there, it is due to a profound and enduring social consensus that life should be made livable based on who they are and not on an abstract moralistic notion of how they ought to be. That conviction, however, rests on another fundamental belief, sorely lacking in America: that our emphasis should not be on doing as much as we can but on achieving a decent quality of life. Maybe quality of life — pure and simple — is what we as women ought to be fighting for these days. Not just for ourselves — but for the men and children in our lives as well.

Out of the Revolution

February 26, 1980

I could taste the creamy strawberry of a *lait fraise*. Hear the crunch of the fine sand underfoot on the sidewalks of the avenue Montaigne. Feel the first savory spoonful of *soupe au pistou vert* against my lips. Picture an afternoon over a *café crème* at the Deux Magots while glancing sideways to see exactly what the *parisiennes* were wearing this spring. I daydreamed of Paris as I stood waiting, surrounded by people escaping the Islamic Revolution.

The noise in Tehran's Mehrabad Airport was deafening, the departures floor a sea of bags filled with treasure — carpets, silver, photographs, painted Persian enamels in blue and green, Korans, anything that could be transported out to create a life elsewhere.

There were no lines, for lines mean nothing in the Middle East. People bunched, surged, shouted, and, when there was space, kicked forward the bags that held their packaged lives. Everyone around me was fleeing forever. Only I was coming back.

My fiancé remained in Tehran. I had a reporter's job lined up with *Newsweek* upon my return. I was going away only for a vacation, to Paris — to shop for shoes, to eat steak tartare, to walk museums, and to see friends and family I hadn't seen while living through the demonstrations and shootings and power outages of a revolution.

I eased at last through the check-in counter with my father's trusted servant Shirghan at my side. He'd bribed someone somewhere and walked into the waiting lounge with me, wheeling my hand luggage behind him. I still had one hurdle to go — the passport desk — and he wanted to see me through. In Iran, unlike anywhere else I've ever been, as a native you don't go to the airport with your passport. Instead, two weeks before you leave, you send it in to the Ministry of Interior to get an exit visa. It was one of the few things that hadn't changed with the shift in regimes: just as you had paid fifteen hundred dollars to the official who had the Shah's picture hanging on the wall, you paid fifteen hundred dollars when that picture was replaced by the scowling portrait of Khomeini. And as in the past, you paid the money without getting the passport back. Instead it disappeared for two weeks — to be checked at least once by Intelligence — until it surfaced at the passport desk at the airport, right next to the security boarding gate. That is, if you were lucky.

These days, many people were not. Instead of receiving their passports and immediately leaving, the passports went missing. Their names would be listed on a grimy sheet of paper as *Mamnoon Khorouj* — "forbidden exit." Bearded police would suddenly appear, and instead of being allowed to board, the passenger would be marched off, thrown into a van, and sent to Evin Prison for trial, and sometimes for execution. The passport desk had become a place of dread. It was where people disappeared, leaving expectant friends and family waiting eight hours later at Charles de Gaulle Airport, or Heathrow, or Frankfurt International, until the awful truth slowly dawned upon them.

Mamnoon Khorouj. It was a phrase of Khomeini's, typical new revolutionary lingo, and it struck fear into us all — even those like me, who, as a member of the younger "revolutionary" generation, had little reason for concern.

Nonetheless, when the Paris flight was called to board, I approached the desk hesitantly. Passengers ahead of me scrambled forward, collected their passports, and headed through security. I could see the plane and the steps leading up to it through the open doorway. I could see Paris, lying beyond.

"Farmanfarmaian, the Lady Roxane," said Shirghan when we reached the counter. A little man in a felt domed hat and day-old whiskers shuffled between the counter and the rows of passport cubicles ranged behind him against the wall.

We could see the letters of the alphabet on the cubicles.

The little man began to scan the cubicles, as did we. At the very same moment, Shirghan and I saw the *F* cubicle. It was empty.

Shirghan's hand clutched my elbow. A wave of heat engulfed me. I grabbed the counter for support. Everything around me seemed to stand out in sharp relief, too bright, hard edged. The man turned very slowly back toward us. I could hear passengers next to me shouting their names.

Shirghan's face was white. He pointed to a handwritten list hanging next to me on the wall. At the top, in big black scrawl, were the words *Mamnoon Khorouj.* The man shrugged. "I'm busy," he said. "Find your name on that." He turned to help another passenger.

Shirghan's eyes tore down the list. Numbly, I watched another passenger collect his passport and step toward the plane.
Shirghan looked over the list again, more slowly this time. At
last, he shook his head. "You're not on the list, my lady," he said.

The little man would not meet our eyes. We called out to
him, but he wouldn't listen. A cobra head of passengers rushed
the counter, all clamoring for their passports. Panicked, heart
pounding, I watched them all — the smiles of relief as the passport was placed in their hands, the angles of expectation as
they passed through the security gate, the lightness in their
movements as they disappeared onto the tarmac. I watched
each one, until the last one passed through the exit, and the
door closed. I was alone, with Paris on the other side. Even my
luggage had gone.

"Khanoum?" "Madam?" The little man had shoved his
domed cap toward the back of his head and was wiping
his forehead with a dirty napkin. He pointed to another list,
this one without a heading. "Maybe you are on there."

The list was short, maybe ten names. Shirghan had to lean
far over the counter to see it, stretching his neck.

"Yes, my lady," he said slowly. "You are there."

"Administrative problem," the man stated flatly. His shoes
were dusty, and though they were leather, he'd bent the back
down so he could wear them like slippers. "Go back to Tehran." He turned his back to us and sat down. "No reason to
stay here any longer."

"But what administrative problem?" I demanded. I was sure
there had been a mistake. Maybe I could take the next plane. I
repeated my question, my voice shrill and rising, angry, shocked,
the image of Paris slipping away. The man didn't budge.

I lingered. I didn't want to go back to Tehran. I'd already said my good-byes. How can you go back when everyone thinks you're gone? It was embarrassing. They have their lives, while yours has been sealed off for a while. They would laugh when they saw me, even if they also felt worried and shocked. If it hadn't been me experiencing this nightmare, I would laugh, too.

"First let's find out what's going to happen to my luggage at Charles de Gaulle," I said to Shirghan. "And then let's pick up a glass of tea somewhere. I can't face going back home just yet."

March 20, 1980

Several weeks elapsed before I stepped into the tubular escalators that crisscross the center of Charles de Gaulle and felt transported, as though through giant intestines, from one world to another. Everything around me was clean, orderly, and, although it was noon, almost empty. The French sun beckoned through the spotless windows. My luggage was waiting at a kiosk, where an efficient woman handed it over. "Ben, Madame! Ça fait déjà trois semaines!" The wheels squeaked as I pulled the suitcase across the deserted floor.

Three weeks. One to discover where my passport was, another two to get the problem fixed. Two years before, I'd had the passport renewed in New York at the Iranian Consulate, and it bore the official seal of the Shah's government. But Khomeini's regime refused to recognize that government and had quietly annulled everything it had done, which meant that my passport was considered expired. Having it renewed again and then affixed with the exit visa had taken lots of steps, and lots of money — in low-denomination bills, passed to officials behind counters and screens, in vast buildings filled with papers and noise.

"How do we know," I asked Shirghan at one point, "that the official we're bribing is someone with any real connection to my passport?"

Shirghan, whose name means Lion Man, had a face pocked with smallpox scars. Longtime family servants were turning on their old masters at the time. The Revolution was for them, after all, not for us. I didn't know if I fully trusted Shirghan anymore. But he was all I had.

Not sure of anything, I had no choice but to wait. At last, one day he called. He said it was finally arranged. I left on the first day of spring, No Ruz, the most celebrated day of the Persian calendar. Aunts, uncles, cousins, were spread out on garden chairs, eating lunch at outdoor tables under the trees, as I left. I barely dared think of Paris this time, and they waved as though I might shortly be back again. Their expressions were like those caught by Renoir in the faces of *The Daughters of Paul Durand-Reul,* relaxed, proper, satisfied, slightly ingenue, the background filled with spring color. It was unreal, a garden party far removed from the Revolution that surged beyond the orchard walls. Here, aristocrats dined among white-gloved servants, as in a painting, while songbirds sang in the trees.

As I emerged from the doors of Charles de Gaulle, the air was cooler, clearer than Tehran's. It would take me some time to realize that I had gotten into the habit of throwing a silk scarf over my head, even when the weather was sunny. "We're going straight to a movie," my cousin announced as he pulled the car onto the highway. "We'll leave your luggage in the trunk."

Suddenly it hit me. After two years of living through a revolution, with bearded young men in the streets, and billboards of martyrs and mullahs on every wall, I was in Paris! I watched the cars around us in fascination. They seemed to move like windup toys along a track — no honking or weaving or speeding, as was par for the course in Tehran. None of the cars were dented or missing a fender, as every car seemed to be back there. The highway signs seemed so big and newly painted — it made me feel as if I'd suddenly shrunk and slipped inside a board game. A woman driver was applying lipstick and chatting to a man sitting next to her. I couldn't stop staring. I hadn't seen a man and a woman together in a car for months.

When we turned into the Paris boulevards from the highway, I caught my breath. I'd forgotten the art nouveau Métro arches and lampposts in filigreed metal, and found them beautiful. The fruit trees were in blossom. "Stop!" I cried as we passed a *boulangerie* where a woman in a white crimped baker's hat was putting profiteroles into a window case. My cousin swerved over so that I could run out to buy six in a box, the aroma filling my nostrils. We ate them all, sitting on a park bench in the dappled sun across from the movie theater, and they were even better than *lait fraise* or *soupe au pistou vert*. I contemplated the garish billboards of actors and actresses on the theater facade as my cousin went in to buy the tickets. In Iran, the billboards had once been even worse than these — the actresses with full-breasted cleavage a story high, lips lascivious and open, arched brows beckoning, but they had been torn down in the Revolution's first frenzy, the theaters set alight and burned to the ground. The last time I'd seen anything on a big screen had been two years before. I was so looking forward to it, I was ready to see anything. Or so I thought.

"C'mon!" my cousin said, beckoning to me from the ticket booth. "It's already started."

We slipped into the darkened hall. The screen was mammoth. The movie appeared to be a regular sci-fi.

"What's the film?" I whispered as we sat down.

"It's brand new," he whispered back. "I've heard great things about it."

"Taisez-vous!" snapped a woman in front of us. All I could think was that I admired her hair. Must get a haircut first thing, I decided.

My cousin made a face. "Typical French!" he whispered. "I'm sure you'll love this flick," he added. "It's called *Alien*." Horrible monsters jumped out of astronauts' chests. They stalked the heroes and heroines through air-conditioning ducts and snapped them up in sudden killer movements.

I emerged into the busy sunshine from the dark theater as though lobotomized. Was this what had been amusing the West while I witnessed a revolution?

April 12, 1980

I barely noticed the weeks slip by. They were, in my mind's eye, filled with uninterrupted sunshine and warm evenings supping outside on the Paris sidewalks. To go to the corner *boulangerie* and pick up croissants in the morning — it was heaven. To walk the avenue Foch and peer into the shop windows. Even to buy a comb or pot of nail polish from the *droguerie* near the Trocadéro — that was heaven, too.

Yet for all the gossamer feel of the city in the spring, in my small circle of family and friends, Paris was tainted by anxiety, becoming oppressive; no longer a vacation roost, it was slowly transmuting into a golden cage. All around me, Iranians were living lives that were momentarily frozen — in their Shah-era pieds-à-terre in the sixteenth arrondissement, spending mountains of cash they didn't have, waiting. No one knew what they were waiting for. The news from Iran did not suggest further change.

I stayed with my aunt in her bijou of a flat around the corner from the Plaza Athénée. My uncle took me to lunch at the Athénée every third day, wearing not only Hermès ties but Hermès belts and Hermès cuff links. In Tehran, everyone in the family had worked — my aunts in design and fashion, my uncles running companies and banks. Now, no one worked. The days of rest had become tedious, the nights tossed with nightmares. Their friends planned holidays abroad, to the beaches of Crete or safaris in Africa. My aunts and uncles, on the other hand, caught like moths in amber, struggled to arrange for new citizenships, unable to escape Paris on their expiring, monarchist passports. They cast lines in all directions, grasping for their spouses' citizenships, collecting on favors from old business contacts. At times it was beyond degrading, and they'd return from lunches with friends glassy eyed, having been treated poorly, as mere supplicants. The shame was unfamiliar. It smarted through long conversations over tea at home among themselves. Dignity kept them aloof: they gradually stopped calling certain friends, and the telephones grew silent. Eventually, one uncle became Spanish; another, Moroccan. My father became Venezuelan.

I, on the other hand, was unencumbered by such worries. My American passport lay safely tucked in my belongings, while my Persian passport, newly renewed, was in good order for my return to Iran. A week before my departure, I wrapped my head in a large, opaque scarf and headed to the consulate of the Islamic Republic to obtain the required entry visa stamp. I was directed to the women's section, where a female consular officer, equally thickly scarved, looked over my papers, filled in various blanks, and told me curtly that the passport could be picked up in three days. Though she did not manage a smile, I grinned widely at her and emerged into the dappled Parisian square beyond the consulate gates with a feeling of elation. As pert French demoiselles click-clicked past me on the sidewalk in strapless heels and bright red lipstick, I knew that this time, all would be well. I even bought a pink rose at the newspaper kiosk on the corner to celebrate.

But that evening, unnerving news came over the radio. I'd been invited to dinner at the home of one of my uncles, and we were sitting around an oval table of milky white glass set with Persian jeweled rice, garlic pickle, the thick eggplant stew called *khoresht,* cucumber yogurt, and a good bottle of Beaujolais. There was a gradual hush as the regular news was interrupted for a special news bulletin: an American helicopter mission to rescue the hostages at the U.S. Embassy in Tehran had crashed in the desert south of Qom. Planes had burned, soldiers had been charred. We listened in silence as President Carter apologized to the American people, his voice dubbed by a French translator.

When it was over, my uncle spoke loudly, condemning the Americans for their incompetence.

"How can you say that?" retorted my aunt, storming from the table. "It is the Iranians that are barbarians!"

"We, too, are Iranians," my uncle said mildly. "We are all of the same cloth."

"We are not!" my aunt shouted. "We are nothing like them! Who are these people, that we must pay for their sins — and who lock us out of our own country?" She sat down heavily in her chair and began to cry.

Suddenly, she looked accusingly in my direction. "And you!" she snapped. "You want to go back to there!"

My uncle walked over and put both his hands on her shoulders. "None of us know who we are," he said. "We cannot judge anything anymore."

In the newspapers the next day there were reports of demonstrations in front of the Iranian Embassy in Paris. Police in riot gear put down the demonstrators with tear gas. I'd seen so much tear gas by now, but still it was a shock to see it billowing through the streets of Paris. Yet demonstrations by Iranians against Iranians had become so commonplace — and sadly violent — by this time that I thought nothing of it.

But when I presented myself at the consulate to collect my passport, I realized that this particular demonstration had been critical to my future. "The demonstrators tried to break into the building," the veiled woman on the other side of the desk explained. It was not the same woman as before; this one seemed kinder. "We became worried," she said, "and we sent all the passports in the consulate at the time back to Tehran the next morning. Yours was among them. You will need to collect it in Iran. We shall meanwhile give you traveling papers for your return."

Traveling papers! What did she mean, traveling papers? I practically spat at her. How could I go back to Tehran on traveling papers? I might get there and they would say no! No passport, or no passport at the moment, or no passport ever!

I walked out of the consulate in a daze. It seemed clear I couldn't go back to Iran. But how could I stay? Where would I stay? What would I do? What would I live on until I found something to do? What would I tell *Newsweek*?

I realized dimly that it was drizzling. The newspaper kiosk had umbrellas. "And a rose?" asked the vendor.

No rose.

I began to walk. I didn't look where I was going. Great drops fell from the trees, and the puddles underfoot grew deeper and more frequent. The moisture seeped through the thin leather soles of my shoes. People on café terraces huddled behind plastic sheeting dropped against the rain. Others repaired inside. At one point, as I stood on a corner, waiting for a red light to change, an empty taxi, windshield wipers slapping, pulled up in front of me, and the driver beckoned. It seemed a miracle, for when is there ever an empty taxi in Paris in the rain?

"Where to, mademoiselle?" he asked as I folded my umbrella and pulled the door shut. I looked at him, bewildered. Where to? I didn't know. I had just lost a citizenship. I could feel my eyes filling with tears.

"Je ne sais pas."

He smiled. "Vous êtes américaine?"

"Oui." And then, I knew where I was going. "L'ambassade de l'Amérique," I said. "The side with the eagle."

He dropped me off at the guard booth in front of the big iron grating. I waited until he pulled away, hiding under my umbrella, and then walked into the square. The embassy was a massive structure, columned and gray. At last I could see the eagle, great wings spread wide, head down, looking out from the helm of the roof. Under my feet the fine white Paris sand of the square filled with rainwater. My shoes were soaked. My umbrella had begun to drip from inside. But I felt none of it. All I saw was that eagle, and at that moment, all I felt was gratitude that that eagle was mine.

July 18, 1980

That summer, it rained more in Paris than it had since records began to be kept. My father's third wife had a two-room flat, it turned out, which she never used, in the Appartements George V, across from the famous hotel of the same name. Great address, horrible flat. Dark, with heavy, old furniture that emitted strange smells and poofs of dust, a galley kitchen with two electric burners, and curling linoleum in the shower. Like so many Paris apartment buildings, this one's elevator was noisy and rickety and made of wood, and it would stay where it was stopped if the inner glass door wasn't shut correctly. The flat was on the fourth floor, and I walked up more than I rode. But though it was horrible, it was free, and it had the great advantage of being three blocks off the Champs-Élysées. Picturesque boutiques lined the *ruelles* behind the avenue. The lady at the neighborhood patisserie became a special friend, calling, "Là voilà!" as she held out the *tarte abricot* she saved for me each afternoon, wrapped in a small square of greased paper. The charcuterie a few doors down was tiny but always had tantalizing offers: quail, rabbit, miniature wood hens.

I spent the days interviewing for jobs, the evenings cooking rabbit stew, or whatever else the charcuterie had had in the
window, and talking on the phone to my fiancé in Tehran. One
Friday night I told him about my interview at the *International
Herald Tribune,* where I had been unceremoniously plopped
down in front of William Safire. Safire had looked menacingly
over his glasses and told me there was no work for Americans
in Paris. "Go home," he said. "I don't care how talented you are,
or not, as the case may be."

Go home? But where was home? I couldn't go back to Iran.
(As it turned out, I never did go back.) The United States was
not really home for me either, despite the clutching moment
when I realized I was down one citizenship and it was the sole
identity I had.

"Maybe we should move on," my fiancé suggested. "I'll ask
for a transfer from Tehran and we can move somewhere new
together. Meanwhile, I'll arrange for some leave from Tehran
and we can go on a prehoneymoon. Then let's get married."

It took several days for me to agree. My budget was getting
increasingly slim; my prospects for work were uninspiring. But
I didn't want to accept the idea that I'd failed in Paris. The city
was too divine, too much a dream. This was my opportunity to
live in Paris — how could I give it up?

The unexpected arrival of another of my many uncles tipped
the scales. He'd never had ample funds, and my father had generously offered to let him stay at the flat I was in for however
long he needed. It was not a good combination. I cooked and
cleaned and bought all the food. He slept late in the living room
and had strong opinions, which he expected me to adopt. He
claimed he'd seen all the Paris sights, and so he stayed inside all

the time. I found myself escaping whenever I could. My fiancé was right: it was time to move on.

Before I left, I had one last task: to buy shoes from Paris for my wedding. I scoured the city, up and down the Champs-Élysées, along the rue de Passy, around the Opéra. It rained every day, torrents that turned the gutters into rivers and infused the Métro with a dank, suffocating heat. I, and hundreds of other Parisians, waited for the trains and steamed. From the gay sommelier at the Hôtel Plaza Athénée to the workmen in drenched blue gabardine replacing the cobbles along the Trocadéro, everyone grumbled bitterly about the rain. I was with them. I was tired of feeling like a sodden rat.

And there seemed to be no shoes in all of Paris. Perhaps that, I thought, was emblematic of it all.

Then, coming home one evening, having splurged on sunflowers, I rounded a corner off the avenue George V and saw my shoes sitting primly in a shop window. There were only three or four pairs on display. I tripped inside, dripping from the rain, my bouquet leaving a wet spot on the carpet.

"Celles-là." I pointed.

"*Ah, oui!* But we have only one pair left." The saleslady herself was wearing lovely patent shoes with cutout toes. I looked at them sourly, knowing they would soon get soaked by the rain. "Your size?"

She shook her head when I told her, but disappeared behind a curtained door nonetheless. The boutique smelled like lavender, and I could see sachets from Provence in a bowl on the counter. When she reappeared, she was smiling. "I found another pair behind," she said. "Maybe these are for you?"

She kneeled down and held one out. I felt like Cinderella,

slipping on the glass slipper. Was it surprising that they were just right? Bursting suddenly with the moment, I leaped up and began to dance around the shop, and astonishingly, she took a step or two, too. Outside, the rain had stopped, and a band of sunset was just visible at the end of the glistening street.

The saleslady folded up the shoes in a delicate paper wrapping. "Merci à vous, et bonsoir!" We smiled at each other like coconspirators. I gathered up my flowers and stepped through the door into the clear, rain-washed Paris evening.

Back in the dark little apartment, I slipped on my shoes. I was going to get married. The shoes would remind me, even as I walked down the aisle, of those tormented but happy days when, for one brief moment, my world was Paris, and Paris was home.

My Literary Paris

IN PARIS, I lived on rue Guynemer. Rue Guynemer, once rue du Luxembourg, is situated in the sixth arrondisse-ment across from the Luxembourg Gardens and is named after Georges Guynemer, a handsome World War I pilot. There is a photograph of Georges Guynemer in the war museum at the Invalides; in it, he is leaning on the fuselage of his biplane; he is wearing a leather helmet with the goggles pushed up against his forehead and looking resolutely away from the camera. According to the caption, the photograph was taken the day before Georges Guynemer was shot down; neither he nor his plane was ever found.

Soon after I moved into my apartment on rue Guynemer, the concierge informed me that the French novelist Françoise Sagan lived a few doors down on the same street.

Ah, oui. Bonjour tristesse.

DIVORCED, WITH THREE small children, I had come to France in the midseventies for a change of scene. Also, since I was born in France, I felt instinctively that I was French. The fact that I did not have any relatives or know many people in Paris, I told myself, did not matter. The beauty of the city would be enough; I would not be lonely. (Strangely enough, there is no specific word for "lonely" in the French language: *seul, isolé, abandonné,* some people even use the word *perdu.*)

Gertrude Stein and Alice B. Toklas famously lived around the corner from rue Guynemer at 27, rue de Fleurus; farther down the street, where rue Guynemer intercepts rue Vaugirard, Zelda and Scott Fitzgerald spent several months in a building with elegant French windows that opened onto the Luxembourg Gardens, which must have been the setting for the North's apartment in *Tender Is the Night:* "high above the green mass of leaves." In addition, not far and within walking distance, there is a place Paul Claudel, a rue Corneille, a rue Racine, and a rue Regnard, streets all named after famous French writers.

I spent the first year improving my French, learning my way around the city on buses and Métros, learning to say "monsieur" or "madame" when I addressed someone, learning how to wrap a scarf around my neck the way French women do, learning to run up the stairs to my apartment before the *minuterie* shut off and left me groping with my key in the dark, and, finally, learning how to order cuts of meat from the butcher around the corner on rue de Fleurus — unfortunately, once, on a Monday, the day French butchers are traditionally shut, I went to a *chevaline* and bought five hundred grams of *viande hachée* before I realized my dreadful mistake. I was, in a word, getting settled in my new life in Paris.

I don't remember exactly how or when I decided to go back to school. I remember that it was a decision taken at the last minute. All of a sudden, I had to fill out forms, assemble papers, copy them: my birth certificate, my transcript from college, my passport, my resident visa. Then I had to stand for several hours in a long line of students to register. The lines were divided according to letters of the alphabet, and I made the mistake of first standing in the line that included the letter E — the first letter of my surname at the time — when instead I should have been standing in the line that included the letter S — the first letter of my maiden name. This error caused me several more hours of standing, and, the last in line, I just made it before the office shut and before I would have had to wait another year to register at the Sorbonne. I was applying for a master's degree, *une maîtrise,* in American literature, at Paris III. As it turned out, my bachelor of arts degree from an Ivy League university was considered insufficient qualification for the French master's program, and I was informed in no uncertain terms that I would have to take an additional undergraduate year and first obtain my *licence.* This news came as a blow — a blow to my pride and a blow, I thought, to the American education system, which was held in so little esteem. It also meant that I had to take eight courses.

That second year is a blur. Looking back, I picture myself hurrying across the Luxembourg Gardens in all types of weather — rain, a rare snowstorm, cold, damp — clutching my bag of books on my way to the rue de l'École de Médecine, where most of the classes were held. (A few were held in entirely different locations, but I have now forgotten where or how I got there.) I also picture myself hurrying back home at noon in time to have lunch with my children and to walk the dog, then, in a still greater hurry, setting out once more across the Luxembourg to yet another class. Thursday was my day of respite. I had classes, but since an afternoon class was followed by an evening class, with just enough time for dinner in between, I had arranged for a babysitter. So every Thursday, promptly, at seven, I crossed the boulevard Saint-Michel to the Balzar, a restaurant, I learned later, much frequented by writers, intellectuals, and professors at the Sorbonne. Each week, I sat at the same table and ordered the same plat du jour and a little carafe of red wine to drink with my dinner. Did I feel *seule, isolée, abandonée,* or *perdue* sitting alone at my table? Probably, but I also felt adventurous — or as if an adventure was possible. While I waited for my meal, I propped a novel by a favorite writer — Donald Barthelme, Nathalie Sarraute, Franz Kafka — prominently in front of me. Someone, preferably a very good-looking, intelligent man, I imagined, attracted by my excellent taste in literature, was sure to seek me out.

The Thursday evening class — one of the eight classes I had to take — was on American economics from 1945 to the present, beginning with a hefty dose on the New Deal, which, according to my notes, FDR introduced four hours after he was sworn into office. For my term paper, I wrote on the controversy then brewing over whether the United States would give the British Aircraft Corporation and the French Société nationale industrielle aérospatiale landing rights for their supersonic aircraft, the Concorde. The issue had yet to be resolved when I wrote the paper, although on May 24 of that year, 1976, the Concorde was due to fly joint inaugural flights from Paris and London to Dulles International Airport. The nominal flight time was said to be three hours and fifty minutes, which meant that the Concorde would arrive in the United States sooner than it left Europe by the clock, since its speed exceeds the rotational speed of the earth. I got a grade of 17 (17 out of 20) on my paper.

I did not do quite as well in my other courses. In one, I had to compare opera librettos to the novels they were based on (I compared *La traviata* to *La dame aux camélias*); in another course I read Shakespeare in French; in another I translated texts (from English to French and French to English — I did well on the latter, not so well on the former); in another, the hardest of all, I studied linguistics (I still have nightmares about linguistic "trees").

A difficulty of a different sort was my age: Although I was in my early thirties, I was always by far the oldest student in the class. As a result, I was considered suspect: I belonged to the other camp. The teacher camp. Then, the division between teacher and student was enormous. The relationship between the two was, at best, formal: one did not speak out of turn, one addressed the teacher respectfully by his or her title. At worst, the teacher was often rudely dismissive or cruel: *Mais non, mademoiselle, votre réponse est complètement idiote.* There was, in other words, no easy camaraderie in the classroom.

The third year, the year of *la maîtrise,* was also the year of Monsieur Le Vot. M. Le Vot, a handsome, articulate man in his midfifties, was my professor and thesis adviser. He taught American literature. M. Le Vot, along with Ferdinand de Saussure, Claude Lévi-Strauss, Vladimir Propp, and Gérard Genette, to name but a few of the famous structuralist and semiotic theorists, were out to demystify literature and to show that like any other product of language, it is a *construct* and can be analyzed and classified. They no longer considered literature to have a vital essence or to be *unique;* they considered literature to be akin to a system of rules. Their clinical approach to literature undermined the reader's cherished belief that what is "real" is what is experienced; it undermined the reader's common sense. And for a time, it undermined mine.

This time I was only required to take a single course, M. Le Vot's. The class met for three hours once a week, on Tuesday afternoons, in a room with a beautiful and distracting view of the Paris rooftops. There were eight of us in the program — all but me were French — and we sat fairly informally at a long wooden table. M. Le Vot began by giving us a brief survey of American literature, whose subjects, he told us, followed a clockwise movement, from the West (wild nature), to the North (metaphysical problems), to the East (urban problems); only the South (its nostalgic quest for history) was different. After that, we were ready to begin. We would read William Faulkner's *As I Lay Dying. As I Lay Dying* was one of my favorite books. I had read the novel so many times, I almost knew it by heart. This would be easy, I thought.

Our first assignment was to draw a diagram. The diagram was to be divided into fifty-nine parts so as to correspond to the fifty-nine chapters in *As I Lay Dying*. Above each, we were to write the name of the chapter's narrator — Darl, Jewel, Tull, Addie, and so forth; underneath the names, we were to write where the action takes place — house, road, river, and so on — and then write in the number of days. The idea for the diagram was based on the five categories central to the literary theory so dear to M. Le Vot's heart (his black heart, I, by then, had decided): time-order, which is divided into prolepsis (anticipation) and analepsis (flashback); duration (length of episodes); frequency (how often an event is narrated); mood (which can be divided into distance; diegesis, recounting the story; or mimesis, representing the story), and perspective or point of view; and finally, voice or the act of narrating, of which there are two basic kinds: heterodiegetic, where the narrator is absent from the narrative, and homodiegetic, where the narrator is inside the narrative (as in the first person).

No, no. Never. I would not make a diagram. Children made diagrams. In addition, I had never heard of prolepsis, analepsis, diegesis, mimesis, heterodiegetic, or homodiegetic. First, I planned to denounce M. Le Vot's and all his fellow structuralists' deluded and pretentious methods; then I planned never to darken M. Le Vot's classroom door again, but M. Le Vot had already put his books and papers inside his briefcase and wrapped his silk scarf around his neck, and with a brief wave au revoir, with one elegantly gloved hand, he himself was out the door before I could open my mouth to object or complain.

I still have my diagram. Three and a half pages that my children and I Scotch-taped together lengthwise on the dining room table, the fifty-nine divisions carefully ruled in red, the rest of the information neatly written below in blue ink.

I made diagrams for William Styron's *Lie Down in Darkness;* Flannery O'Connor's *Wise Blood;* Carson McCullers's *The Heart Is a Lonely Hunter;* Tennessee Williams's *A Streetcar Named Desire;* Joyce Carol Oates's *Expensive People;* Fitzgerald's *The Great Gatsby;* Nathanael West's *Miss Lonelyhearts;* John Gardner's *Grendel* (I would write my thesis on John Gardner's novels); Robert Coover's story "The Babysitter," in *Pricksongs and Descants;* Richard Brautigan's *Trout Fishing in America;* and a few of Donald Barthelme's stories in *City Life.*

I learned a lot that year. In, for instance, our first assignment, *As I Lay Dying,* I learned that by studying the nineteen contrasting voices — Darl's objective listing, Vardaman's senseless "My mother is a fish," Dewey Dell's subjective meditation — how and why Faulkner so mightily succeeds in representing both an emotional reality and the simultaneity of an experience. In our second assignment, Styron's *Lie Down in Darkness,* another favorite novel, I could make out how, by making a diagram showing the progression of the seasons, of time, of place, and of the longer and longer use of analepsis, a pattern took shape, a kind of spiral indicating a nostalgia for a lost paradise, emblematic, perhaps, of that felt by the author for the lost grandeur and dream of the American South, and I could begin to understand how Styron was able to write so movingly and convincingly. I learned, in other words, that a careful, analytical, and even technical reading of a novel, instead of — as I had initially feared — spoiling the pleasure of that novel, greatly enhanced it.

M. Le Vot was an excellent teacher. He was passionate about his subjects. His English, though flawless, was spoken with a slight, appealing accent. He encouraged us to speak up and was never dismissive or rude. He graded fairly. He wore elegant English tweed jackets, cashmere V-necked sweaters, highly polished shoes, and a wedding ring. Nonetheless, I fell deeply in love with M. Le Vot. I also fell deeply in love with American literature.

On a warm June day, after I had handed in my thesis and passed the oral examination, I went to say good-bye to M. Le Vot. I crossed the Luxembourg for almost the last time, as I was soon going back to America, and I walked slowly. I admired the tall chestnut trees and the flowers in bloom and stopped for a moment to watch the children sailing their boats in the boat basin. M. Le Vot was sitting behind his desk in his office and he stood up to greet me. He told me that my dress was pretty and that I had gotten a *mention bien* on my thesis. I told him that, inspired by his teaching, I now wanted to write fiction. "Courage," he said, smiling, "et bonne chance." Then, in what I interpreted as a blessing of sorts, M. Le Vot kissed me lightly on both cheeks.

ZOÉ VALDÉS

The Tribulations of a Cuban Girl in Paris

THE FIRST TIME I visited Paris — what a lovely, unreal phrase! — I was just twenty-three, I had never in my life been on a plane, and the only idea I had of the City of Light was just that: a sort of vague glow imported from my readings of Balzac, Flaubert, Rabelais, Proust; by the paintings of the impressionists and Fantin-Latour, Gustave Courbet, Marie Laurencin . . . ; by the songs of Claude François (although Lully's opera *Atys* had come first, as had Umberto Giordano's *Andrea Chénier*), Edith Piaf, Maurice Chevalier, Juliette Gréco, Barbara, and Serge Gainsbourg; by the movies shown in Havana movie theaters and sometimes, from Easter to the Día de San Juan, on Cuban television — *Les demoiselles de Rochefort, Le gentleman de Cocody, Fantômas, Rocco et ses frères, Fanfan la tulipe, Le samouraï, Les tribulations d'un chinois en Chine,* and my favorite, *La belle et la bête.*

I wanted my voice, my hair, to be like Françoise Dorléac's; I yearned to seem as melancholy as Catherine Deneuve, to feel loved by Jean Marais, and to be kidnapped by Alain Delon, though rescued by Jean-Paul Belmondo. I longed to write and direct movies like Jean Cocteau, and I dreamed that my grandfather was a very funny old gentleman named Fufu — Louis de

Funès. In real life, it was my grandmother who bore an eerie resemblance to that brilliant man, who in my opinion was one of the greatest actors ever seen by humankind.

From all these works and people I had acquired my first notions of Paris, and of France. Ah, but I mustn't forget my then husband's uncle, one of those exile *gusanos* — worms — excoriated by Castro but transformed by the magic of Jimmy Carter into a butterfly, who on his first trip from Puerto Rico to Cuba, his second home — he'd been born in Spain but raised in Cuba — stepped off the plane with suitcases filled with Chanel No. 5. The family was expecting chorizos or, if not chorizos, something equally suitable for satisfying its Communist hunger, but he showed up with Chanel No. 5, and I, at least, appreciated it enormously. Since we had nothing to eat, or nothing but shit, I'd lost interest in food. It was the first time anybody had ever given me French perfume; the fact is, it was the first time I'd *seen* a bottle of French perfume, or smelled it. Till then the only thing I'd worn was Red Moscow, which stank, and Paris, a Bulgarian cologne named for the hero of the *Iliad*.

That first trip of mine to Paris was not a pleasure trip, exactly. I should make it clear that in 1983, very few Cubans could travel outside Cuba, and those who did travel invariably did so for the same reasons: they were either representatives of the regime who were authorized to travel, or "traitors" to the regime who were departing, lugubriously and forever, into exile. Only a handful of marriages to foreigners were beginning to occur at this time, and the *jinetes* and *pingueros* — whores and hustlers — had not yet come on the scene, at least not like now, in such extraordinary numbers and under such abusive conditions for themselves. I was a member of the first category above, those "authorized to travel," although I was not a government functionary — I was actually a student at the university. But I was *married* to a functionary, the editor of a film magazine that I myself, several years later, would edit. It seems my husband had fallen out of grace for having defended a movie that Fidel Castro hated. In Cuba, when one of the Castro brothers hated somebody, the person in question knew there were two possible fates for him from that point on: a velvet-box exile in an embassy somewhere abroad (the famous *traversée du désert,* as the French so elegantly call it), or the firing-squad wall. There was a third option, though it was the least attractive of them all: being "sent to the tank" — prison.

My functionary-husband was sent off to an embassy, as first secretary. His boss at the magazine was made ambassador, and all the others on the boss's staff were sent abroad, too. The men weren't allowed to travel unaccompanied, since the government argued that the CIA might send a spy in the guise of a lover, to entrap them and force them to desert. That was when they decided we had to get married, so I could accompany my functionary-husband on the new assignment he'd been given by the Revolution, as far as possible from the world of Cuban culture. Anyone in their right mind would say that a trip to Paris was a reward. But in the mind of the Communists, the reward was Moscow — Paris was a punishment.

And that was how I came to board a plane run by the most religious airline in the world — Cubana, which flew when it was the will of God to fly. That was the saying, anyway. So I abandoned a room in Old Havana — no water, no electricity, no stove, with a collective bathroom down the hall — to move to a city that I had been dreaming about practically since I was born. My grandmother never stopped telling us that babies came from Paris, wrapped in a diaper and brought by a stork. That meant that I — in my fantastical mind — was making a journey back home.

In Havana I was always very Parisian; in Paris, I've always been very *habanera*. But I only realized that years later. I left in December of 1983, alone with a man I'd married overnight who'd been turned overnight into a diplomat. I left without my mother, virtually alone. (Traveling with a man is traveling alone.) I knew nothing about the world; all I knew was what Fidel's daily news programs told me: The world was a bad place, the worst of humanity. Cuba was a gem, a paradise. Outside, the entire world wanted to be like Cuba. Traveling in those days, at the age of twenty-three, was for me like a trip for a three-year-old today. My sixteen-year-old daughter knows more about the world than I could even imagine when I was her age. But then she doesn't know Cuba. Although she was born there, it's the only country she doesn't know anything about.

The first problem in traveling to a cold country in the middle of December was clothes. I had two summer dresses, two pairs of jeans, two light turtlenecks — that was it. We were taken to a store, called La International, where the only people who could make purchases were the functionaries being sent to the Communist countries of Eastern Europe. The only things in the store for sale were bolts of gray or brown wool cloth. I picked out six yards of brown wool, and my mother-in-law made me a coat copied from an old French magazine. The lining was made from a burlap sack, dyed, and it was so stiff that when I wore the coat it looked like I was disguised as a transatlantic steamer — which seemed to my mother-in-law the right sort of look for crossing the ocean.

The first few weeks I wore that coat in Paris, there wasn't a person on the street who didn't stare at me, and anybody who knows Paris knows that in Paris, nobody looks at anybody — nothing is striking enough to draw a true Parisian's second glance. Except, that is, for me in my boat disguise.

The first night I spent in Paris, I fainted twice. Dropped like a chicken with its neck wrung. The lights, the perfumes — so much light, so many lovely fragrances at once, just literally bowled me over. The second time I fainted was as I was walking past one of those little ovens they have in the street for roasting chicken. The smell of that chicken entered my nose, went up to my brain, passed through my arteries, and bang! — I hit the sidewalk. I'd never smelled so much roast chicken in my life. The last time we'd had chicken in my house in Havana was when my grandmother was sick. I was ten years old. Six months later we couldn't go to pick up the rest of the chicken we were entitled to on our ration card because my grandmother had the bad luck — for us — to die two days before the next shipment to the store came in.

The day after my fainting spells, the ambassador from the Cuban Office to UNESCO insisted that I go to the hospital. Everything went smoothly there — I had a blue diplomatic passport, I was seen immediately — under the fixed gaze of a Spanish Communist driver sent precisely to keep that stern eye on us. It turned out the Spanish Embassy was on the verge of firing him, as they'd discovered he had a "vice," as they termed it: he played the *tiercé,* the French version of the horseracing trifecta. But the Spanish Communist said his mea culpas or mea Cubas (thanks, Guillermo Cabrera Infante) and they reinstated him in the service of automobiles and surveillance of the embassy and the Cuban Office to UNESCO. At that point he became more of a Castroite than Castro.

I weighed forty-three kilos — less than ninety-eight pounds — and had full-blown anemia, and when I told the doctor about the circumstances under which I'd lost consciousness the second time, he smirked and said — obviously, said the driver later, that doctor was no Communist, and was probably actually an enemy of the Revolution — that instead of smelling the chicken, what I should have done was buy some and eat it. And that was what he prescribed for me: Eat chicken, meat in all its many varieties, and fruit. And he assured me that this was the first time he'd ever recommended this to a woman in France, but he ended by saying, "Fatten yourself up, madame, or the next time you fall you will break a bone!"

Which is exactly what happened. The third time I fell, I broke my coccyx. So I was confined to my bed for two months, with my ass in state, eating, reading, watching French television, where everybody talks and I could hardly understand a word. That was another thing — I spoke exactly zero French. That's why when we left the hospital and I listened to that driver spewing fire and brimstone against the doctor, I couldn't understand quite why he was doing it. Until, that is, he translated what the doctor had said when he said, "Les gens qu'arrivent des pays communistes atterrissent d'abord chez le médecin, et ensuite, vous allez voir: attendez-vous à une crise de foie": "People arrive from these Communist countries and the first place they wind up is at the doctor's, and then, you wait and see, prepare yourself for a liver crisis." And as a matter of fact, after two months being laid up in bed eating everything, or almost everything, I did have a liver crisis. When the doctor advised me to eat meat, I'd forgotten to explain to him that with what the Cuban government paid me each month for being a Cultural Documentary-Film Maker I could buy only four chickens (one per week) and not much else. But that was fine with me — since in Cuba I couldn't eat a chicken even once a year and hadn't actually tasted chicken since I was ten years old, I spent my Paris money on cheap chocolates from Ed l'Épicier. Not for nothing was my liver ready to pop. When I got to the hospital, the doctor on duty asked if I was an alcoholic. "No," I said. "Chocoholic."

Once those first hospital traumas were behind me and my tremendous sense of melancholy, homesickness, missing my mother, had become less intense, I started sneaking out. We weren't allowed to go out alone; we had to be accompanied by two of the embassy's policemen-with-diplomatic-passports — nice guys at first glance but, especially the Asturian driver, grouchy as hell. But I started taking on jobs that nobody wanted to do: taking the mail to *la poste,* being a messenger between the embassy and the offices of various UNESCO countries. Between one visit and another, I'd go out to the street, breathe some fresh air, smoke a cigarette, and walk two or three times around the Métro entrance. I'd never entered the Métro; I was terrified of entering the Métro. The Communists said women were raped and murdered there. The other thing I was terrified of was shopping. To Communists, shopping was an illness, a disease. And I wanted to go home to my mother in the same condition she'd seen me leave in: healthy, perfectly healthy, although with an almost chronic anemia and less meat on my bones than it would take to make a meatball.

Finally I was given the assignment of carrying some secret correspondence between the UNESCO office and the Cuban Embassy. That day the Asturian driver was working with the ambassador and the diplomatic police in an important meeting to prepare for the visit of a high-ranking French government official. There was no help for it: I'd have to take the Métro. The Spanish secretary — another Communist — walked with me to the entrance of the Métro, showed me how to buy a ticket, how to slip it into the slot, and how to quickly slip inside. I got stuck three times. I looked around — I was more embarrassed than I'd ever been in my life. People couldn't understand why I couldn't get through the turnstile. I banged into that turnstile so many times that the ticket seller finally came out of his booth and opened the handicapped entrance for me, thinking I had some sort of brain malformation that prevented me from entering the Métro like a normal person. Once I'd delivered those important documents that made me incredibly nervous because everywhere I looked I could see the Enemy that was going to snatch them out of my hands in broad daylight — of course I didn't open the envelope (it's best to remain ignorant of a dictatorship's secrets), although I admit I was tempted — I left the embassy and walked back. It was then that I felt — that I breathed — free. I was alone, apparently nobody was watching me, and if I felt like it, I could take off running to the American Embassy and ask for political asylum. I didn't; I wanted to see my mother again and I was too in love with my husband. And when you're too in love, the other person oftentimes isn't, but that's another story.

From a room in Old Havana we moved to an attic on the

rue Saint-Dominique — after living with the ambassador in the ambassador's residence for a year, that is, putting up with his rudeness, his snide remarks, his foul moods. I spent a year being his maid, without being paid a cent, in addition to my work at UNESCO. After we moved, he decided that I would continue to be his maid, and I agreed because having won his trust through my silence — at the time, I didn't talk — the job allowed me a degree of freedom. I was able to move between his residence, the office, and the embassy without being so controlled; I was given permission and a Carte Orange to use in the Métro, and I could meet with certain trusted Latin Americans without having to turn in reports on them to the embassy's counterintelligence people. Playing stupid is always the right thing to do with Communists.

What did they consider stupid? I spent my days reading newspapers in French and trying to learn the language by watching television and listening to the people talking, not trying to insist on speaking Spanish — excuse me, *Cuban* — or pretending that the French were under the obligation to understand me just because I was a Cuban "revolutionary." And I'd pick up all the invitations to art exhibits and museums that came into the office — activities that the Castro officials avoided like the plague. I was stupid because instead of visiting the city's stores and shops like all the other wives accompanying their diplomat-husbands — and never buying anything, because what would they use for money? — I would go to museums, try to learn French, and socialize with the Latin Americans friendly to the embassy, or at least the ones the embassy thought were still its friends.

Five years went by like that. I loved walking through the

Champ-de-Mars, the Champs-Élysées, loved going into bookstores to hide in a corner and read books forbidden by the embassy — that's how I got to read the books of Armando Valladares and some of Reinaldo Arenas's and my maestro's, Guillermo Cabrera Infante. The people in the embassy pressed me, since I liked books so much, into throwing out all the books that Alejo Carpentier had written when he was cultural attaché in the Castro embassy — thousands of titles! I didn't do it; instead, I organized a library that they later proudly showed to all their visitors.

I loved the libraries, the museums. For several months the Louvre was a very special refuge, as were the Musée Gustave Moreau and the Jeu de Paume. I would lean back on a bench in the place de Furstenberg for hours, smoking; I would walk the streets of the Latin Quarter passionately, like something out of a François Truffaut movie; I would drink *kirs* in the bistros and nourish myself on baguettes slathered with butter and Bonne Maman strawberry jam! I smoked and smoked and smoked, like my idol Serge Gainsbourg. And read and read and read, like my other idol Bernard Pivot. And so I gradually acquired more freedom, although more than once, looking over my shoulder, I discovered that some official from the embassy was following me. I became an expert in messing with their heads. I would carry wigs, hats, scarves in my purse; I'd gotten a new coat. And whenever I could, I'd slip into a stairwell to put on a disguise to throw them off, or sneak down a corridor to the building's back exit.

As I gained more freedom, other things began to draw my attention. First, money. I discovered that in order to have all the things I liked — books, records, that sort of thing — I first had to learn to respect and like money. Before, it hadn't mattered to me, or I had actively disliked it. Now I wanted to save money so I could take presents back to my mother in Cuba, and the only way to get the things I liked was to do what in Cuba had become the only way to live — become a criminal. Another diplomat's wife invited me to sell the cases of rum that the government sent to be given out as gifts for New Year's. We set ourselves up in the busiest corner of the Barbès-Rochechouart Métro station and started selling rum for twenty francs, then moved on to Cuban cigars and gasoline chits. The rum was a hit among the Muslim population.

One afternoon I went to rent *Le grand Meaulnes* in its old version — the movie based on the Alain-Fournier novel — and the clerk asked me if I'd let him take nude photos of me for his customers. I said OK. Later I modeled for painters, among them one very famous one, Monsieur B. My baby face and teenager's body were perfect for his paintings. What I'm saying is that I led a double life, and on a diplomatic passport.

I figure the dossier they have on me in the offices of the Sureté is as thick as a brick. The ambassador, playing dumb, would praise my job performance — and in every conversation with his illustrious visitors he would say that I'd learned more than anybody in the embassy about this city. At one of those moments I was wearing a tulle skirt I had found in the *marché aux puces* at Porte de Clignancourt and a velvet jacket I'd bought for almost nothing at a Guerrisol — an Arab shop that sells dead people's clothes — and Alberto Moravia, his hand beneath my tulle, was stroking my behind.

"What a lovely outfit!" crooned the publisher Ingrid Feltrinelli, eyeing my costume. "Who is it?"

I didn't know a thing about labels or designers; all I knew was that my fingers were throbbing from all the needle pricks I'd given myself that afternoon as I'd sewn up the skirt. So I lied.

"Dior, it's Dior." (Dior, forgive me — I can't ask forgiveness of *Dios,* another designer that's done pretty well for himself.)

I loved Paris with all my heart. But I had to get a divorce and flee the city I loved best for that other one, which I also loved very, very much, though with increasing reticence. I returned to Havana. I couldn't imagine that I'd be going back to Paris six years later, married to a Cuban filmmaker, with our year-and-a-half-old daughter (what I had to do to take her with us!), on a three-month visa. I knew that *that* departure would be the last . . . I sensed it. My passport was no longer that magical shade of Prussian blue that symbolized the diplomatic corps. My passport was gray, like any other government official's. I had been invited to Paris as a writer and the assistant publisher of the journal *Cine Cubano*, and I carried several novels and poems in my suitcase filled with books. My mother stayed behind, alone. I'd charged her with taking care of my library.

I breathed the winter air of Paris and felt that I'd been reborn. We stayed with a painter in the Marais. My husband, my daughter, and I slept on an IKEA sofa until somebody gave us a crib for the baby. We lived for three months with no money, boiling spaghetti — no sauce — and drinking milk, both of which the painter bought us. Fortunately, friends I had met during my previous sojourn in Paris often invited us out for dinner. On April 5, 1995, when my second novel, *La nada cotidiana,* was published by Actes-Sud, those friends, or almost all of them, cut off my lights and water — they stopped speaking to me. The embassy sent an emissary to warn me that I would not be allowed to return to Cuba. At that, the French authorities informed me that they would never give me political asylum *or* legal residency, that I either had to go back to Cuba or go to the United States. I spent many long days in the police station on the rue de Lutèce. After hours of interrogation by a lieutenant and the chief of police himself, I would return to the Paris streets, step into Notre-Dame, light a few candles stolen from the dead, and go back home, feeling a little better. For ten years we paid taxes and waited for French citizenship. My books sold very well and my face was on ads in the Métro. I was a member of the Cannes jury, and I was still "undocumented." Once I became a Spanish citizen, the French made me a French one. But none of that kept me from loving this city. When I felt lonely and miserable, I'd go down to the Seine with a white plate of meringue and leave it for Oshún, the mother-goddess of rivers, the goddess of love, an offering so that she would help me. Now that I think of it, that may have been one reason they wouldn't give me the papers, because if some gendarme saw me leaving a plateful of meringue on the bank of the Seine, he must surely have said that I was absolutely out of my head, batty, *alienée*, ready for the insane asylum!

The fact is, I *was* mad — mad for Paris. In the bookshops of the rue Beautreillis I learned what freedom was, talking to the people there. Yes, I know, Parisians are difficult, but you have to prod them. Here, I realized that the words the French use most are "découragé," "solitude," "ridé" . . . The phrase inevitably used by men to reply is "Oui, mais non . . ." My greatest problem was water and the use they made of it. They've not only replaced water with wine, but they shower very infrequently. The

BO in the Métro killed me — it still kills me — not to mention the smell of rotten cheese between the teeth, the wine on the breath, and the clouds of dandruff, which looks like snow in the middle of summer. I didn't have too many problems in the winter. Although I'm not cold natured, I adapted by wearing caps, gloves, scarves, and all the paraphernalia that goes with overcoats. It wasn't easy — when I didn't lose my gloves, it was my beret, and I still have the sense sometimes that the umbrella is my third arm, because when it starts drizzling, it drizzles! And with that irritating *drip, drip, drip* that would make you think that half a dozen drummers were playing a rumba beat on your head with their fingertips.

I must say that I've gotten along well with the Parisian men. With the Parisian women it's another story. Those women are tough. If I were a man, I wouldn't have all that patience. If men's stinginess is proverbial, women's is biblical. I remember the time that painter we were staying with introduced us to his girlfriend. We invited her to dinner; I made *arroz con frijoles negros* and *picadillo*, with *platanitos fritos* — practically the Cuban national meal. She looked at the plate as though instead of a Cuban dinner she was standing before the Wailing Wall in Jerusalem. The painter had warned us that the surprise of the night would be left to his girlfriend. We thought he was talking about the wine, but no — she proceeded to drink all our wine, and then our rum, and then absolutely all our liqueurs. The surprise of the night was (Beethoven, please — da-da-da-*dum*) . . . cheese.

She took from her bag a small silver package, a little wrinkled and not a little mashed, opened it before our astonished eyes, cut us each a tiny piece of camembert as though slicing up a gold nugget, rewrapped her cheese, and tucked it back in her purse. The only reason my husband and I didn't burst out laughing was out of respect for our friend the painter.

What do I love most about this city? Its passion for art, its resistance to anything that's happening to us in the present, when the discourse is increasingly political and/or religious. Paris resists, with its art exhibits, its editions, its bookstores, its museums, its designers, its artists, its writers. Paris resists in art, no doubt about it. Though Paris no longer functions *because of* its artists. Paris is not just the center; it's also the suburbs and their infinite anguish, racial problems, stories of abandonment, of unemployment, of inability to "fit in." But I'm not going to tell any politically correct stories. What I'm interested in is the cultural life of this city — its theaters, its movie houses. That's why I stayed here; that's why I decided to create and make a life for myself in Paris. That's why I had to give birth to Paris — a difficult childbirth, no question, but in the end, the child has brought exceptional love into my life.

Translated from the Spanish by Andrew Hurley

Montparnasse and Beyond

I HAD AN INSTANTANEOUS connection to Paris. All the clichés applied. I loved it and thought it was great. I liked every part of it, including my tiny room on the boulevard Edgar Quinet. It was a typical nineteenth-century working-class building — one room, no heat, and a communal toilet in the stairwell. The hallways were dark and you had to turn the light on when you left or entered the building. The room had a single bed and a propane gas cooker. There was only cold water running out of the sink, and in the wintertime even that stopped at nine. It became a real stopping-off point; at one moment I had five people sleeping there. I had a generous concierge, Madame Fernandez. I thought it was all wonderful. I was living the dream.

Montparnasse was still as it had been in the early part of the century. The boulevard Edgar Quinet was easy to live on. It had its own subway stop and there was a food market twice a week out in the center. Le Monocle — the biggest lesbian bar in Paris — was also on the street. There were very friendly prostitutes on the nearby rue Delambre. I didn't patronize them, but they would help me out by cashing traveler's checks for me from time to time.

I went to classes at the Sorbonne and to the École du Louvre. Because of the French system with student passes, I could wander freely in the museums. It was months of looking. I wasn't particularly predisposed toward pictures; it was a slow conversion.

I used to go to the Louvre to escape from the cold of my room. This was a reversal of what had happened in the previous four years when, starting at the age of fourteen, I'd lived in Washington, D.C., for one full year and three summers as a page in the U.S. Senate. There, because it's so hot, I'd flee to museums to go to the coldness. In Paris, where there was no heat at all in my room for part of each day, this was how I would stay warm.

I became a deep museumgoer. For me it was a refuge, an escape, and on the way to warming up, I saw several other universes. The Louvre was a typical destination. It was delicious and huge. I loved the classical part — the Poussins seemed wonderful to me, and the Watteaus. Then it all came into full blossom for me with the nineteenth century. I'd also go to the old Musée d'Art moderne de la Ville de Paris and, frequently, the Rodin Museum. Rodin, for me, conformed to my most romantic expectations.

Of the French artists, I liked Poussin in particular. I have a bad contrarian streak in me, so I really appreciated his sense of order. The eye-openers for me were the more florid works, starting with Rubens — this isn't a style that most Protestants are accustomed to! That carried over to Delacroix. Looking at his work, I felt that I'd never seen excess before, that I was seeing it for the first time. That, in turn, led me to Courbet, which I saw frankness. Each one of these artists made a different kind of impression. And, of course, Courbet led to Cézanne.

When I'd go into the old Musée d'Art moderne, it seemed as if there was a chorus of people there who were willing to reinvent the wheel. Braque, Picasso, Picabia — I felt intrigued by all of them. That urge to be modern and to reinvent — it so impressed me. At a certain point it stops being about just one work of art or artist; rather it becomes about how an aesthetic vision is the universe. Artists believe in the completeness of their world and they want you to enter it. It's an exciting invitation.

I did a lot of hitchhiking in and out of Paris, so I saw the city from the front and back of *camions* and other unlikely vehicles. I hardly ever took the train. I just didn't have the cash. I sometimes had good-looking girlfriends around and they acted as bait. We'd get a ride that much faster.

I had a taste for the French countryside. I'd spent months in Burgundy and thought I was in the Garden of Eden. It was so beautiful. We were studying Romanesque architecture in a very desultory way; we'd go from one great site to the next. When you see towns like Autun and Auxerre — they're captivating. They really arrest you. They stay in your imagination for your whole life. Even if it wasn't misty or if the sycamores didn't quite line up perfectly, you'd imagine that they did. It's so synesthetic, that part of the world. That wet air carries everything with it. Those places are so humid and damp and all the antiquity lingers in the air.

One night, many years after I lived in Paris, when I finally had some cash, I was a little bit loaded and riding through the city in a friend's convertible when I realized that Paris was meant to be viewed from a carriage. When you're moving above the crowd, seeing the buildings from a few feet up, you really appreciate how distinguished the tops of the buildings in Paris are. Driving around that night in an open convertible and stopping at traffic lights gave me a view of the city that approximated how Haussmann meant it to be seen. It was a dream night, recognizing that this was the other 85 percent of what you're supposed to be experiencing as you go through the city.

One of the things I admire most about Paris is that the task in front of you is the central task. There's no displacement. Even when people are sweeping the stairs, the task at hand has to be accomplished with a high level of perfection. A mere errand has to be accomplished with great élan. There's all the dressing up. You can't just slouch around — everything has a certain correctness to it. You feel like you're in the present and therefore you're living.

I miss the rigor of it all, the way that when you go into a shop there's the standard greeting and the impossibility of leaving the shop without saying, "Au revoir, monsieur," or whatever. All that handshaking! They greet and say good-bye to everyone.

It really doesn't hurt if you don't know anything about Paris when you arrive, because it's all visibly legible. The French mark their houses in a uniform way; they even pile fruit up in a way that makes it legible. They have outfits for each task. Anyone with any sense can see the logic of the street. Their phenomenal ability to organize things and make them legible makes the whole thing somewhat theatrical — and quite memorable.

I'd imagined myself being a politician, but then that morphed into my thinking I'd be a journalist. Then, in Paris, I started looking at pictures. It was a whole period of sorting out where I wanted to put my energy. I didn't even make a choice. It was all done accidentally. I went to the Sorbonne, I got the diploma. But I never really took studying very seriously from then on. I felt that life was meant to be empirical. I still wanted to be a writer, but in the end I wound up writing about pictures.

As told to Penelope Rowlands

Guillaume à Paris

M Y SON, WILLIAM, celebrated his second birthday on
the evening that we arrived in Paris, with twenty pieces
of luggage, for a year's stay. The first Gulf War had just begun,
and the dollar was worth four francs. I had come to do archi-
val research for a biography of Colette at the Bibliothèque na-
tionale, which was still in its grand nineteenth-century palace
on the rue de Richelieu. The librarians had only just begun to
computerize the catalog, which, I discovered, was arranged not
by author, title, or subject but by the date a book or a manuscript in the collection had been acquired. Why come to Paris,
though, if not to lose oneself in its labyrinths?

I had sublet a furnished apartment on the rue de Rennes,
almost directly across the Seine from the library. Its creaky
parquets gave off a scent of beeswax, and the Haussmannian
plasterwork was a bit too grand for the rooms. There were two
chambres, each with a marble fireplace and a lumpy mattress.
The French doors in the small oval salon opened to a narrow
balcony. A two-year-old could easily have scaled the railing,
although I told myself that the awning of the café below might,
with luck, break his fall. In the building next door, Simone
de Beauvoir had spent her unhappy adolescence. Around the

corner, on the rue Cassette, was the barracks of a firehouse, and Will loved the handsome young *pompiers,* who sometimes let him try on their casques. Saint-Sulpice was around the corner, and it was a pleasant walk to the Luxembourg Gardens.

My maiden aunt Charlotte, who was known as Arkie, an intrepid world traveler of eighty-one, had come to France with us, mostly, as she put it, "to be useful, which is much more satisfying to an old woman than being happy." When she tried to speak French, no one — not even those rare, gallant Parisians who tried to respond, and who tended to be North African — understood a word. "Djuh vux doo reez," she would say to the Algerian grocer on the corner, meaning, "Je veux du riz," "I would like some rice." Then she reverted to her pidgin/ pantomime routine: "Reez: petite, blank, boilay danz oon pot. Manjay avec burr. Mercy bowcoo." But when she pushed Will down the boulevard in his stroller, she cut the figure of such a proper old *grandmère* — in a neat plaid skirt, lisle stockings, sturdy brogues, and a twin set — that they always received po- lite nods of approval. One of her particular "friends" in the neighborhood was the pastry chef at the cafeteria of Le Bon Marché, the department store on the rue de Sèvres, convenient to the carousel of miniature racing cars in the square Bouci- caut. She and Will lunched at the buffet three times a week, and the chef doffed his toque to them. My son's French was quickly much better than his great-aunt's. "Mousse au choco- lat!" he could say, with the proper inflection of culinary admi- ration, and then he would add, to anyone, for whatever reason: "En garde!"

As the child of a taxpayer in the sixth arrondissement (the taxes on my electric bill apparently entitled me to more social benefits than I had ever received as an American citizen), Will was welcome to attend the local *halte-garderie,* on the rue Chomel, a state nursery school for children. The teachers were gracious young women with advanced degrees in education; there were two of them for every small class, and one for every three of the infants who spent the hours of their parents' workday in the crèche. The *garderie* was housed on the ground floor of a forbidding fortress with a wrought-iron porte cochere, but its big windows overlooked a sunny courtyard where the children spent their recess. It was Will's first experience of school, and we had a long conversation about a subject I would never have had to address in New York. Every other two-year-old in the class had, according to the custom of the country, long since outgrown his *couches.* Will, to my surprise, used the lavatory with his classmates (visits were, like all the activities, strictly scheduled), and he never had an accident. But as soon as he got home, he asked for his diaper, and he told me that he wasn't ready, yet, to be *propre* out of school. Since *propre* was the word he chose, I supposed that one of his teachers had tactfully introduced the subject. I didn't want him to feel unclean because he wasn't *propre,* but he seemed amused by my reassurances — a faintly Gallic smile played on his lips — and he gave me to understand that *propre* was just a silly French notion one pretended to accept.

There are, in fact, no precise translations, because there are no pure human prisms who refract a text or a speech without distortion. Rendering a word into another language is a mysterious process, and just as the noun *mystery* is religious in origin, so is the verb *to translate.* Its first meaning is "to remove the body or relics of a saint or hero from one place of interment or repose to another." Its second meaning is "to carry or convey to heaven without death." That, of course, is what one aspires to do when one translates a work of literature: to convey a vital essence that has been buried in the crypt (encrypted) of an alien lexicon, to a place in the light where it can endure.

It is enthralling — especially, perhaps, to a writer — to watch a child acquire two languages at the same time, his supple mind (the capacity of the human brain, and the speed of its synapses, apparently peak at about thirty months) parsing the world as he discovers it, according to separate protocols, and keeping them straight. I had learned French as a teenager, and while my French is fluent, no one French mistakes me for a native speaker. After a few weeks in Paris, I can pass as one for about five minutes, until I misuse the subjunctive, or attribute a noun to the wrong gender. Even after forty years, I can still stupidly say "le fin" — the end (it is, after all, *le pin* — the pine tree — and *le lin* — flax or linen). "On n'est pas née femme," de Beauvoir wrote, "on le devient." (One is not born, rather one becomes, woman.) *Mais,* "on le devient"? French is not as rational as the French like to believe, and where caprice or intuition trumps reason, their myths about sex are often the culprit.

In researching the life of Colette I was, of course, translating her, literally and metaphorically, eight hours a day, and in my social life in Paris, I was translating myself, literally and metaphorically, to whomever I met. Biography and translation are related enterprises. In neither case does a word-for-word transcription produce the most desirable result: it refuses the challenges and the risks — the deep adventure — of the poetry. The transcription school of biography sticks timidly to the shore of fact, accounting for every petty quarrel, doctor's appointment, cup of coffee, thank-you note, orgasm, and pair of gloves. Such biographies may be useful to the scholar, but they cheat a lay reader of something more vibrant and sensuous, which only comes through an imaginative connection. When one translates the story of another life — an epic with many ellipses, lost passages, and obscure references — it is always into one's own sentences, and if the essential question of biography is "Who are you?" the only way to hold a steady course toward the answer is to keep asking, at frequent intervals, "Who am I?"

THE FRENCH ARE, as one knows, appalling snobs about foreigners, especially Anglo-Saxons, who mangle their language, but one also discovers that they mistrust anyone whose polish, in French, has no little cracks that flatter their sense of superiority. One summer after college, I took a job at the State Department as an escort-interpreter, and I was one of two guides attached to a group of French journalists, guests of the government, on an official tour of America. My senior colleague was an obese Hungarian polymath who traveled everywhere with two heavy leather suitcases, which he said were filled with the manuscript of a thousand-page novel that was better than *À la recherche du temps perdu*. I discovered, however, that the suitcases contained two portable fans.

The journalists marveled at — which is to say resented — the seamless perfection with which my colleague interpreted the half-finished sentences of their American interlocutors in elegant Cartesian paragraphs. His French seemed inhuman to them, or, as one of them put it, "inauthentically objective." Later in my twenties, reading Walter Benjamin's great essay on

Nicolai Leskov, I would understand why. Benjamin describes two classes of storytellers: the "resident tiller of the soil" and the "trading seaman," who are merged in the figure of the artisan. Every master was once an itinerant journeyman before he returned to settle in his village, and this description also fits the translator, who brings to his work both "the lore of far-away places" and that "lore of the past" that, Benjamin writes, "best reveals itself to the natives of a place." It reveals itself in and through their mother tongue, and one cannot translate literature — connect with the deep taproots of meaning — without having one. Those suave polyglots who speak ten languages without an accent but are at home in none do not, as a rule, make great translators. A smudge of one's native soil on the pristine surface of a translation is a signature — both a flourish of pride and a mark of humility — proper to an honest artisan.

On a visit to Paris a few years before I moved there with Will and Arkie, I had made what I thought was a galling mistake on a live French television broadcast, *Apostrophes,* a famous book program that ran for ninety minutes on Friday evenings, in prime time. I was telling a story about Isak Dinesen's Swedish husband, Bror Blixen, a white hunter of whom she wrote, "He did not know whether the Crusades came before or after the French Revolution." She intended the remark as a compliment — it came from a bluestocking who suffered for her cleverness in the patrician yet philistine society of Kenya, and who revered conspicuous virility. But when I came to the Crusades (*les croisades*), I called them "les crosières" (a *croisière* is a pleasure cruise). There was polite hilarity on the set, and a friend who had seen the program promised me afterward that the slip had been "utterly charming." He then dared to surmise — as only, perhaps, a Frenchman would have — that it had been intentional.

"PEOPLE HUGGING — *embrasse-moi*!" That was Will's first observation of and in the Luxembourg Gardens. The day had a desolate, winter beauty: earth and sky were the same Parisian *gris de perle*. We were making our way down a long allée of plane trees, toward a cluster of shaggy ponies stamping their feet. The tennis courts were empty, the fountains were dry, the waffle stand was shuttered, the boccie courts lay under a crust of snow, and the only evidence of life was, in fact, the passionate young couple (if indeed they were young — an assumption one should not make of the lovers in Paris parks). He had buttoned her inside his overcoat, their bodies were swaying, and the wind mingled strands of their hair. Will studied this wooly beast with its two heads and four legs, intrigued but a bit doubtful.

There are many rules of conduct in the Luxembourg, but none that I know of pertain to displays of affection. Two of you may share a single garden chair, entwined like the figures in a Moghul painting. You may also pull two chairs together to make an impromptu divan. You may strike the classic cinematic pose, bending your lover half backward, in full view of the Senate and its armed guards. You may stop suddenly, in the middle of a path, in the middle of a sentence, and fling your arms around each other, obstructing the passage of flâneurs, who will make a silent, uncomplaining detour around you. You may neck at a café table, or perched on the rim of a fountain, or astride a balustrade, or pressed against a chestnut tree, or on a bench inside the children's playground, provided you have paid your entrance fee and have a child with you. You may not, however, take any sort of carnal liberties on or with the grass.

When the bare trees are coated with hoarfrost, the Luxembourg has the air of a vast, dust-sheeted summer palace. Even in summer, the precise allocation of space, the maniacal tidiness and symmetry, are somehow those of an interior — a very grand, formal French salon where, as a guest, you are invited to have a good time, but where you are also on your best behavior. The Luxembourg, one should note, is a *jardin.* It is not a *bois,* or even a *parc.* While dogs are welcome in most French restaurants, they are forbidden in the Luxembourg. The tulips grow in perfectly weedless, monochromatic beds. The lawns are as smooth as cashmere, and Will could have told you what happens if you dare to dip a foot — even an adorably infantile little *pied* — into those inviting, forbidden pools of green. "Policeman blow whistle! *En garde!*" Indeed, a *gardien* in a smart blue uniform, with gold epaulets and a legionaire's hat, is instantly upon you, scowling under his mustache and wagging his finger. The presumption, under French law, is always of guilt: "Vous savez très bien, madame, que la pelouse est interdite!" ("You know very well, madame, that the lawns are off limits.")

The Luxembourg is a great rectangle, but its corners are soft — it feels circular once you are inside the gates. A dirt track runs around the periphery — delicious for jogging. You can smell the hyacinths from the rue de Vaugirard, and the damp, faintly sour scent of the well-turned-over soil, and as you move from sun to shade, the smells change, as does the temperature of the air. If you run, as I did, early on weekday mornings, you will have the paths nearly to yourself — everyone French is at home smoking. The Parisians are, or at least were, twenty years ago, weekend athletes. Nevertheless, they pride themselves on their form. There must be some unwritten code about who may *faire le footing* in the Luxembourg and who must stay at home on the treadmill. No one shuffles or groans. No one wears old Camp Minnewaska T-shirts, cutoffs, John Deere caps, or Kool-Aid-colored nylon boxers over baggy sweatpants. There is no more flab or cellulite on view than there are dandelions among the grass blades. The muscles are firm, the flesh is rosy, the outfits are soigné, and the brows, only a little moist.

Will went to the Luxembourg whenever it wasn't raining, after lunch with Arkie, and a nap. He was generally accompanied by the lovely dark-haired girl from the Dordogne whom I had hired to give my aunt a few hours of well-earned rest before I came home from the library. The French referred to her as his *jeune fille,* precisely defining the romance of their relationship. They fed the goldfish in the sailboat pond and watched the "dancers," as Will called them, practicing tai chi in beautifully laundered kimono jackets. He played in the crumbly brown sand of the *bacs à sable* — six neat little boxes that must look, from the air, like an expensive tin of shortbread from Fauchon. Was this deluxe sandpile, I wondered, tucked behind the labyrinth of hedges because the architect of the Luxembourg thought that *les petits* needed privacy? Or because he thought that the inevitable disorder of their games, quarrels, picnics, and toys was so unseemly?

I was always impressed when my son nodded to someone whom I didn't know — the pony driver, the ticket seller in the playground, a gardener at the Orangerie, an old man playing chess — and said, "Bonjour." (His *jeune fille,* I suspected, was as popular in the Luxembourg as she was at the firehouse.) By the spring, his grasp of French, while focused mainly on bakery products, was deft enough for the odd joke, as when I caught him at, and scolded him for, a piece of mischief, and he replied, with a sheepish grin, "Touché!"

Will does not, he says, remember much of Paris, although I hope that his senses do. Perhaps the city and its labyrinths figure in his dreams, and perhaps, when he is Arkie's age, the smells of hyacinths, waffles, or Gitanes will suddenly bring the scenes of that year back to him, miraculously fresh, like the disinterred body of a saint. But one of the greatest charms of having lived next door to the apartment of Simone de Beauvoir, chased the pigeons of Saint-Sulpice, and played in the Luxembourg as a little boy is the Proustian glamour of being able to claim that one did so.

Ma Vie Bohème

SOMETIMES, WHEN MOST in the city lay sleeping, I would rise from the mattress and slip over to the window to watch the slate rooftops turn silver in the moonlight. I didn't have to slip far. The room measured about three by three and a half meters — perhaps more, perhaps less. There was enough space for the bed, sagging toward the wall with lumps pressed in by generations of strangers, a slender armoire supporting the ceiling, and a chair. The remaining floor planks stored the odds and ends that accumulate in the course of a student's life. Bathed in ethereal light, the room seemed suspended, safe, even cozy.

On warm nights when we left the window open, the roofs across the way appeared to beckon, daring me to climb out and dance barefoot under the Parisian sky. It was only as the stars faded and the day dawned that the reality of the room under the roof grew clear. Generally it reached its full glory at noon, when the sun was closest and most merciless. The walls and even the sloping ceiling of this nineteenth-century maid's room seven stories above avenue Malakoff, in the sixteenth arrondissement, were covered with a relic of what had once passed for elegance downstairs. Styles had changed in the decades since the Haussmannian construction of the building.

Meters of cloth deemed out of fashion had been ripped from the walls of a dressing room in the master apartment below, then pressed into service in the servants' quarters. There the glistening satin, with its jacquard motif of golden florals, received a new raison d'être far removed from its earlier elegance. When we entered the room, it was like coming home to a pulsing liver, pink and raw and oozing with pus.

I was not alone up there. Aside from the inner chamber in which I slept with *mon amour* — we, the lucky ones, with a door that could close out the world — the quarters included the entrance area, where J. and M. had their mattress shoved against the adjoining wall. The drama of their daily battles about nothing, peppered with fiery curses, was as heated and audible as their reconciliations in the dark. From here, a doorless entryway led to the kitchen, with its floor of grizzled tiles. This room contained a tilted table, a sink, two hot plates, and, center stage, a shower cubicle. Unlike many of those found in the low-end lodging of some other European countries, this spartan concession to twentieth-century hygiene wasn't coin-operated. You didn't need to have a franc or two lying next to the soap, ready to slip into the slot when suddenly the water went from sublime to ice. No, the temperature in this shower simply went from hot to horrible, and that was it — unless you cared to wait twenty minutes for the tank to reheat.

Mornings were struggles for civility as, stressed and squeezed, we vied for space and water. Reduced to laughter, we learned to manage. Then, too, there were not just the four of us, as Gaston seemed to live here also, appearing and reappearing like a young bird flitting back and forth to a nest under the roofs. Perhaps he slept in the shower; I can't recall.

The other facility we shared was the toilet. Squat-type, it was equipped with a water tank that might have dated from the Second Empire, with a chain dangling and a sunken enamel basin with footrests on either side. A cracked window under the ceiling was good only for letting in the cold. There were actually two tiny rooms with toilets, separated by the long and narrow hallway that ran like a brittle spine under the roof. Doors lined either side of the hallway, but these portals stayed shut. The other residents came and went mysteriously; the only traces of their existence were brisk steps at decidedly odd hours along the creaking wooden floorboards, strains of music — Sylvie and Johnny and Maghrebian crooning — through the cracks beneath their doors, and the infrasound from the toilet closest to our quarters. (This one was to be avoided, except in emergencies.)

The trip to the far end of the hall was easy to accomplish during the day, but at night the passage was disquieting. The murky light from two low-wattage bulbs . . . the whispering in the woodwork . . . all those doors with unknown occupants . . . Past midnight, showing his true colors, *mon amour* would make the trip with me, standing sentry in the gloom of the hallway.

I had seen *La bohème* some years earlier, as a child. The romance and tragedy had awakened me, not just to opera, but to greater possibilities. One day I would be an artistic soul in a Paris garret; love and creativity would see me through everything. And now, here I was, living high under the eaves in Paris, not unlike Mimi, although I hoped that the coming winter would not see M. or me felled.

I had been lulled by the ease with which the bohemians

flitted in and out of their charming garret onstage. The opera hadn't prepared me for the reality of reaching my own Parisian idyll: a climb of seven stories, day in, day out, often several times a day. If the dim upstairs hallway was the dislocated spine of our domain, then the coiled servants' stairwell, deep within the building's interior, was its digestive tract. We would begin our descent in the morning, laden with textbooks. The journey was a dizzying circle; only the landings outside the kitchen entrances of the apartments en route provided space to breathe. This was the route the garbage took, too, and its scent often lingered long after the bags had been carted to the *poubelles* in the courtyard.

The evening return could be arduous. Our shoulders sloped under the weight of the books. In one hand we might clutch shopping bags from Félix Potin filled with bottles of cheap wine and jars and canned goods on sale; in the other, there might be fragile packets from the *fromagerie,* wrapped in stenciled paper. One of us almost always had a baguette or two under an arm. In the ascent, the timing of the light switches was crucial: you could easily be stranded midflight in the near blackness of the stairwell, then have to grope along, guided only by the grudging red glow from the single button on each floor. To avoid this, we pressed the buttons ardently at each landing. It was a long trek upward, but we were young.

Some of us were familiar with Hemingway's belief that if you are lucky enough to have lived in Paris as a young man, then wherever you go for the rest of your life it stays with you, for Paris is a movable feast. We weren't impressed. We were a part of Paris; it was all around us. What we needed was real substance, for our bodies, now. While most of our meals were taken in various eating places in the city, dinners were often shared at the kitchen table with anyone — friends, classmates, old boyfriends — who happened to be around. On the upstairs budget, nearly anything was edible. We were carnivorous, we children, but rarely bought fresh meat. When we did, it was usually horse — the cheapest cut at most butchers. The table was crowded: elbows and a wild assortment of cutlery, courtesy of previous tenants, collided as we touched on as many subjects as our youth could conjecture. We argued and tested, dissolved in mad laughter, ate what was in front of us, and drank something red from dark green bottles.

The quarters under the roof were our haven, but we didn't hide there. Each day we strode forth into the city, claiming it as our own. Being on time for classes was de rigueur; otherwise we lived by the timetable of the Métro. If you missed the last one, you had to walk home, even if it was from all the way over at Nation. Our search for good but cheap food and drink took us all over the city. We would often march through the night, walking westward along the Seine from Boul'Mich', cutting down from Clichy, up from Montparnasse.

We adored the restaurants that specialized in couscous: its meat-flavored sauce was served with limitless grain. Then there were the little Tunisian shops with their sticky sweets and rolls packed tight with tuna and olives. We loved the coq au vin at Chez l'Ami Jean, a hole-in-the-wall in the seventh arrondissement. Rue Cler was the place to go for *mimolette ancienne* and grapes, comely cucumbers, and freshly baked baguettes from which we would rip off chunks, still warm, to eat as we walked. Sometimes we would stand at a certain window on the corner of that street, where Normandy butter and cacao from the former colonies scented the air. We let our eyes feast on the seductive array of mille-feuilles and *tarts* and a dozen types of patisserie before breathing in deeply and continuing on our way.

As students, we felt little anxiety or stigma about doing without. Student discounts were matter-of-fact, our bodies were strong, our minds inquisitive, and as for clothing, we were young and could wear what we pleased. We were, after all, the future. Our egos didn't suffer, even when we got a one-day job cleaning a penthouse on avenue Pierre 1er de Serbie. *Mon amour* washed the windows, I the toilets, and we were each paid one hundred francs.

When I left to visit my parents and uncle in Hamburg, *mon amour* rode to the Concorde Métro station, where he laid down his beret and played his guitar in the windy passage. For a few days he worked on the ledge of the thirty-seventh story of a building rising up on the western front of the city in La Défense. Yet there he was, waiting safely at the Gare du Nord when I stepped off the train laden with care packages teeming with North German goodies, and we returned to our room under the roof.

Daughters of conservative parents, M. and I did not technically live in the servants' quarters on avenue Malakoff. Only J. and *mon amour* were the bona fide tenants. M.'s official residence was a room in an apartment on rue du Faubourg Saint-Honoré, while mine was quite a bit closer. Actually, it was downstairs. It measured about eight by five and a half meters — perhaps less, perhaps more — in the fourth-story apartment of the woman who owned the servants' quarters in which we spent most of our domestic hours. How could I have explained to my parents that I was living with *mon amour*? Impossible. Our clandestine arrangement seemed ideal, indeed, rather *parisien*.

It was in the 348-square-meter home of Madame, a widow with a long name that had known better times, that I kept the bulk of my possessions. Entrance to my room, which looked out upon some plane trees on the avenue, was not by way of the servants' door in the kitchen but through the front entrance, easily accessible from the red-carpeted, cream-colored stairwell with its tidy brass-fitted elevator. The stairwell's scent was of polish and the perfume of the building's other residents, who lived, apparently in utter silence, behind their own heavy doors. Our occasional exchanges were brief: "Bonjour, monsieur." "Bonjour, mademoiselle." The latter was sometimes accompanied by a slight tip of an elderly gentleman's hat.

In the downstairs room, nothing was permitted to fall into disrepair. Although never used, the marble fireplace was dusted each day by the maid, who lived in a *banlieue*. The bedding came from one of the finest shops in Paris. The mattress was flat and firm and the headboard could have welcomed Napoleon III himself — in style, not in age. The room's palette was cream and pale blue, like the light that flooded in through the three windows at the far end. Two armchairs, upholstered in silk the color of that Normandy butter, seemed to wait attentively near a round mahogany table. I sat at a lady's writing desk, also from the Second Empire, to pen my letters home. Several meters above me, stucco detailing wound along the perimeter of the ceiling. And just outside the door was the bath room, clean, spacious, and for my use alone.

My landlady was often away at the ancestral home deep in

the Dordogne; her long-winded descriptions made it sound as if she journeyed there by calèche. In her absence, I was welcome to use the kitchen, which retained no vestige of the previous century. I could eat in the vermilion-paneled dining room, at the massive table gleaming with lacquer. Yet I remember taking only one meal there.

On the sunny day my father stopped in Paris for a visit en route from the Amazon, I showed him my virginal chamber. He pronounced it neat as a pin and suggested we meet again for dinner. "Invite a friend," he added, smiling. Later, when I arrived on my own at the restaurant high up on the Eiffel Tower, he looked surprised. "But where is your young man? I thought you would bring him along," he said, and I realized that, of course, he was aware that I wasn't alone in Paris. Clearly, I did not know my father as well as I had thought.

Family and friends passing through Paris were our tickets to the city's finer cuisine. We weren't mercenary, and enjoyed their company as much as the food. Cousins of *mon amour* took us to some of the best-kept culinary secrets on rue Mouffetard; a friend's uncle offered Maxim's. There were creamy hot chocolates at the rue de Rivoli, oysters at École Militaire. Sometimes we ate well even without being guests. It was lovely when it happened, but gone the next instant. Paris was about so much more than food.

The postal system went on strike. No letters entered the city from October to the beginning of December, and none went out; we hoped our families were well. But the Métro still ran and garbage was collected, at least most of the time. It was the season, so, dressed in our best, we made our entrance at the opera house, climbed its Grand Staircase, and kept climbing.

Arias rose to fullness, we found, even where we sat — up high,
near the ceiling. Somehow, when Nureyev came to town as
Tristan, we managed tickets. At the Musée Rodin we wandered
in the rain under trees that had lost most of their leaves; at the
marché aux puces we strayed through the lanes, bargaining for
trinkets while "Padam, padam, padam" sounded in the background from a distant accordion. We played pinball in Gitane-
clouded cafés where radios aired Georges Brassens singing "Les
amoureux des bancs publics." *Mon amour* shot pool with old
men. I browsed the stalls along the Seine, finding treasures. All
of us studied and wrote, laughed and loved. On the eve of my
twentieth birthday I wept into the monogrammed pillowcase
on the fourth floor with a melancholy that was bittersweet,
mon amour at my side.

A light snow fell in early winter. In photographs taken then,
Paris looks as it did in images surviving from the turn of the
last century, grainy and shadowed. I wear an ankle-length coat;
his hair is long and dark against the snow. We are turned in-
ward. A short time later, I lay gasping for air in our room under the roof, hearing voices singing "Sono andati? Fingevo di
dormire" inside my head. *Mon amour* took me to the hospital
and waited for the IV drugs to work their magic, his face as
pale as the snow had been. "Don't worry so," I whispered, smiling up at him from the narrow cot in the emergency room. "It's
only asthma. I am not Mimi."

Eventually we moved across the city to Nation where twice
a week the morning market sprang up beneath our window,
rough voices extolling the creaminess of the brie, the deep purple beauty of the aubergines. The refrigerator in the kitchen
was actually a cupboard; its back was a screened opening in

the building's outside wall. It worked well in winter, but with spring the ice melted, the milk turned sour. The kitchen sink doubled as the bathtub — but the place was ours alone. Meanwhile, still battling, J. and M. rented a studio on rue Mouffetard until, at last, the fire died out and they went their separate ways. Gaston spread his wings and disappeared south.

The following year we moved again, this time west to a ground-floor studio that faced south, overlooking a garden. We slept on a water bed. Here the building's garbage was tossed down a chute straight into the giant *poubelle* in the basement. Our concierge was Madame Hiret, plump and high pitched, her hair tightly coiled, and she spoiled and petted us almost as much as she did her fat little dog, Voyou. *Mon amour* and I gave each other one of our own, an Afghan. We folded her into a canvas bag to take to classes on rue de Varenne. We chased her across the Pont-Neuf and through the Bois de Boulogne, kicking up leaves, and one day we knew that no matter where we might find ourselves in the world, Paris would be an ache in our hearts.

Yes, we were young students in Paris. We had gone there because we knew it was the city of love and learning and light. Where it would lead was not as important as where we were at the moment. Looking at the city, we thought we saw our whole lives. Perhaps we did.

A Mild Hell

I N MY FIRST years in Paris I felt a shyness about going into cafés where I wasn't known — a timidity peculiar, admittedly, in a man already in his forties. I preferred to wander the streets in the constant drizzle (London has the bad reputation, but Paris weather is not much better). The whole city, at least *intra muros,* can be walked from one end to the other in a single evening. Perhaps its superficial uniformity — the broad avenues, the endlessly repeating benches and lamps stamped from the identical mold, the unvarying metal grates ringing the bases of the trees — promotes the dreamlike insubstantiality of Paris and contributes to the impression of a landscape "stripped of thresholds." Without barriers, I found myself gliding along from one area to another. (This inside/outside dichotomy of Paris as experienced by the flâneur keeps showing up in [the German essayist Walter] Benjamin's notes: "Just as '*flânerie*' can make an interior of Paris, an apartment in which the neighborhoods are the rooms, so neatly marked off as if with thresholds, in an opposite way the city can present itself to the stroller from all sides as a landscape stripped of all thresholds.")

Eventually I was able to distinguish what Parisians had labeled a "stuffy" quartier from a "happening" one, a workers' neighborhood from the home of the young and up-and-coming, but these distinctions were all acquired later and in conversation. At first, when I had to depend on my own observations, Paris impressed me as a seamless unity in which, by American standards, everything was well tended, built to last, and at once cold (the pale stone walls, the absence of neon, the unbroken facades never permitted by city ordinance to pass a certain height or to crack or crumble without undergoing a periodic facelift) *and* discreetly charming (lace curtains in the concierge's window, the flow of cleansing water in the gutters sandbagged to go in one direction or the other, the street fairs with rides for kids, the open-air food markets two days out of every week, segregated into different stalls under low awnings: this one loaded down with spices, that one with jellies and preserved fruits, not to mention the stand of the pâtissier and the baker, florist, butcher, fishmonger, the counter selling hot sausages and *choucroute* — or two hundred kinds of cheese). That water in the sandbagged gutter reminds me of something the great American poet John Ashbery once said in discussing the peculiar unaccountability of artistic influence: "I found my poetry being more 'influenced' by the sight of clear water flowing in the street gutters, where it is (or was) diverted or dammed by burlap sandbags moved about by workmen, than it was by the French poetry I was yearning to read at the time."

Imagine dying and being grateful you'd gone to heaven, until one day (or one century) it dawned on you that your main mood was melancholy, although you were constantly convinced that happiness lay just around the next corner. That's

something like living in Paris for years, even decades. It's a mild
hell so comfortable that it resembles heaven. The French have
such an attractive civilization, dedicated to calm pleasures and
general tolerance, and their taste in every domain is so sharp, so
sure, that the foreigner (especially someone from chaotic, confused America) is quickly seduced into believing that if he can
only become a Parisian he will at last master the art of living.
Paris intimidates its visitors when it doesn't infuriate them,
but behind both sentiments dwells a sneaking suspicion that
maybe the French have got it right, that they have located the
juste milieu, and that their particular blend of artistic modish-
ness and cultural conservatism, of welfare-statism and intense
individualism, of clear-eyed realism and sappy romanticism —
that these proportions are wise, time-tested, and as indisputable as they are subtle.

If so, then why is the flâneur so lonely? So sad? Why is there
such an elegiac feeling hanging over this city with the gilded
cupola gleaming above the Emperor's Tomb and the foaming,
wild horses prancing out of a sea of verdigris on the roof of the
Grand Palais? This city with the geometric tidiness of its glass
pyramid, Arch of Triumph, and the chilly portal imprinted by
the Grande Arche on a cloudy sky? Why is he unhappy, this
foreign flâneur, even when he strolls past the barnacled tow-
ers of Notre-Dame soaring above the Seine and a steep wall so
dense with ivy it looks like the side of a galleon sinking under
moss-laden chains?

WHEN I ARRIVED in Paris I was a fairly young-looking forty-
three and when I left I was nearly sixty, snowy-haired and jowly.

In the beginning I'd cruise along the Seine near the Austerlitz train station under a building that was cantilevered out over the shore on pylons. Or I'd hop over the fence and cruise the pocket park at the end of the Île Saint-Louis, where I lived. There I'd either clatter through the bushes or descend the steps to the quay that wrapped around the prow of the island like the lower deck of a sinking ship. Garlands of ivy dangled down the white walls from the deck above. I kept thinking of those lines in Ezra Pound's Second Canto where a Greek ship is immobilized at sea and transformed by the gods:

> And where was gunwale, there now was vine-trunk,
> And tenthril where cordage had been,
>   grape-leaves on the rowlocks,
> Heavy vine on the oarshafts,
> And, out of nothing, a breathing,
>   hot breath on my ankles,
> Beasts like shadows in glass,
>   a furred tail upon nothingness.

I had to step over the giant rusting rings on the quayside to which boats could be roped — though I never saw a boat moored there. When the *bateaux-mouches* would swing round the island, their klieg lights were so stage-set bright that we'd all break apart and try to rearrange our clothing. I kept hoping I'd run once more into an ardent, muscular lad who came home with me several times but never told me his name or gave me his number; all this boy would admit to was that he was kept in great style, in a town house in the Marais, by a German businessman who greatly resembled . . . me. (Busman's holiday, apparently.)

Of course most people, straight and gay, think that cruising is pathetic or sordid — but for me, at least, some of my happiest moments have been spent making love to a stranger beside dark, swiftly moving water below a glowing city. If you're a history buff, you can look at men (but don't touch them) in the late afternoon in the Tuileries Gardens up and down the gravel walkway behind the Orangerie. At night the whole place rocks — or did, at least, when I was still motivated to jump over fences and prowl (illegally) the moonlit pathways between ancient and modern statues or circle the mammoth round pond in which prehistoric carp doze in the ooze and surface in a feeding frenzy only when someone scatters breadcrumbs.

I CAN REMEMBER the heady days of 1981, when I paid a long visit to friends in Paris. When I moved to France in 1983, the euphoria was still in the air. I'd been conditioned by three decades of gay life in America to be in a permanent state of alert about possible police raids of bars, baths, and cruising places; equally feared were roving gangs of queer-bashers. But in Paris the streets and parks and saunas and back rooms seemed positively tranquil by contrast.

Socially, gays were treated differently as well. In New York, at least in the 1960s and 1970s, gays seldom ventured to gatherings out of the ghetto, whereas in Paris my American lover and I were invited everywhere and received as a couple, even if sometimes we were the only gay males present. In New York, liberal straights would have found a way to reassure us that we were really, truly welcome, whereas in Paris (at least among the well-heeled, sophisticated, arty people we were meeting) no one ever mentioned our sexuality. Or if someone did, it was in a general spirit of ribaldry, which so often presided over those worldly, lighthearted conversations.

FOR ME PARIS lives in its details — the blue windows set in the doors of the boxes at the Opéra-Comique, the only (and magical) source of illumination during that moment just after the house lights are lowered and before the stage curtain is raised. The drama with which the waiters cluster around a table in a first-class restaurant and all lift the silver bell-shaped covers at the same moment to reveal the contents of the plates — and the pedantry with which one of the waiters explains in singsong detail exactly what each dish contains. The pleasant shock of the klieg lights that suddenly turn night into day when a *bateau-mouche* glides by. The melancholy mood (worthy of an old-fashioned production of *Pelléas et Mélisande*) of an autumn day when one rows over to one of the islands in the Grand Lac of the Bois de Boulogne in order to have lunch in a deserted restaurant — or the squalid excitement when one staggers through the bushes nearby at night to see the theatrical costumes and maneuvers of glamorous transvestite prostitutes from Brazil striking poses in the glare of passing headlights.

The Sky Is Metallic

THE SKY IS metallic and draped over a square dome of the École Militaire. There are cobbles on the boulevard, and a Parisian in her mid-fifties walks by wearing a navy blue blazer, an imaginary crest of belonging on her breast pocket, shiny red padded ballerina shoes to offset her shiny blond padded hair. She walks with tailored yet wary purpose, as one who has spent a lifetime being what her status and looks demanded.

Four people, two male-female couples, also in their fifties, stop to look at a street map on the avenue de la Motte-Picquet. Their waistlines, their roomy shorts in September, their open-toed comfort nylon footwear, and a royal blue golfing visor propped in female hair identify them as North American. One of them, a white man wearing a knee brace, says something out loud, and all four turn to one another and laugh loudly together, on the street, showing all at once their teeth, the inside of their mouths, gray tongues, unconscious, easy pleasure, camaraderie. This communal laughter between couples, between male and female, signals tourists, *étrangers*. The sound of Paris is not laughter. But it is not only their laughter; there is a plate-glass optimism to their faces that is not from these parts.

Across the road and outside the military academy there is a plaque behind the number 82 bus stop. On it is written:

On 12 December 1941, the German military police, assisted by the French police, arrested 743 French Jewish people, the majority of whom were war veterans and *professions liberales*. They were held in the riding school of the Commandant Bossut of the École Militaire. The 743 were interned in the German camp of Royallieu in Compiègne, where some died from hunger and cold. On 24 March 1942, most of the 743 were deported on the first convoy to leave France for the destination of Auschwitz, where they were executed.

From the road you can see the green roof and concrete facade of the riding school where these French citizens were held. There are 332 plaques outside schools in Paris commemorating the eleven thousand Jewish children taken from Parisian schools during the Occupation who never returned.

There is a fault line to the city that weighs heavy. Paris and its people were occupied. They were a people that fought, fled, surrendered, resisted, rescued, collaborated, kept silent, watched, much as any occupied population does. De Gaulle's defiant rhetoric on the steps of the Hôtel de Ville on the day of the city's liberation could not erase the humiliation and compromise of four years of Nazi occupation. Parisians do not assume a moral zone of black and white. Nothing is unequivocal, absolute, indisputable.

Paris is grayness and fractured humanity, an acceptance of fault and frailty that is disconcerting and disorienting to the Anglo-Saxon system of beliefs. It is easy to confuse the French propensity for doubt with moral escapism. In 2003, France objected to entering the war with Iraq; they questioned the very existence of "weapons of mass destruction," those imaginary stockpiles of chemical, biological, and nuclear weapons that proved so effective in rallying public support for an immediate invasion of Iraq. For their objection and doubt, the French government was denounced by a swath of politicians and media commentators: the London *Times* predicted France's diplomatic future in "unsplendid isolation in the anteroom occupied by history's losers," while the *New York Post* derided France as "the axis of weasel."

I came to Paris fifteen years ago, aged twenty-six, with an English sense of right and wrong: self-righteous, simplistic, judgmental, puritanical, an island mentality. The English belief system has long found perfect expression in the myth of King Arthur and the Knights of the Round Table, in the chivalric code of honor, the valiant knight, the concepts of feudal courtesy and unquestioning courage. When Gawaine, Arthur's well-loved knight and nephew, manages to fatally wound his own cousin Uwaine in a jousting contest and a case of mistaken identity, Uwaine forgives his cousin with the dying words, "Do not grieve, for all men must die sometime, and I could not have died by a nobler hand than yours." When I came to Paris, I believed in queuing, apology, duty, ideals. I believed that life could be achieved by will.

I traveled recently to England for a wedding service that took place in the chapel of an Oxford college. The bride and groom, thoroughly modern media and medical professionals, chose "Jerusalem" as one of their hymns. Written by William Blake in 1808 as a prelude to his epic *Milton,* the words were set to music some one hundred years later, in 1916, for a Fight for Right campaign meeting, in an effort to rouse toppled morale and reignite stoicism to continue fighting the First World War. The opening stanza is

> And did those feet in ancient time
> Walk upon England's mountains green?
> And was the holy Lamb of God
> On England's pleasant pastures seen?

Perhaps not surprisingly, over the years Blake's words have been reappropriated for their patriotic and nationalistic symbolism. "Jerusalem" has been used as the official anthem for English sports teams, boarding schools, political campaigns — wherever there is a need to stir up a sense of right or righteousness. Hearing the surge of voices in the chapel, I was struck by the gust of pride and sentimentality and I considered that Paris and the French would never dare to indulge in this level of delusion.

The English want to know that what they are doing is right; the French cannot permit themselves this lofty moral high ground. The English want their leaders and heroes faultless, morally impeccable, and those who are not must fall. Paris does not require the unimpeachable. President Mitterrand had a secret family, an illegitimate daughter, and a post in the Vichy local administration. President Sarkozy is twice divorced. His second wife left him after he had been in power for three months; four months later he married a woman he had known for three months. Carla Bruni, his new wife, has a habit of crashing in on marriages and a past of rock-star lovers. Paris does not even require consistency. Napoleon's empress,

Joséphine de Beauharnais, was the daughter of a nobleman, married a nobleman, and used to hunt with the king's brother. During the Revolution she was imprisoned, but she escaped the guillotine, although her first husband did not. She survived the carnage, whereupon she reinvented herself as a society hostess under the Directoire before marrying Napoleon. The French are endlessly subtle in their embrace of humanity and the mutations of a life. They accept human fault. They expect it.

Recognition of human frailty brings with it an inevitable sadness; there is no joy to Paris, no helium of optimism. I am not sure Barack Obama could exist in France, because I am not sure the French would ever let themselves believe in the ideal, the virtue and hope, that people have instilled in him. I remember a lunch with several women; the husband of one of them had left her six months before. She was in her late fifties and had been married for over thirty years. Her silver blond hair curled over the collar of her suede and fur *gilet,* her wrists were slim, her sorrow sheer. At the lunch it was obvious that her Parisian friends had decided the time of grieving was over. "You've got two children, a granddaughter, a lovely apartment. You're invited out to dinner parties," they said, as if this was enough to salvage from a lifetime of marriage and trust. "It's true," she said. "I go out a lot. I've never had as many *Brushings* as since my husband left me." Paris is no place for idealization; sorrow and depression are accepted parts of life.

I live in the south of the sixth arrondissement, a quartier populated by schoolchildren, students, and the bourgeoisie. On a Wednesday in Paris, children do not go to school, and I spend much time crossing the streets and squares and the jardins du Luxembourg on foot with a stroller or a child's hand in mine. At around three in the afternoon I stop beneath the windows of an apartment building on the rue Joseph Bara to listen to a person who is practicing the piano. I can't work out which floor the sound comes from; I'm not even certain which side of the road the piano is on, only that it is high above and I stand beneath. The music is soulful, classical. I cannot tell you which piece of music it is, only that the person is always there at this time playing. The sound of Paris is this melancholy, exquisite gift, this person playing, alone. Doubt is everywhere. "You always want to master it," my piano teacher said to me, "but you have to feel it first." Paris has taught me my will alone cannot get me there.

I pass by the sculpture of le capitaine Dreyfus, who stands on the boulevard Raspail. A young French officer of Alsatian Jewish descent, he was wrongly convicted of treason in 1894. He was sentenced to life imprisonment for allegedly having passed French military secrets to the German Embassy in Paris. Dreyfus suffered falsification of documents, wrongful imprisonment, a military cover-up, and rampant anti-Semitism. In 1898, after Dreyfus had spent four years locked up on Devil's Island in French Guiana, Émile Zola exploded the military cover-up and forgery with his famous open letter to the president of the republic, Félix Faure, in the newspaper *L'Aurore,* which began "J'accuse." The statue of Dreyfus shows him standing in all his humility and humiliation, at the moment when he was publicly stripped of office on the parade ground of the École Militaire. His sword is broken, but he still holds it to his face in salute, and the gesture is one of pathos and dignity. It is a remarkable sculpture in that it expresses both the offense against the person and the admission of fault within the French establishment.

I walk across the boulevard Montparnasse, where my child has a rendezvous for a vaccination with a pediatrician, Dr. Jean-Claude Moscovici. I have been bringing my children here for five years but have only recently read Moscovici's memoir of his childhood, *Voyage à Pitchipoï*, which was published in 1995. Dr. Moscovici's father was the doctor in a village in the French countryside. His father and uncle were arrested by the Gestapo and French gendarmes in 1942, having been denounced by villagers. They were deported. Two months later the Gestapo returned to the house and took his grandparents. As soon as his sister reached the age of two, his mother was arrested. She escaped at the moment of arrest and remained on the run for the next year. Jean-Claude Moscovici, aged six, and his two-year-old sister were then imprisoned and taken to Drancy, a French concentration camp to the northeast of Paris, directed by SS officers and administered by French gendarmes, from which prisoners were deported to concentration camps, principally Auschwitz. Miraculously, Moscovici and his sister were released. We talk of the Occupation of France on a Wednesday afternoon as his hot waiting room fills with children and sighing mothers and my son deconstructs the playhouse. Moscovici, his mother, and his sister returned to the family house after the war, finding it shut up, emptied. His father and grandparents never returned. He still owns this house; it is where he spends his holidays, the last place he saw his father.

Still, the instinct to judge surges up in me — the Englishness, the need to know who was right and who was wrong.

And how could you carry on living there, go back among that village, those people? I ask. He shrugs and tells me his mother used to say that every time she was on the run during those years, one door would close in her face and another would be opened.

I walk home through the jardins du Luxembourg; it is brown and humid. They have placed warning posters at the gates, signaling strong winds and the possibility of falling branches. Beneath the warning text is a line drawing in black ink of a Parisian dressed in a winter coat with an umbrella turned inside out; she walks bent beneath a swooping tree, shards of branch flying. She walks through the *jardins* knowing that a branch can strike, asking if she will be strong enough to resist. Always this doubt. Paris knows that human failing is part of human endeavor.

STACY SCHIFF

In Franklin's Footsteps

THE OBSESSION TOOK hold in New York, which posed
a problem: what I wanted to write about next was Ben
Franklin's eighteenth-century adventure in France. On some
level, I knew from the start that the only way to research that
book was to move our family, for some period of time, to Paris.
And from the start — even as friends enviously asked if we
would do so — I dreaded the prospect. Generally Paris is not
considered a hardship posting, save to someone who values ef-
ficiency, candor, and Szechuan takeout. Nor was this to be a
larky, lighthearted school year abroad. Paris means Angélina's
chocolat chaud and the Tuileries at dusk and the Rodin Museum and Pierre Hermé, but it is also a city, I had come to learn,
of phone repairmen, plumbers, and dentists, the vast majority
of them French. With age, the dislocations tend to announce
themselves less as bracing, extracarbonated mental states than
as crippling tornadoes of small details.

In part I suppose I dreaded what can only be termed my
own devolution. Whereas at home I am organized, competent,
and semiarticulate, I am in France awkward and incapable. I
can be deaf to nuance. Some frequencies elude me entirely.
Franklin was very clear about the fact that a man sacrifices

half his intelligence in a foreign language, but he had plenty of intelligence to spare. (He bemoaned especially that his humor fell flat on the page, as indeed it did.) Even without a language barrier, I knew myself to be handicapped. At any moment I am likely to revert to my Anglo-Saxon habits, to forget not to lay a finger on the greengrocer's tomatoes, not to reach for my *boulangerie* change before it is counted, not to order my sandwich before my *café crème*. (My husband falls in a different category. A Frenchman raised on foreign soil, he passes for a native until confronted with a cheese tray, at which juncture his passport is nearly revoked. He once left a Normandy inn-keeper dumbstruck by asking, in unaccented and syntactically impeccable French, what precisely *un potage jardinier* consisted of. Imagine a native New Englander inquiring after a definition of clam chowder.) There was one other deterrent, too, one that the biographer Richard Holmes has identified: "Writers of course are always slightly ashamed at not being at their desks, especially in Paris, where they might be out — having a good time, *mon dieu*."

We figured that the one-year-old wouldn't object to the plan but assumed that some finessing might be in order for the eight- and ten-year-olds. Which may explain why we broke the news at the Café de Flore a semester beforehand, over *cafés liégeois* and *éclairs au chocolat,* the blackmailing parent's best friends. The eight-year-old was an immediate convert. The ten-year-old succumbed neither to the sugar rush nor to the pandering. He made it clear that he would not be decamping to Paris until France fielded a major-league baseball team. And it was he who — on the August day we headed off to JFK with our 15 suitcases — planted himself on the steaming sidewalk and refused to budge. It was also he who planted himself on the sidewalk and refused to budge a year later, when we headed to Charles de Gaulle with more bags than any of us bothered to count. They were at least fewer than the 126 with which Franklin headed home in 1785, baggage that included three Angora cats, a printing press, a sampling of mineral waters, and a variety of saplings.

By a happy quirk, we found an apartment in Franklin's old neighborhood, less hilly today than it was in the 1770s. There were other modern-day advantages as well. No fewer than six *boulangeries* stand along the mile that separated Franklin's home from that of John Adams. Franklin had to make that walk on an empty stomach, something I never did. There was, after all, pressing *pain au chocolat* research to be done. We lived fifteen minutes from Versailles, an expedition that took Franklin two dusty hours by carriage. When we bicycled in the Bois de Boulogne, we crossed the lawn where Franklin followed the first manned balloon as it rose into the sky in 1783, something he did with considerable anxiety. We were two very different Americans in Paris, but I delighted in the overlay of our lives. It did what a foreign adventure is supposed to do — it made the mundane thrilling. Along the route Franklin traveled twice every week, to the home of the woman he hoped to seduce (as opposed to the one he wanted to marry), was the lovely Congolese tailor who lengthened our son's pants before the start of the school year. Picking up the dry cleaning qualifies as less of a chore when you are doing so on ground you know Ben Franklin and John Adams have trodden before you. And I could always justify shopping at the pricey ice cream shop on the rue Bois-le-vent. It seemed nearly obligatory to do so, given that the shop stands where the back door to Franklin's home once had. Moreover, it seemed dangerous not to, as the shop hours were erratic, a universal signal of artistic integrity but a guarantee of greatness in France.

To France America sent as its first emissary a man who confessed he was wholly indifferent to food. (And one who was ignorant about it in the extreme: it was his conviction that there was no butter in French sauces.) Franklin ate well but pined for a good Indian pudding, a piece of salt pork, Newtown Pippin apples, and walnuts. We had an easier time fending off homesickness. Never has our family eaten as many H & H bagels as we did in Paris; they can be had, frozen, at a little store on the rue de Grenelle, conveniently on my way home from the diplomatic archives. And so breakfast became an odd binational affair — bagels with Kiri, the French spreadable that most closely resembles Philadelphia cream cheese. One thing that immediately fell off our radar was Chinese food, much though the cravings for sesame noodles and pork dumplings continued. Just as the word *teamwork* is missing from the French language, so are the concepts "family style" and "for the table." To attempt a Szechuan or Hunan meal without sharing is to defeat the purpose of the exercise. Inevitably one is left to covet one's neighbor's plate.

On the other hand, Thanksgiving in Paris was a dead ringer for Thanksgiving at home, save for the much-missed butternut squash and the fact that everything tasted better. I don't know whom we have to thank — I fear it may be Hallmark — but Parisian butchers have come a long way since the first time I ordered a *grosse dinde* in November, nearly twenty years ago. "Oh, is it for your American rite?" asked the butcher, with a

squint of the eye generally reserved for Jewish-Masonic con-
spiracies. Now those *grosses dindes* come with a side order of
miniature American flags. In New York we are Pilgrims, but
in Paris we are Americans.

We had one great advantage over Franklin: we spoke French.
Franklin rarely acknowledged that minor handicap, although
he did refer to contracts that had been signed in his first year,
when misapprehension was the order of the day. Even a bilingual family came in for its share of surprises, however. There
was the hockey coach who chain-smoked on the ice. (There
were also the unforgiving stares to be endured in the Métro
when traveling with an eight-year-old in full hockey equip-
ment, especially as that child was a girl.) School recess may well
have taken place in the magnificent parc Monceau, but one
did not (a) set foot on the grass, (b) throw a ball, or (c) throw
anything resembling a ball. In turn, the flying scarves, the
chestnuts, the bottle caps were confiscated. The school week is
cleverly configured to keep mothers from working (home for
lunch; half day Wednesday; four-hour birthday parties). The
academic calendar is configured to keep teachers from having
to work more than three weeks straight.

Some of the frustrations were maddeningly familiar. The
problem is less one of language than of the sterling example
set — and the expectations harbored — by North American ef-
ficiency. It is almost impossible to shake the Anglo-Saxon concern that you are holding up the line, a qualm that does not
exist in France, where it is one's privilege and responsibility to
do so. Quite simply, ours is a service economy. France's is not. A
café waiter is meant to do his job, but that job is most decidedly
not to guarantee the satisfaction of his customer. Rather it is

the customer's job to admire the professionalism of the waiter, the expertise with which he can flick a baguette crumb into oblivion, his unerring capacity to make change. Stocking the larder is a full-time job, more so even than in Franklin's day, when the fruit seller and the pâtissier and the *laitier* delivered their goods to the door. (Judging from his household accounts, Franklin had a hearty and prescient taste for apple pie.) Early on the ten-year-old delivered up the paradox of Parisian life: In that city, one accomplishes precisely half of what one sets out that morning to accomplish. Which means that if one heads out with only one thing to do, one has a problem.

France is a country hidebound by regulations; the national sport consists of gracefully subverting them. The trick is not to follow the rules but to avoid getting caught breaking them. It is Casablanca on a grand scale. One adapts quickly but some-times ambivalently, especially since this is not necessarily the lesson one cares to impart to one's American children. Two thousand two was an election year in France, which meant several things. It meant there was a strike of some kind pretty much every minute; one might call the Louvre to confirm that the children's weekend class was in session, only to hike across town to discover that, indeed, class was not canceled, but that the building was locked tight. (The opposite might also be true: the post office was open, but the employees were on strike.) The library staff might well be in place — except those who delivered titles from shelves *L* through *S*. Under the highly regulated exterior all is chaos: The order at a piano recital is whoever wants to go first. The TV news starts at a set time — and continues until the news is finished, a signal triumph of content over form. There may be a hockey bus to convey the team to Meudon, or there may not. (Naturally this nontruth requires three phone calls to establish.) There is no such thing as a Gallic work ethic, and in an election year there is no constituency that is too dignified, or too disenfranchised, to strike. In the course of the year, the emergency room doctors, the gendarmerie, the teachers, the unemployed, all walked out on strike. Everything is predicated on the crucial "except," and *exceptionellement* quickly became our favorite word in the French language. The exception of the day became a staple of the dinner conversation.

Election year brought with it lessons apart from the political ones. As every Frenchman knows, all driving violations are promptly pardoned by the incoming *président de la république*. It is his gift to the people of France; it is the modern-day version of royal prerogative; it is the tradition every candidate must vow to uphold. Which means that for the months leading up to any presidential election, all speed and traffic laws are de facto suspended. (Road fatalities rise accordingly.) Essentially what this means is that any piece of Parisian surface — sidewalk, driveway, bus stop — suddenly qualifies as a parking space. Quickly we went native; our children seemed ambivalent about what they termed our "rural parking." What kind of lesson, they asked, were we imparting? The lesson we were imparting was, should our children ever settle in France, they had better get with the program, or they will be circling the block eternally.

And then there is that staple of French life: the specious argument. After a full day's drive to the country, fully wilted, we inquire in a restaurant at 5:00 p.m. if there might be anything on hand to eat. No, is the answer. Not even an ice cream? Well, yes, of course, comes the reply. We got very good at playing Go Fish. Also at heading off the brand of logistical display we had encountered years earlier on an Air France flight, when we attempted to settle the firstborn in the airline's bassinet. He did not fit. The bassinet was for children under two. Ergo, reasoned the indignant stewardess, the child was not under the age of two. (As his passport duly attested, he was nine months old. Under other circumstances, my outsize American children have elicited plaudits, of the kind a Great Dane wins in a city of poodles. "Ça, madame," offered a well-dressed gentleman in the jardin du Ranelagh one day, pointing to a different nine-month-old, "Ça, madame, c'est un bébé.")

Go Fish is a game I can play. A different tournament will forever stand between me and French nationality. That is the sport essential to French life: I pontificate, therefore I am. Between Passy and Saint-Germain, a royalist taxi driver worked himself into a fever one night over Chirac's misdeeds and the pressing need to reinstall the Bourbon heir (rather than the Orléans pretender) to the throne of France. His diatribe, and his reliquary of a taxi, may be the last thing our children forget about the year abroad.

Some mysteries of our new life went unsolved. Is there anything the French can't advertise with cleavage? How is it possible that twenty-first-century Paris could still boast Turkish toilets? Why does the milk not need to be refrigerated? Why does the shampoo not lather? Certain things were best left unexplained, like the gaggle of short-skirted teenagers who congregated across the street from the apartment, rain or shine. "Have you ever wondered when those girls go to school?" asked the eight-year-old. Fortunately, she never noticed that those prodigies spent their day getting in and out of cars with out-of-town plates, cars that reliably delivered them back to the corner an hour later. At least they dressed respectably, as opposed to their sisters (and faux sisters) a block deeper into the Bois de Boulogne. There were two jogging itineraries: my Felliniesque own, and the less scenic route, which I took when running with the children.

In the end, though, the pleasures exceeded the familiar physical glories and culinary delights. One lives better in Europe, not only on account of the cheeses and the three-hour lunches and the enforced weekend. One does so thanks to SOS Couscous, whose deliverymen ladle dinner from dented metal casseroles; on account of pediatricians who pay house calls and orthodontists who take appointments until 9:00 p.m.; because the playgrounds are vastly superior, free as they are from liability issues. There is good coffee and *steak frites* even at the hockey rink, where the adults are blessedly oblivious to the game. And the parent of a school-age child saves countless hours: there are no bake sales, no safety patrol, no home games. The last thing any French school administration cares to encounter in its hallways is a parent. We came nearly to take for granted those built-in privileges of a socialist country: when making travel arrangements, when buying shoes, when visiting a museum, we were entitled to a discount as a card-carrying *famille nombreuse*. (Woe to any *famille nombreuse* that attempts a dinner in a good French restaurant, however. At least until the two-year-old orders oysters.)

As it happened, we had something else in common with Franklin. While I waited to pick the children up from school one fall afternoon, my Parisian sister-in-law called to report that a plane had flown into the World Trade Center. I assumed she meant that a crazy student pilot had done so until I got home and turned on the television. From that moment on Americans in Paris were few on the ground. As it had been in the eighteenth century, America was naked and vulnerable again. "Nous sommes tous américains," blared the headlines, and any cabdriver who heard a whisper of English was happy not only to ask where we were from — for once New York was the proper answer, rather than California — but to offer sympathy and thanks for 1945. For the worst reasons imaginable, we enjoyed a taste of the fervor for the New World that Franklin had so effectively cultivated in the Old. A friend who was treated to a rare viewing of original Proust papers asked afterward why he had been so lucky. "Consider it repayment for June sixth," he was told, just after the fiftieth anniversary of D-day. Say the words "Benjamin Franklin" and you elicit a smile from a Frenchman. On days when I wasn't smiling, I made a point of coming home via the place du Trocadéro, over which a bronze Franklin presides. Sometimes I felt closer to him there than I did in the archives. That is the blessed thing about France: the history is always close to the surface. I suppose it was why we went.

Litost

I T BEGAN WITH a word: *litost*. My six turbulent years in Paris were launched by a reading of Kundera's *The Book of Laughter and Forgetting* and, specifically, by this one word. Described in Michael Henry Heim's translation as

> a Czech word with no exact translation into any other language. It designates a feeling as infinite as an open accordion, a feeling that is the synthesis of many others: grief, sympathy, remorse, and an indefinable longing. The first syllable, which is long and stressed, sounds like the wail of an abandoned dog.

Kundera, in trying to describe the elusive sense of this word, touched a nerve deep within me.

> Under certain circumstances, however, it can have a very narrow meaning, a meaning as definite, precise, and sharp as a well-honed cutting edge. I have never found an equivalent in other languages for this sense of the word either, though I do not see how anyone can understand the human soul without it.

Suddenly, my quest to understand my own indefinable sorrows and longings came to include a desire to learn this language, one that had a word for this range of human emotion that English and all others lacked — a set of emotions so close to my heart. How could I think and write without knowing it? An aspiring poet and language autodidact — I had taught myself bits of Gaelic and Latin in addition to my high school French and German — I craved something from language and literature. I just didn't know what.

Michael Henry Heim happened to be visiting Harvard at the time, and a friend studying at MIT, who'd been having trysts with members of the Cambridge literati, connected us. I went to meet him to describe my love of Kundera and to ask how he'd learned the language, and how I might. "Do you speak French?" he asked me, seemingly nonsensically. Passably, I replied. "Well, you can't go to Prague" — this was 1985, and the wall had not yet come down — "but you can go to Langues O' in Paris and they'll teach you Czech." Langues O' was the nickname for INALCO, the l'Institut National des Langues et Civilisations Orientales. Kundera was living in Paris by then and had begun writing in French. "You might meet him," Heim added. And that was that.

I was amused to find that *orientales* for the French meant anything east of Germany, and south as well — dozens of African dialects were taught at Langues O'. It was ridiculously cheap: fees for the year were less than two hundred dollars. Where would I live? My MIT friend — we ourselves had met by chance on a train to Berlin in the mideighties, each on a postcollege European tour — had a friend who had studied abroad and could connect me to one of her friends there. This man was incredibly helpful and spoke great English; he developed software and so was usually up half the night, convenient for calling from the States. A friend of his was on sabbatical in Silicon Valley; I could rent his studio, just south of Paris but with a view of the Eiffel Tower. Would that be OK?

So much of this story is incredible, who could have imagined it? Even more so because I did not have any great Francophilia in my heart. I grew up with a sort of split-screen idea of the French, with a father who came of age on a dairy farm in Depression-era Georgia but graduated at the top of his high school class and made it to the Naval Academy, studying, among other things, French; he was posted to Saigon in the early 1960s, within a decade of the French departure, and conducted intelligence there. From him I acquired a sense of France as a place of culture and fine things in life. My mother, on the other hand, is an Anglo-Canadian who grew up in Halifax. Her father was twice premier of Nova Scotia and minister of the Canadian Navy during World War II. For my Canadian side, the French represented a threat to their country's unity and to the well-being of the impoverished Maritime Provinces, which would be cut off from the rest of Canada should Quebec ever succeed in seceding. Our summers in Halifax had included mutterings about the rabble-rousing French, oaths against bilingual road signs and cereal boxes, and ridicule of de Gaulle and his call to arms for the Québecois.

So I had conflicted feelings about going to Paris, and about France, but surely I could put up with anything to reach my dream of understanding the language that created this amazing word, *litost*. How bad could it be?

I arrived in Paris loaded down with books and an antique Royal typewriter. I'd been delayed two months while Langues O' came back from vacation and sent me the necessary papers.

The friend of my friend who'd arranged my apartment was to pick me up at Charles de Gaulle Airport, so after my plane landed, I gathered my luggage onto a *chariot* and waited. And waited. When he finally appeared, tall and handsome and close to an hour late, his first words were, "Where were you?" I was speechless. If I'd known the role lateness would come to play for us, I might have grabbed my *chariot* and run the other way. But late as he was, he *was* handsome, with the suggestion of great charm, and, crucially, I'd been told he had a great mind. He also had the keys to my apartment, and so when words returned to me, I replied that I'd been there all along, and where was he?

We got into his big, beautiful old Mercedes sedan and headed to his office, a town house off the Champs-Élysées, and had lunch, prepared by the in-house chef, with his charming but somewhat geeky — though geeky in French was really pretty adorable — fellow *polytechnicien* colleagues. He had been born the same year as I but seemed older and had already started a successful business. If *Sex and the City* had been around back then, I might have called him Mr. Big. Or in this case, Monsieur Grand.

Paris is beautiful in the autumn, at least until the rains come, when you want to sit in a café reading and nursing a cognac. I had several weeks until classes began and so I familiarized myself with my neighborhood, a sort of nice middle-class suburb immediately south of Paris, and with the city itself. And all the little details of life in *la belle France*. That everything closes between noon and 2:00. Or 1:00 and 3:00. Or thereabouts — you had to pay attention. No grocery shopping at 11:00 p.m. — everything closed by 7:30. The pharmacies were one of my favorite discoveries. They were beautiful emporiums of fine soaps, baby food, even beautiful Band-Aids, and housed homeopathic and naturopathic remedies as well as being places to have your prescriptions filled. You could go to your pharmacist as you would your doctor, just about.

Sure enough, the Eiffel Tower was a giant nightlight in the distance from my studio balcony, blinking off at 1:00 a.m. Having left a complicated relationship behind, I was in no rush to start up something new, but M. Grand was a great tour guide. Among other things, he taught me the difference between *savoir* and *connaître,* because of course the French have two verbs for "to know," and he shared with me the highly useful and consolatory fact that stepping in dog poo in France is considered a stroke of luck. He was hoping for a more elevated status than guide, but this time, he was waiting for me.

I remember a lot of walking on my own and a lot of language shock — my high school French was like another language altogether. I also remember going into a patisserie and ordering "un Napoléon, s'il vous plaît," and the girl looked at me as if I had two heads. (The rich, layered pastries known in the United States by the name of the famous French general and emperor are known in France as mille-feuilles — "a thousand leaves," appropriate to the many layers of puff pastry therein.)

I ate a lot of cheese, discovering some of the hundreds of varieties of which France is so proud, and bread, so excellent and cheap, and washed it down with good wine that was cheap as well. I discovered how delicious French pizza is, and even canned French vegetables (I was pretty poor). I read a lot of *journaux* to bolster my vocabulary and watched some fairly bad French TV. I kept trying to hold M. Grand at bay, but it seemed clear that it would be only a matter of time before he wore me down. I didn't really know how I felt about him — he was so easy to be with, charming and smart. For a variety of reasons I thought love had to be hard — but I liked how much he liked me. And he was on a mission to take care of me.

One of the anthropologist Raymonde Carroll's American subjects described her relationship with a Frenchman thus: "If I had wanted to have a child, I would have liked to have it with him, but never in a million years would I have wanted him to be the father of my child." This paradoxical statement came to make perfect sense to me. The brilliance of the graduates of the *grandes écoles,* the savoir faire inculcated from birth, the near-suffocating sense of history, legacy, and birthright that Americans, in comparison, lack — all this is entirely seductive, something you would want to pass on to your child. The deeper you dig, however, the more those subtle, charming differences take on a different cast . . . But I'm getting ahead of myself. *Revenons à nos moutons . . .*

I had found out that my image of Langues O' as a beautiful gothic building in the center of Paris — I knew that their offices were on the rue de Lille, in the seventh — was just a hopeful fantasy, and that each language was taught in some peripheral cluster, usually in university buildings around the edge of the city, built in the sixties. They were probably already somewhat grim then; now they were outright bleak. Czech was taught in Clichy, a working-class northern suburb. Bare-bones does not begin to describe the facilities. Having come from the aesthetically beautiful American university system, especially my alma mater, which could define the term *ivy-covered halls,* this was a shock. Also, the location could not have been farther from where I lived, south of the city.

I soldiered on, meeting interesting young French students who were intrigued by this *américaine* who'd come all the way to Clichy, God forbid, to learn Czech, of all things. They loved the literary reason behind it, and I loved that they loved it — I was used to things literary being treated at best like a dalliance or at worst like a waste of time, and here I was in a country that held literature up on a pedestal, where the publication of a new literary work was treated with reverence, and where there was a prime-time, must-see weekly talk show dedicated to recent books and their authors. It blew my mind. Truly, this was the land of milk and honey. And mille-feuilles.

Six months later, I had stopped going to classes and had moved in with M. Grand. I rented a small studio from an American painter near the Bastille in order to write. One day, my work of several years disappeared — my work-in-progress, poems typed and in longhand, journals, Czech dictionaries and books — stolen by an unstable acquaintance of the painter's. He took them, and later admitted he had, but couldn't tell us where. We never understood why.

Then I learned that I was pregnant, and everything else in my life seemed to stop. I did not know if I could be both poet and mother. Here, in a foreign land, these two realities strained my sanity.

The gendarmes called just as we were leaving to drive to the south to visit M. Grand's parents. Some of my papers and books had been found on a train near Lyon; they would hold them for us to claim. Driving to pick them up was a surreal and symbolic experience, mimicking so much else of my life in France, where I was continually challenged to stake and claim my identity in situations of cultural divide, emotional stress, personal turmoil. Retrieving some of my poems — there were many I would never get back — I realized, standing in the *gendarmerie lyonnaise,* M. Grand by my side, our Franco-American child on the way, that it was entirely up to me which of these pieces of my identity I wanted to continue holding in my hand, and which I should set free.

Our baby boy was born the following New Year's Day. He was a magical baby, sweet tempered and beautiful — a family friend joked that he was *une fille manquée* — a near-miss girl. He was born in the States but flew back with us to France at three months. Life there with a baby was an entirely new chapter of *la vie française.* The beautiful clothes (but no snaps between the legs!), the beautiful parks (but children not allowed on the grass!), the wonderful restaurants for tired parents to dine (dogs, OK; kids, no thanks!). On the plus side, good health care, childcare immediately, paid time off, and the most beautiful baby food: puréed *artichauts, petits pois,* the tenderest spring vegetables, and, at the appropriate age, delicate cuts of meat (the French take palate development quite seriously).

From being a writer-in-progress I became a full-time *maman,* and I reveled in it at first. But we were living in a western suburb that first year and the loneliness and isolation took its toll. *Les beaux-parents* — I use the term for in-laws loosely, as I did not marry M. Grand, instead choosing, to the chagrin of all, to continue in the dreadfully termed state of concubinage — were wonderful, for the most part. I actually loved the *déjeuners en famille le dimanche,* which lasted till 5:00 p.m. When the baby was four months old, we drove to the Île Saint-Louis in my favorite of M. Grand's car collection, a 1970s navy blue Jaguar with white leather interior, and baptized the baby in the lovely Église Saint-Louis-en-l'Île. The enormous family gathering afterward at M. Grand's parents' house west of Paris brought American and French families together in the closest thing we would have to a wedding reception.

The summer was split between the family's house on the Côte d'Azur and the States. We moved into Paris the following spring, somewhat controversially, as it was out of the rent-free family-owned apartment in the suburbs into a paying situation (*horreur*!). We took an apartment that had to be completely redone — it did not in fact have a bathroom — but it was lovely Belle Époque.

Part of the reason for the move was to be closer to M. Grand's office — he continued to work long, grueling hours, having shuttered one business and started another, and family time was nonexistent. His chronologically challenged aspect, which I had seen even before we met, as I waited at the airport with my *chariot,* did not improve with the birth of our child. But otherwise, life was delightful in the seventeenth, next to the Église Suédoise with its pealing Sunday bells and beyond-charming Christmas bazaar. I joined British and other American mothers in playgroups, where we commiserated about our outsider status and traded tips on where to find the foods and other bits from life back home that we missed.

I became attached to this *vie parisienne,* getting to know my little quartier: the excellent *fromager,* the two *boulangeries* — both good, but I had my favorite — the *épicier,* the many Arabs who sold a little of everything, the Nicolas wine shop, which held an all-out spirited Beaujolais day when it arrived in November — "Le beaujolais nouveau est arrivé!" By then I'd returned to Clichy, now taking Russian, and I was on my way out of the Métro around 6:00 p.m. when I stopped in for a glass, or two . . . It took me a while to get home.

I spent many happy hours pushing the little one in his lovely *poussette,* at the marché rue Poncelet or in the exquisite parc Monceau, embarrassed to be continually mistaken as his au pair. I wanted to be the sophisticated *parisienne* but instead looked as young and as English as the wonderful gap-year girls who babysat for us.

It was one of these girls, a beautiful young Irishwoman, who described to me her perception of something I'd long felt but could not yet admit about Paris: its distinctly sinister side. Something about its history—more than in London or other European cities—oozes from its Haussmannian boulevards and wedding-cake buildings and makes you feel the blood that has run in the streets, during the Commune and the Revolution and for centuries before. Dickens's image of a peasant woman knitting the names of the condemned into her work feels all too believable once you have spent any length of time among Parisians. It is why fresh-faced Americans don't stand a chance. To play the Parisian game, you must become sophisticated, with haste.

I was increasingly uneasy, as well, with the self-satisfied confidence of the French, which could swiftly veer to arrogance. Quick to tell the historically young Americans how to right the wrongs of racism and the like, they are quite often unable to recognize their own national shortcomings, such as the disenfranchisement and impoverishment of the ranks of Arabs and Africans segregated to the *cités* around Paris and the subtle and not-so-subtle anti-Semitism evidenced in strains of historical revisionism and the rise of the Far Right.

On the personal plane, I recognized a growing inability to

cohabit with M. Grand, whose obliviousness to time and schedules became acute with the pressures of family and a growing business. Saying he'd be home for dinner by eight could as well mean eleven or one, and it was wearing me down. We had passionate, terrible arguments, about time and space and other Kantian issues, until finally it became unbearable to stay.

Only recently, M. Grand used the term "irreconcilable differences" to describe what happened to us. It's an expression that has long made me queasy, but it's entirely apt in our case. So, not a year into our beautiful apartment with *cheminées* in every room, parquet floors, exquisitely carved ceilings, Habitat kitchen, and Bellini crib for *le petit,* I left it all and fled, toddler in his Maclaren, back to the United States. It was not a definitive break — there would be some years of back and forth — but something in me knew there was an end here. I felt an unbearable, deep piercing sorrow as I pulled away from this man, this home, this city, this country. I was pulling away our child, as well, and that was an enormous piece of my broken heart. But I had to go.

When people ask why, even if I had to leave M. Grand, I didn't remain in Paris with the boy, I have a hard time explaining. I felt profoundly that it was not home. As an expat, you are never completely *chez vous,* anywhere, again. However long you remain in your adopted country, you are always at least a little *étranger.* Returning home, you no longer quite belong, either.

Now let's revisit that word, *litost.* The second sense Kundera speaks of is one that involves resentment, "a state of torment caused by a sudden insight into one's own miserable self . . . *Litost* works like a two-stroke motor. First comes a feeling of torment, then the desire for revenge."

This second sense, from what I have come to understand, refers to a set of emotions usually limited to one's youth. In full maturity, the *litost* that operates is that of the first, broader meaning. This word that led me to Paris, to study, fall in love, have a child, also describes the continuing arc of my departure. The resentment for what I lost — though it was I who chose to leave — evolved through the cycles of grief, remorse, longing, ebbing away into inflected memory. I don't feel any pull to return to the city that remains an important part of who I am. Our son has grown into a young man who is his French father and his American mother in equal measure and, along with two passports, carries two cultures and two very different families within. And he will have his own Paris.

It may have been Gertrude Stein who wrote that to lead a life of any interest, one must first spend time in Paris. It is a place that defines and shapes like no other; its Aphroditic nature can overwhelm or inspire, but it can't leave you indifferent. Nearly twenty years after leaving, I still feel the deep rivulets Paris made in my heart and in my mind, and they flow on.

La Bourdonneuse

TWENTY-FIVE YEARS AGO this month, I watched the streets of Paris erupt on the television screen. I was lying on a living room floor in California, but as I watched the fires burn and the cobblestones fly I felt an extraordinarily intimate connection with it all, as though I were seeing the meaning of my own dream.

Only it was not a dream but, rather, a symptom that I suddenly understood. The year before — my fifteenth — I had spent in a girls' school in Paris, and what came back when I thought of that year was a strange sensation at the base of my throat.

People said it was a lycée in decline, but it was in a fairly elegant neighborhood and it certainly looked impressive. It had a high stone wall with an immense wooden door. If you were as much as a minute late, you had to ring a buzzer, which echoed through the inner court, and then a scowling man opened the door. He was the only male in the building, and this made his presence all the more fearsome. Recently, I saw again the French film *The Red Balloon*. When the boy, Pascal, gets to school, he has to let his balloon go. That's exactly how it felt when you got to that door — you had to let something go. You hoped that it would still be there when you came out.

Once inside, we sat for hours, mute as stones, in drafty, high-ceilinged rooms. The teachers spoke endlessly, and as they spoke we wrote down what they said word for word on graph paper in small plaid notebooks. We wrote in our "Sunday handwriting," with a pen in one hand and a ruler in the other, and every now and again, when a teacher felt she'd made an important point, she'd say, "Underline and make a box around it." The only times we spoke were fraught with terror.

"Lamontier!" a teacher might call out. "Stand up! Button your smock! To the blackboard!"

"Yes, madame."

"The Jura Mountains are composed of what kind of rock?"

"Boulders, madame."

"*What?*"

"*Large* boulders, madame."

If you shamed yourself in front of the class, you might try to make up for it by keeping your notebooks impeccable. At the dime store, the Monoprix, you could buy small packets of pictures to paste in at the relevant points: "View of the Jura Mountains," or "Crowd Storms the Bastille."

I still remember how we were assigned our first composition that year: " 'The love of risk has its advantages and its disadvantages.' Begin by folding your paper in two. At the top of one column, write 'Advantages.' Underline and put a box around it. At the top of the next column . . ."

In science class, we never touched a plant or stirred a solution or peered at an insect through a microscope. We sat silent in the dark, watching slides of plankton, Louis Pasteur, and cowpox projected onto brown peeling plaster walls that made everything look like fried chicken. The teacher droned on in the background, but all I've retained is a single sentence, perhaps because it struck me as oddly heroic: "Drop by drop, the urine forms itself in perpetuity."

In sewing class, we made gray wool jumpers for nonexistent babies; it must have been a way of saving cloth. The teacher said we could bring our own fabric, but I was the only one who did. She hated me for my small piece of blue-flowered flannel, because it meant she had to change the thread on the one machine. Each time I came up, trembling, to have her sew a seam, she stooped and made runs in my stockings with her needle.

In art class, we had two projects the entire year. We had to draw a stuffed bird "feather by feather" and a moth-eaten corncob "kernel by kernel." "But, mademoiselle," the teacher cried one day, seizing my pencil. "You must be more free!"

English class was the one relief. The teacher was kind, and was somewhat embarrassed to have a native speaker in the room, but I never corrected her — not even on the day she had us reciting "Negroes have crispy hair." This was the one time we could let our voices go without restraint, and we belted out phrases like war chants: "Grandfather, won't you have grilled kidneys for breakfast?"

Often, there were tears. That year was a crucial one for the girls: if they didn't pass that grade, it meant they were out of the lycée and into the working class. When exams were handed back, the teachers read out names in order of declining marks. As the list went on, there were cries of "Mouchoir!" — "Handkerchief!" Since my own future was not at stake, I took to bringing a stash of handkerchiefs for the others, and handing them out soon became one of my more important functions.

At the end of the year, several girls who were being dropped were called before the class. Their faces were crimson, and they looked down at their feet.

"And what will you do, mademoiselle?"

"I will work as a baker's assistant, madame."

"And you?"

"I will learn to cut hair, madame."

These were the moments of drama in a tedium so extreme that it was — for me — almost exotic. I lived for the moment, around three o'clock each day, when the man in the adjoining building leaned out the window in his undershirt and watered the plants in his window box. It was a sign that outside the high stone wall that enclosed us, living things were growing. One afternoon, he didn't appear, and I was overcome by utter desolation. Then I became aware of a catch in my throat. It wasn't pain but something that demanded release. With my face carefully composed and my lips closed, I made a sound. It was a strange sound, and at first I wasn't sure whether anyone had heard it or not. But the teacher fell silent. "Qui vient de bourdonner?" she asked in an icy voice. "Who has just —— ." I didn't know what *bourdonner* meant. I looked it up in my pocket dictionary after class and found that it meant "to hum" or "to buzz." That's funny, I thought. I wouldn't have known what to call it. But I knew it was something more drastic than a hum or a buzz.

Thereafter, the sound issued from me at least once a day. It wasn't something I planned; it had a life of its own. Though the teacher tried to remain impassive, as the weeks went on she grew increasingly enraged. "We are not going on until we find the *bourdonneuse,*" she would say, her eyes narrowed to slits as she scanned our faces, row by row. The girls all knew that I was the guilty party, but they would never tell. After class, they teased me in an affectionate way; they were amused and somewhat awed by what they saw as a peculiar form of American bravery. I pretended that it was a kind of joke I performed for them, but it disturbed me. I'd heard of disorders where words came flying out of one's mouth at inappropriate moments. Was this the beginning?

Lying on the living room floor in California, watching the students' shouting faces, I had an impulse to look up *bourdonner* in the big dictionary we kept on the mantel. Under the noun, *bourdonnement,* I found "a buzz . . . a hum." Then it went on: "a drone . . . a boom . . . of bells . . . bees . . . a swarm of insects . . . a buzz in the streets . . . a crowd."

So that's what it was. The teacher had been more right than she knew. That strange sound was the crowd in my throat — and there it was, wild in the streets of Paris.

Paris Is Gone, All Gone

SINCE I BEGAN teaching Proust's *In Search of Lost Time,* my occupational hazard has been nostalgia. Every fall, alongside my New York University freshmen, I reread Proust's immense novel, the most potent advertisement ever devised for the concept that "the only paradise is paradise lost." Every fall I am back there, in Proust's Paris, not just the place of my birth, that is, but the real Paris, as I now see it, the world capital of memory and desire, the ineffably beautiful Paris of pure, eternal childhood yearning. It's been ten years since I began to teach the Proust Freshman Honors Seminar, and every year that part of it gets more painful.

Paris's beauty is of the heartbreaking kind. After all, so much of it was designed or ornamented by artists. In many ways, Paris itself is a work of art and, like all great art, it succeeds in drawing forth intense emotion. I'm sure that's one important reason it acquired a reputation for romance. Romance, yes, but also tragedy, betrayal, profound disappointment. It's true that Paris is a great place to fall in love, to eat, drink, and be merry. But it's also the perfect city in which to be depressed or, even better, melancholy. There's never been a better place to be lost, displaced, and bereft, and it's always been home to any number of soulful exiles. You don't have to be French to smoke a Gitane and notice the falling leaves drifting by your window.

Any number of ingredients have gone into that magic and potent Parisian elixir of hedonism and loneliness. Of course, my pick for first place in creating that exquisite contradiction is the weight of the past, the city's history. Centuries of French gallantry are compressed within Paris's walls, but also centuries of despair and failure. You can see that contradiction expressed by the tremendous extremes of scale: everywhere you look, the picturesque tempers the sublime and vice versa, the quaint and the monumental coexist in what we have come to believe is perfect harmony. But there is something disequilibrating about Paris's combination of discreet charm and crazy French grandeur. The French have always loved glory too well, and their penchant for excess seems to have been poured into every Paris monument, every wide avenue, every majestic site, and every noble vista, rendered all the more poignant by our knowledge that French history (like all others) has failed to deliver on its glorious promise. That failure may be what gives Paris and Parisians their irony and their poetry, making the vestigial bombast seem not so much arrogant as touching.

All of this, or something like it, is echoed in Proust's work. One of his favorite subjects was, as it happens, disappointment, and how art springs from it. And my freshmen get it. People I know who have not read Proust (or tried and failed) think it's insane to even try to teach it to kids who are just starting college, but my students really get it   Proust, Paris, childhood yearning, and lost or artificial paradises, the whole thing. After all, they've just left home and their own childhoods behind. It's true that when we start out, many of them, fresh from Iowa, Illinois, even Tennessee, have never heard of the Faubourg Saint-Germain, the Champs-Élysées, or the Bois de Boulogne. They may know the terms *art nouveau* or *La Belle Époque,* but never anything about the Third Republic or about the final, saddest, and most gorgeous hurrah — the end of the French aristocracy. When we start out, most of my students can't tell a marquise from a madam (of course, this will turn out to be a confusing distinction, halfway through volume 3, *The Guermantes Way*), and it's only when they're deeply into the text that they discover this is something that they are missing in their lives. That is, if I've done my job well enough.

To help them out, I put up images on our class's Web site, and as the semester progresses, I imagine I see Paris 1900 taking shape in my students' imagination. I link to reproductions of paintings, old maps, posters. There are plenty of early photos; the fin de siècle was one of the new medium's first heydays. The work of Eugène Atget, for example, is easily found online, on the Web site of the Bibliothèque nationale and others. I've spent a great many hours staring at the deserted sepia streets, the dusty shop windows, the merry-go-rounds, the old blind organ grinder with his laughing daughter. I suspect I spend much more time looking at them than my students do.

It's not necessary, of course. Paris is evoked for Proust's readers even if they never look at a single photo, and it can be imagined in infinite detail (often more detail than my students ever bargained for, at least at first). I do believe that these visual aids facilitate the reading, but the truth is that I've fallen in love with those images and that particular iteration of my city. And just as one eventually becomes confused, while reading Proust,

about which are his memories, and which our own, which are
his reveries alone and which are the daydreams in which we
lose ourselves time and again when one of his sinuous, seductive sentences leads us to some wish we had forgotten we were
hiding from ourselves, so, too, has my own Paris become somehow merged with his, as if the decades between his descriptions
and my birth had really caused only a bit of cosmetic change
here and there. Long after every student in my class can recognize the Champs-Élysées, where M. first heard Gilberte's name
(when both were children and she played with a shuttlecock,
watched over by a governess wearing a hat adorned with a blue
feather), long after they can identify Sarah Bernhardt from her
Nadar photographs, or the Eiffel Tower in construction for
the 1900 Exposition universelle, I find myself still collecting.
I can't get enough of the glistening pavements at night, of the
allées of chestnut trees, of Verlaine, looking dazed, sipping ab-
sinthe at a corner table in the Café François, circa 1890, of the
moody waitress at the Moulin Rouge. I'm amazed at my own
obsessive collecting.

And yet I cannot describe the mood I'm in as I click through
images of Paris as anything but painfully, almost unbearably,
homesick. Homesick for what, exactly? It's true I have family
and friends there, whom I miss, but it really is more of a longing for something unnamable, very old and hard to articulate.
Maybe for longing itself, that state of pure hope that children
have and then are nostalgic about for the rest of their lives. Or
should we call it pure illusion? Something about Paris awakens
that nostalgia, somehow. And surely I'm not the only one who
has felt it or who has, indeed, sought that incomprehensible
and irresistible sensation. "For regret, like desire, seeks not to

analyze but to gratify itself," writes Proust in *Within a Budding Grove,* the second volume of *In Search of Lost Time.*

My Parisian friends — those in whom I confide, anyway — tell me I am lucky to be in New York. (Though I don't think they say this as often as they used to.) But still, especially the ones who have spent some time in the United States console me for my homesickness by pointing out how rigid a place Paris can be, how much less mobility there seems to be than in New York. True, true, all true. I know that the everyday variety of rabid ambition one encounters every moment in Manhattan seems downright naive by comparison with the sort of Grand Guignol snobbism everyone in Paris takes for granted, that it is perfectly possible to feel stuck and stranded in Paris, that shoes are too expensive, and that the subway doesn't run all night. True, all true.

My friends laugh at what is left of France's *folie de grandeur.* And as for Paris. Don't get them started! The crowds, the prices, the brittleness, the stupidity! The deterioration of the butcher's skills and the pastry shop's display, *le fast-food,* the vulgarity of the Champs-Élysées, the museums packed with exasperating idiots, the gentrification — or as they call it, *boboisation,* for *bourgeois bohème* — the loss of the ateliers, which have all become expensive lofts, of the working-class cafés, indeed of the old working class itself, of the old dingy neighborhoods, of the bistros with the zinc bars where you could once get a brilliant lunch for next to nothing, briskly served by an expert waiter who spoke with a populist accent. "Now everybody sounds the same," someone will always say at around this point.

Yes, it's gone, all gone, even if you've never left Paris. My friends who live there, I've discovered, are as nostalgic for Paris as I am. In a way the extraordinary efforts of the city of Paris to keep the city clean, all the sparkling monuments' facades, the orderly parking, the kind of efficient garbage collection that would make New Yorkers weep with envy, all that takes away Paris's grime and shabbiness also robs it of itself. Perhaps the best-maintained, the best-functioning, the most pleasurable city in the world, Paris may face the future more optimistically and with more beauty and comfort than any other world capital, but the price is a constant severing of its own past. But of course that is the very definition of renewal, and it is always accompanied by nostalgia, emotion, and, perhaps, romance.

And so it was in Proust's time, as well. He was born in 1871, just after the siege of Paris. Less than twenty years earlier, Napoleon III, obsessed with hygiene, had hired Georges-Eugène Haussmann to modernize the city. "Paris embellie, Paris agrandie, Paris assainie" was the campaign's slogan: Paris was to be embellished, made bigger and more salubrious. All that was dark, dirty, stinking, was to disappear, down to the very belly of the city, which was disemboweled to make way for a sewer system such as the world had never seen, and a vast transportation system, the Métropolitain, over which were paved wide avenues supporting row upon row of new, opulent structures. Within a few years, the medieval city had been torn apart, most of its buildings destroyed or renovated. More than 60 percent of Paris is estimated to have been altered. Innumerable small streets were gone, replaced by the aforementioned noble vistas — incidentally providing clear paths for the army, in case any insalubrious insurrections should occur and crowds had to be strategically herded away

Nothing stood in the way of this raging urbanism. Haussmann was obsessed with perpendicular lines — *le culte de l'axe.* The Luxembourg Gardens, which had not respected the right angle, were amputated. Twelve avenues were carved out around the Arc de Triomphe to make la place de l'Étoile. One of the oldest and most populous parts of Paris, in the center, was razed to make way for the new opera house, flanked by a Métro station. The poor were pushed out to newly created zones outside the center. The bourgeoisie moved in en masse and set forth with alacrity upon the pursuit of so-called leisure-time activities — a brand-new concept in the 1870s — which the Baron de Haussmann had carefully segregated, away from residential quarters. The aristocracy still hovering in the Faubourg Saint-Germain, on the Left Bank, also caught the fever of modernity. Paris was soon studded with department stores, restaurants and cafés, *cafés-concerts* and concert halls, cabarets, theaters, indoor and outdoor dance places, and innumerable brothels catering to every imaginable taste, where the beau monde met the demimonde on a regular basis.

For all their storied gaiety, Parisians in Proust's time must always have been aware that the city's past had been lost, that they were unmoored, exiled. This seemingly definitive sense of loss must have receded in Parisian consciousness during the disastrous Prussian siege of Paris, and even more with the advent of World War I, when the concepts of loss, disappointment, destruction, and the unmooring of sensibility acquired their most gruesome and modern meaning.

Proust spent most of his war years writing and revising, feverishly adding thousands of pages to his work about the destruction of both the past and our fantasy of the past, and about the problem of hope that takes the form of illusion. The mourning that Proust expresses most eloquently is not for the loss of what was possessed; it is for the loss of what was, on the contrary, never possessed, but profoundly desired. Here is what he writes in *The Fugitive,* the penultimate volume of *In Search of Lost Time:*

> We do not succeed in changing things in accordance with our desires, but gradually our desires change. The situation that we hoped to change because it was intolerable becomes unimportant to us. We have failed to surmount the obstacle, as we were absolutely determined to do, but life has taken us round it, led us beyond it, and then if we turn round to gaze into the distance of the past, we can barely see it, so imperceptible has it become.

As for me, I'm still waiting for that acceptance which seems to me to be a kind of paradise, even if it's drenched around the edges with nostalgia and regret. I can wait in Manhattan as easily as anyplace else, perhaps, and teaching Proust is not a bad way to savor some of the hours, in the meantime. Or some of the years, I guess. Ten years! As it happens, I was ten years old when my parents first brought me to New York, so I've been teaching now for as long as I lived in Paris as a child. But of course, in so many ways, I never really left.

Every fall, I show my students how to levitate there, if they're willing, without ever leaving our classroom. Unfortunately, I've stopped smoking and cannot have a Gitane. But in Manhattan the memory of blue smoke wafting toward the ceiling is just another detail from a distant, other world. Still, in so many ways Proust's Paris lives on in the lives of my students even if, in spite of all my efforts, it's a city that's very different from my own.

Enfin

THE IMAGE PEOPLE have of my life in Paris is that each
fabulous day begins with a trip to the bakery for my morning croissant, which I eat while catching up with the current
events by reading *Le Monde* at my corner café. (The beret is op-
tional.) Then I spend the rest of my day discussing Sartre over
in the Latin Quarter or strolling the halls of the Louvre with
a sketchpad, ending with my sunset ascent of the Eiffel Tower
before heading to one of the Michelin three-star restaurants
for an extravagant dinner. Later, after toasting the day with
glasses of cognac in the lounge at the George V, I stroll along
the Seine until I'm finally home, when I tuck myself into bed
to rest up for the next day.

One of my character flaws is that I'm not very nice in the
morning, so as a courtesy to others, I refuse to leave my place
until fortified with coffee and toast, which I eat while scrolling
through the *New York Times* online and reading e-mail. And
believe it or not, I've never been to the top of the Eiffel Tower.
After the few hours I spent stuck in the claustrophobic elevator
in my apartment building when the woman on the other end
of the emergency phone told me to call back later — because
everyone was at lunch — you can understand why I avoid eleva-
tors as much as possible around here.

As for starred restaurants, I can't justify a bowl of soup for a hundred bucks — unless a visitor is footing the bill. And you can imagine how many of my friends are going to visit me now, knowing how I feel about visitors.

ONE OF THE first words I learned in French class was *râleur,* which means "someone who complains." Maybe it's *la grisaille,* the dull, gray skies that hang over Paris, causing *la morosité ambiente,* the all-encompassing gloom that blankets the city at times. Complaining is such an important part of life here that my first French teacher felt it's a word we needed to learn right off the bat.

But living here, I now understand the pouting and the infamous French reluctance to change. From my daily baguette being baked just the way I like it, to the tomato vendor at my market who sings the James Bond theme song to me (even though I tell him that Mr. Bond is actually British), I like things to stay the same. And let's face it: most visitors come to Paris to bask in the glories of its past, not to marvel at the modern innovations of the present.

So it's annoying when you head to the market, clearing a path with your basket, and the tomato guy doesn't serenade you, and treats you just like any other customer. (And worse, you discover a couple of rotten tomatoes at the bottom of the bag.) Or worst of all, your corner bakery, where you go every day, has changed bakers.

When I first moved into my apartment, its biggest plus — aside from sporting the world's most meticulous paint job — was the fantastic baguettes from the bakery just across the street. Each slender loaf was a dream, baked to a rough, crackly brown finish with little bits of flour clinging to the sharp ridges, which swooped down the loaf at curvy intervals. The counter clerk would rifle through the basket to make sure to pick out an especially good one for me, because she knew how much I appreciated it. Then she'd wrap a small square of paper around the center, give it a few sharp twists to seal the ends, and hand it over with a genuine, "Merci, monsieur, et bonne journée!"

The moment I grabbed my loaf, I could feel the heat radiating through my hand and could barely wait until I was outside before I tore off and devoured the prized crusty end, *le quignon.* By the time I reached the top floor of my building, I had polished off half the baguette, and there was a telltale trail of little flaky crumbs behind me to prove it.

One late summer morning, a few years later, the bakery reopened after *les vacances.* Excited they were finally back after their annual month-long holiday, I nearly burst through the door as soon as it swung open, but was startled to see a new woman behind the counter. After I ordered, she brusquely slammed on the counter a baguette she absentmindedly plucked from the basket, one that was remarkably smooth and pale, with nary a blemish. When I hefted it, I felt like I was lifting a sledgehammer. I didn't need to take a bite to know that something was wrong.

Outside, I ripped off the end and popped it in my mouth; the floury taste and gummy texture were a few steps in quality below what was on offer at my local Franprix.

DESPITE MY SETBACKS, I was proud I had survived *le bizutage,* the hazing you must endure when you move into a new neighborhood in Paris, spending a solid year befriending the local merchants so you get good service. Sometimes you're successful, like I was at my local *boulangerie;* other times, not so much, like with the nasty lady at the chocolate shop a few blocks away, whom I was never able to crack.

I knew I had made it here when the woman at the charcuterie finally responded to my friendly overtures and actually carried on a conversation with me, one that lasted for a couple of minutes, instead of her usual grunt in my direction. And our chat consisted of more than how many *saucisses* I wanted and if I wanted regular wieners or the ones *aux herbes.*

That was after five years of visiting her charcuterie twice a week, which means I shopped there over five hundred times before I was met with something other than a disdainful grimace. No longer does she see how thick she can get away with cutting my four slices of *jambon de paysanne,* and sometimes she even lets me get away with giving her a €10 bill on my €8.50 purchase, without making me rifle through all my pockets for exact change. (The French like taking money, but they don't like giving it back.) Funny how one measures success around here — by no longer needing to have exact change, and by the thickness of ham.

Parisians have a reputation for being difficult, and sometimes kindness seems to be a priceless commodity, doled out parsimoniously to the lucky few. Yet I've managed to survive any wrath I've invoked with my special brand of American optimism (and brownies). I'm also grateful that I'm probably treated better than someone who moved to America would be, not speaking a word of the native language, trying to get by in a foreign land.

What helped was that I understood the food and tried my best to adapt to the culture, rather than trying to make the

culture adapt to me. I arrived knowing a fair amount about
the pastries, cheeses, chocolates, and breads, which impressed
the French, and I also soaked up as much as I could. More important, though, I learned to take the time to get to know people, especially the vendors and merchants, who would patiently
explain their wares to me. Plenty of people who move here arrive wide eyed and excited, only to leave after a year because
they miss their favorite brand of shampoo, or air-conditioning,
or customer service, or 110 cm shoelaces (which I finally found
at Target, in Houston). I'll admit there are plenty of things
that I miss, too, but I have also made new friends, had quite
a few unusual experiences, and feel much more a part of the
global community than I would had I stayed in the States.

Once I learned the rules and got past the inevitable emotional
bumps and bruises that an outsider anywhere must endure, I
became a regular fixture in my neighborhood: *l'américain* and
chef pâtissier. (I'm pretty certain the first distinction wouldn't
have worked out quite so well if I hadn't had the benefit of the
second.)

I do my best to act like a Parisian: I smile only when I actually have something to be happy about, and I cut in line whenever I can. I've stopped eating vegetables almost entirely, and
wine is my sole source of hydration. I never yield to anyone
else, physically or otherwise, and I've gotten so good at giving myself a shot that I'm beginning to think my mother was
right — I should have been a doctor.

But I make sure to always stop for a handshake and a chat
with the vendors at my market, who have become my friends —
Jacques, who sells the best olives and tapenades from Provence,
and José, at the Graineterie du Marché, whose bins are stocked

with all sorts of lentils, grains, salts, *pruneaux d'Agen,* and *le pop-corn,* which I think he carries just for me.

My Sunday mornings wouldn't be complete without picking up a *poulet crapaudine,* a spatchcocked salt-and-herb-crusted chicken, roasted to a caramel brown crisp by Catherine, the wacky chicken lady who loves to yelp over the other shoppers clustered around her fired-up rotisserie: "Daveed — howareyouIamfine!" in one nonstop greeting. And since the pork lady decided I'm okay, my life's become not just sweeter, but richer, too. There are lots more pâtés, *boudins blancs,* and *saucisses aux herbes* in my life, plus an occasional *goûter* of *jambon de Bayonne* when she's feeling generous.

And, of course, there are the fish boys. Because of them, I now enjoy more fish than ever.

I've been fortunate enough to experience things that very few outsiders ever get to see in Paris: early mornings hefting slippery eels, overseeing chocolates at one of the finest boutiques in Paris, and an educational trip to harvest salt off the Atlantic coastline, which included a delicious detour (of which there are many in France) where I learned the secret of salted butter caramels from a native Breton chef.

I'll know for sure that I've made it here when I buy outfits specifically for taking out the garbage. And when it seems to make perfect sense to me that the switch that turns on the light inside the bathroom is located outside it. When during the stifling heat of summer, I know enough to keep my windows firmly closed at all times, to avoid the possibility of coming into contact with any fresh air — which would make me very, very sick. And when the gap-toothed vendor at the marché d'Aligre stops feigning surprise when I point out that the bag of cherries on his scale is (courtesy of his thumb) off by more than just a few grams — a benefit of my pastry chef training.

I know I've finally arrived when my doctor no longer wonders why I've brought a flashlight to my appointment. When the change from my €1 purchase is 37 centimes, and the cashier doesn't hand me back 37 individual centimes as punishment for not having the exact amount. And if someone says to me, "That new shirt looks terrible on you," I take it as a compliment — because in that special French way, they're actually doing me a favor.

On visits back to the States, I always anticipate the trip, thinking, "Ah, I can't wait to be around people who understand me." But that isn't always the case anymore, and nowadays I'm not quite sure where I fit in: here or there. And I'm okay with that.

Every day in Paris isn't always so sweet. Although I've tried my best to fit in, no matter where you plant yourself, there are certain to be ups and downs. I embarked on a new life in Paris without knowing what the future would hand me. Because of that, my life has turned into quite an adventure, and I often surprise myself when I find I'm easily mingling with the locals, taking on surly salesclerks, and, best of all, wandering the streets in search of something delicious to eat.

It's the bakeries with their buttery croissants served oven-fresh each morning, the bountiful outdoor markets where I forage for my daily fare, the exquisite chocolate shops that still, after all these years, never stop astounding me every time I visit one, and, of course, the quirky people that really make Paris such a special place.

And I can now count myself as one of them.

Le Départ

IT WAS AFTER nine when we headed into the Bois de Boulogne that evening, yet, since it was northern Europe and
midsummer, it was still only dusk. It was, in short, *about to be.*
Which pretty much described the state of everything, on this
night, for us. We were about to be gone. I'd ordered a taxi to
the airport for the next day, sold our appliances and household
things, dispiritedly, to strangers for outsize, brightly colored bills
with writers on them — Voltaire on the hundred-franc note,
Saint-Exupéry with his spritelike Petit Prince on the fifty —
noting with irony that this currency, too, would soon be disap-
pearing, supplanted by the euro.

I'd felt invaded, irrationally, by people who'd arrived by way
of a classified ad, picking over our possessions in a manner that
seemed brutal, ripping them from us, taking away the television
on which Julian, my seven-year-old son, had watched strange
marionette shows on Wednesday afternoons when the schools
were closed and I'd tuned in to Arte, the Franco-German
television channel, with its sometimes startling avant-garde
programming, in the evenings after he finally dropped to sleep.

Gone was the cassette player on which he'd listened to E. B.
White, more Wednesday afternoon fare, intoning over and

over his joy at having found — in a spider! — someone who was both "a true friend and a good writer." The final words of *Charlotte's Web* had sounded delightfully discordant the first time I heard them, hardly less so in the dozens of times since.

I'd implored friends to take all that wasn't sold, the pots and pans, the bunk bed from IKEA, which I'd painted a shade called Breton blue. I'd rolled up the large Persian carpet, ancient, threadbare, beautiful, an heirloom that a friend had passed on to me before he, too, left town. I sold the much-too-big-for-me man's bike — gift of another departing friend — on which I'd wobbled through the Bois, to a businessman who gave me a deposit, promising to send on the rest. (Ha!) Julian's bright red bicycle went, too, the one on which he'd ridden beside me on so many Sunday afternoons, past the roaring smog of the *périphérique,* into the strange, almost artificial-looking countryside that was the Bois, desolate and far flung.

The young mother who bought Julian's bike paid in full, I'm glad to report, although at first she refused the training wheels. (French children hardly need them; they begin riding miniature two-wheelers while still tiny themselves.) I offered them again anyway and she took them then, to humor me, I guess, and I still remember standing next to her, in the long, angled courtyard of the Villa Chanez, where Julian had zigzagged back and forth on a succession of damp, gray winter Saturdays, learning to ride without them, and hearing her say that she lived in a nearby suburb with a surprising name, a place called Paradise.

So do I, I thought, as it all began to dissipate around me.

All that was left, besides our suitcases, were our mattresses and a telephone, a particularly complicated French variety — is

there any other kind?—that seemed to require a degree from
MIT or, more fittingly, the École Polytechnique, to operate.
It was the final vexation, burlesque in memory: I'd turned its
ringer off long before, since the fax machine in the same room
rang loudly enough. But now that was sold and the phone's
ringer couldn't be reset without a screwdriver and a complicated set of instructions, both of which were packed away . . .

The curtain was coming down on the Villa Chanez, with its
six identical golden brick buildings curving gracefully around
a bifurcated central courtyard. Every detail of our cul-de-sac
seemed iconic, from its rows of tall, balconied windows to the
vast, geometric-patterned front gate through which people
flowed each day, like the tide, greeting one another incessantly,
"Bonjour, monsieur," "Bonjour, madame." Very little beyond
these words broke the courtyard's habitual, almost unnatural
silence. The iron gate would click open and shut, the *gardien*
might sweep the courtyard, and every few months a discordant
ringing bell indicated that the itinerant knife sharpener had
arrived. Otherwise, it was just soft footsteps or clicking heels
and "Bonjour, monsieur," "Bonjour, madame."

Children were forbidden to play alone in the courtyard, and
on the rare occasions when Julian tried to slip out by himself, to
bounce a ball, say, or ride his bike, it was never long before some
ancient crone or another clacked open her shutters to tell him
to stop, in one case even reciting the number of the ordinance
forbidding such behavior. The *gardien* kept his eye on everything and Julian and I realized early on that he wasn't nice, and
discussed it, but I don't think either of us could have said how
we knew. He was also, as everyone else apparently understood,
receptive to bribery — the classic *pot de vin* — something I only

pieced together later, after wondering innocently for months why I never seemed to receive the afternoon mail (there were two deliveries a day, when there wasn't a strike), never quite had a key that worked for the storage room, and on and on.

There was a pervasive reserve to the Villa Chanez, its residents, its very air. Life there seemed to take place at one remove, as if wrapped in organdy or mousseline. Each building had a tiny, creaking cage elevator in its stairwell. Inevitably, I came to see these as symbolic. The trip from one floor to the next felt like moving through life itself. Each day we stood inert, all manner of people — rarely more than two, never more than three — crushed within these small wood-and-metal capsules: the Korean couple from the floor below; graduates of the *grandes écoles* — you could tell, somehow — in outer jackets with corduroy collars; solid, authoritative women of indeterminate age. There we stood, as close as lovers, ascending and descending ceaselessly, in silence. As the physical space between us shrank, another kind of distance, a psychological one, always grew — I never quite understood how. At nighttime, when the *minuterie* that ran the hall lights snapped off, we would rise and fall wordlessly, ever more distantly, in the dark.

In all my time there, I spoke to only a handful of neighbors, and never about much. One was a widower who seemed always to be going in and out. "Bonjour, madame," he'd greet me — surprise, surprise — when we ran into each other on just about every morning as I returned from the arduous round-trip Métro voyage that delivered my son to his bilingual school. My reply was hardly earth-shattering: "Bonjour, monsieur." And yet I always felt a complicity between us. It certainly existed with another neighbor who was, like me, a foreign woman in her forties — Austrian, I think. She and I kept up a running conversation in and around the elevator, about our neighbors, about Paris, about life. It was she who pointed out how liberating the carefully prescribed French rituals could be. The rhythm of the greetings, the close, yet anonymous proximity to other lives, "give you a certain freedom," she said. And I saw that she was correct.

It was so hard to leave. Yet it seemed right to go for many reasons. And a permanent move had never been part of the plan. "I don't want to grow up to be French," my son remarked at some point; in many ways, neither did I. For two years he had skipped along beside me or clattered at my side on roller skates as we walked through the neighborhood, to the shops, the bus stop, the twice-weekly market near the Métro stop with the artist's name: Michel-Ange–Auteuil. Now he seemed to fly at my side, singing, "California, here I come!" joyously, as I moved, increasingly disconsolate, beside him.

It felt mournful to pick him up from his summer program on that last day, to take our last bus home together, the same one on which we used to go over his French homework — about a frog named Toulalou? — then his English, as it lurched along, past the playground where even the very young mothers sat formally on benches, never slipping down a slide or venturing into the sandbox themselves.

Like most Parisians, we'd wander the distance between bus and Métro and home on foot, often making the same trajectory many times in a day. It doesn't take many such journeys for a Paris quarter and its inhabitants to enter your heart, and stay. It seemed almost obligatory to set out together on a final round, to say good-bye to the neighborhood, from the ever-changing cast of dark-haired young women at the *boulangerie* ("Au revoir!" they sang out in unison), to the almost manically groomed couple who owned the stationery store — caricatures of the French bourgeoisie. Even visiting the fierce toy store owner who'd hit Julian on the knuckles, hard, with a pencil on his first visit — *bienvenue!* — felt momentous; through repeated visits we'd come to treasure her, along with her handmade wooden toys, Tintin paraphernalia, and more.

Julian even requested a final day at the hated, chaotic *centre de loisirs* in the neighborhood, where I'd parked him, on some Wednesday afternoons, until too many stories of unchecked playground cruelty came home. Late in the afternoon, when I picked him up, he called "Au revoir!" to a cluster of boys who replied "Good-bye," in English, of all things, with sudden kindness. It always disarmed me, the way the French could abruptly change emotional tack, shifting from *froideur* to something warm and real. On the way home we were startled by the sight of my once-exquisite Persian carpet wrapped around a homeless man in a crawl space beneath a building just a few doors from ours.

How to say good-bye to Paris? How to acknowledge all that it had done for us, lulling us with its constancy, marking our time? How to thank it for teaching us how to stand close, how to give way, how to do all at once when ascending in the dark in a burning cage? How to mark occasions such as this?

I presented a bottle of calvados to the *gardien* — too late! a friend pointed out, in vain — too late, certainly, for the afternoon mail, which, after all, never did make its way up to our apartment on the *quatrième à gauche*. But so much else came to that door. People I was writing about: a young artist carrying his portfolio and trembling with ambition and hope; an industrial designer who told me that when I turned my head in a certain way he could visualize me as a lamp(!); countless messengers, including one from *Vogue* — Mount Olympus to me — for which I'd begun to write, bringing an envelope of bright currency, petty cash for a trip (and, on every level, a beautiful sight). Babysitters I relied upon: a young Tunisian woman who spoke five languages; an Italian man, an actor and dancer, who spoke four. Friends who tumbled in and out.

In those days before e-mail was widely used, the phone rang and rang. Writing about culture unleashed an army, a largely female one, of press attachés, publicists, fashion house assistants, gallery owners, museum personnel. A disproportionate number of these women had aristocratic names, a fellow journalist pointed out; I was amused to find, over and over, that this was true. In any case, they all called all the time. These were crisp women, so confident it was terrifying, and they all sounded the same to me at first, challenging and superior, that is, until a perky, funny remark slipped through. (There was almost always a sense of humor underneath.) As so often with the French, they could turn on a centime, dropping into a sudden, disarming humanity as abruptly as if they'd tripped into an oubliette. "You're leaving for good?" one particularly ferocious press agent asked, sounding bereft, when I told her my news.

The phone brought the world beyond France to us, too. America arrived each evening in the form of calls and faxes from editors, family, friends. And there were unexpected juxtapositions when work and home would mix, such as the time when a famous artist called for an article I was working on and

Julian, then six, took the message, writing his name painstakingly in his newfound letters on a scrap of paper I've kept ever since.

You might be depressed in Paris — had to be at times — but never disoriented. You could always tell the time of year quite precisely by the light flooding through the immense apartment windows: deathly gray and scarce in December, endlessly long-lasting at the other side of the year. In winter, Julian and I would leave for school in the mornings when the streetlamps were still on, only to arrive back home each afternoon in the same voluptuous, inky black. Sometimes, when I headed out to see friends in the evening or left, early, on work trips — always amazed that such exotic places as Tunis and Genoa could be reached after just a short flight — Julian would stand in his pajamas on our balcony as I passed through the courtyard, calling out, "Good-bye, Mommy!" in conspicuous English, over and over, for all the villa to hear.

I'd hear him in my mind even after reaching the Métro station at the corner, as I stepped onto a train full of people who seemed alive with anticipation, particularly on the *ligne 10,* as it slipped into the Latin Quarter on a weekend evening, everyone on it searching for the thing that everyone in Paris was always after, *le plaisir.* It was what we all wanted, a grab at happiness in fast-moving time, and it was there for the taking in disconcertingly easy ways: in an aperitif drunk on a café terrace; in friends around a table; in endless talk slipping, twistingly, from one language into another; in the passing parade of Parisians, with all their armor and style.

Before I moved to the Villa Chanez, I'd eschewed domestic life, rebelling against an overdecorated childhood. But sitting at a desk each day by tall windows overlooking the apartments across the way taught me how rugs, furniture, lamps, could impart a sense of life unfolding, calmly, forever, on and on. This permanence seemed catching; I could almost feel my nomadic self stealing away. And while nothing about my bank account explained how this might take place, I began to imagine living a more rooted life among long-rejected household accoutrements. (And soon enough, I did.)

I left Paris with an encyclopedia of images to draw from, faces to remember, vignettes large and small. Although I'd spoken French for my entire adult life, I'd had a crash course in new vocabularies this time around, ones centered on children and work. And some words had achieved new prominence. The adjectives *morose* and *stressé* seemed to be on everybody's lips in a city apparently full of people having nervous breakdowns, including, most memorably, a press attaché of about thirty who informed me that she'd be spending her Christmas holidays in a darkened room — recovering from *la stresse*, of course.

I lived my share of it, working at a freelance trade in what was then a hugely expensive, tough city, carving out a life while wondering each day if I wasn't too sensitive to live among Parisians — I was routinely reduced to tears and/or outrage by, say, the shop assistant who refused to let me try on a third pair of shoes ("I've already brought out two pairs!"); the battle-ax — there was no end to these — who swatted Julian with her umbrella for the crime of speaking English on the number 52 bus, the one that ferried the snootiest passengers in all of Paris; the enormous woman who sat on him — sat on him! — on the Métro as we pulled out of the Duroc station, on purpose, we were both sure, although we couldn't have said why. And on and on.

But there were endless rewards. There was a pervasive sense of adventure, that a surprise was just waiting to be discovered in the next encounter or at the end of the next street. There was the food, of course — even the most banal café seemed to serve something exquisite — and the artistry with which it was all done, right down to the tiny scenarios in bread and chocolate that were unveiled fortnightly in our *boulanger*'s window. I even came to appreciate — in memory, to bask in — the flirtatious comments made by men in the street, bending every rule in my postfeminist, Anglo-American playbook as I did so, seeing it all as just more joyous street theater in a city that was alive with it, especially in warm weather when everyone was out. I knew that I would remember all of it always, that Paris would be there forever in sharply delineated images, a pack of mental cards to be shuffled through, rearranged, anytime I liked.

In our last month in the villa, a new neighbor moved across the hall. She was, like me, a single mother, and she'd just returned to Paris after a decade in Rome. "But you must go to your destiny!" she exclaimed authoritatively as I told her how wobbly I felt about leaving town. Such offhand wisdom had also become familiar; it was another French surprise. And her verbal push helped me along the way. But soon this brief, shared camaraderie, this friendship that could never bloom, would enter into the realm of might-have-been.

If you're seven and living in a country like France where fireworks are legally sold, there's really only one way to say good-bye: Julian and I had long decided to set off a rocket to mark our departure. Which is why we found ourselves on this last night heading into the Bois. It wasn't black enough for rockets, really, but we had to get moving, we had to go. Julian took the tiny firework from his school backpack, a miniature paper rocket on a slender stick, and twisted the latter in tiny back-and-forth motions until it stood upright in the soft summer earth. We lit the match together, held it to the wick, then pulled back as it began to sizzle.

I wish I could write that the rocket shot skyward, limning this scene by the fire of its propulsion, silhouetting our lives, this moment, this place that mattered so to us. But in truth it sputtered out after rising only a few feet, crashing anticlimactically back to the ground, and I steered a weary seven-year-old — my son, my light — out of the park, past the Métro entrance with its exuberant Guimard ironwork, and into the Villa Chanez as residents for the last time. Tonight, of all nights, we needed our sleep. We were just two people, just two lives — Paris had reminded us of that, every chance it could — and on the very next day we'd be repositioning ourselves on earth. There was nothing left to do but leave. Just go. *Au revoir, messieurs. Au revoir, mesdames.*

Richard Armstrong is the director of the Solomon R. Guggenheim Foundation and Museum in New York. Before joining the Guggenheim, in 2008, he was the Henry J. Heinz II Director of the Carnegie Museum of Art.

Marcelle Clements's most recent book is a novel, *Midsummer.* Her articles and essays have appeared in many national publications. She teaches a course on Marcel Proust's *In Search of Lost Time* at New York University.

Janine di Giovanni, the author of *The Place at the End of the World* and other books, is a reporter who has covered numerous war zones, including Chechnya and Iraq, for such publications as the *Times* of London and *Vanity Fair.*

Brigid Dorsey lived in Maine, upstate New York, and New Jersey after Paris. She is a writer and editor who lives in Columbia County, New York.

Alicia Drake wrote *The Beautiful Fall,* a nonfiction account of fashion in Paris in the 1970s, which was published in 2006. She is working on a novel.

Roxane Farmanfarmaian was born in Salt Lake City and raised in Holland and now lives in England, where she is a lecturer at the University of Cambridge. A former editor and journalist, she wrote *Blood and Oil: A Prince's Memoir of Iran, from the Shah to the Ayatollah.*

Natasha Fraser-Cavassoni is a Paris-based journalist and author of a biography of the Oscar-winning film producer Sam Spiegel. She has worked at Chanel and *W* magazine and was European editor of American *Harper's Bazaar*.

Mark Gaito is a television producer and writer who lives in Paris.

Andrew Hurley (translator of Zoé Valdés's text) has translated numerous works of fiction and poetry from the Spanish and is perhaps best known for his rendering of Jorge Luis Borges's *Collected Fictions*. He is a professor emeritus of literature and translation at the University of Puerto Rico.

Diane Johnson is a novelist (*Le Divorce, Lying Low,* etc.) and critic who lives part of the time in Paris. Her latest novel is called *Lulu in Marrakech*.

Alice Kaplan teaches French at Yale University. Her recent books include *The Collaborator: The Trial and Execution of Robert Brasillach* and *The Interpreter*.

Patric Kuh is the author of *The Last Days of Haute Cuisine: The Coming of Age of American Restaurants* and is the restaurant critic of *Los Angeles* magazine.

Julie Lacoste began her blog, Un temps de retard (A Delayed Time: The Diary of a Homeless Mother), in September 2008. She ended it the following year after moving into a subsidized apartment in Paris. She works at a university library.

David Lebovitz lived in San Francisco for twenty years and worked in the pastry department at Chez Panisse. He currently lives in Paris and blogs at davidlebovitz.com. His memoir, *The*

Sweet Life in Paris, was published in 2009. His latest cookbook is *Ready for Dessert.*

Janet McDonald was the author of a memoir, *Project Girl,* and six novels for young adults. Her last book, *Off-Color,* was published in 2007. She died that year, at the age of fifty-three, in Paris.

Jeremy Mercer is the author of four books, including *Time Was Soft There,* his memoir of life in a Parisian bookstore, and *When the Guillotine Fell,* a philosophical investigation of the last execution in France. He lives in Marseilles. www .jeremymercer.net.

Noelle Oxenhandler is the author of three books, including her recent memoir *The Wishing Year: A House, A Man, My Soul.* She teaches creative writing at Sonoma State University.

Christina Phillips (translator of Samuel Shimon's text) has translated a number of works from the Arabic, including, most recently, Naguib Mahfouz's *Morning and Evening Talk.* She lives in London.

Joe Queenan is the author of ten books, including *Closing Time,* a memoir that was published in 2009. He lives in Tarrytown, New York, and has returned to Paris on at least twenty different occasions.

Penelope Rowlands is the author of, most recently, *A Dash of Daring: Carmel Snow and Her Life in Fashion, Art, and Letters* and is the editor of this anthology.

Stacy Schiff's year in Paris resulted in *A Great Improvisation: Franklin, France, and the Birth of America,* winner of the

George Washington Book Prize. Schiff won the 2000 Pulitzer Prize for *Véra (Mrs. Vladimir Nabokov)*. Her most recent book is *Cleopatra: A Biography*.

Karen Schur was born in South America and has lived in North America, Europe, the Middle East, Asia, and the South Pacific. She now lives in Thailand, outside Bangkok, and is at work on a novel.

David Sedaris is the author of numerous books of personal essays, including, most recently, *When You Are Engulfed in Flames*. He won the Thurber Prize for American Humor in 2001. He lives in Paris.

Samuel Shimon is an Assyrian writer and editor. Born and raised in Iraq, he has also lived in Damascus, Amman, Beirut, Nicosia, Cairo, Tunis, and Paris. He has been based in London since 1996. His novel, *The Assyrian Guerrilla,* has just been published in Arabic.

Valerie Steiker is the culture editor at *Vogue* and the author of *The Leopard Hat: A Daughter's Story*. She coedited the anthology *Brooklyn Was Mine* and has worked on the editorial staffs of *Artforum* and the *New Yorker*.

Judith Thurman, a staff writer at the *New Yorker,* is the author of *Cleopatra's Nose: 39 Varieties of Desire; Isak Dinesen: The Life of a Storyteller,* which won the National Book Award in 1983; and *Secrets of the Flesh: A Life of Colette*.

Lily Tuck's novel, *The News from Paraguay,* won the 2004 National Book Award. Her most recent work is a biography, *Woman of Rome: A Life of Elsa Morante*.

Zoé Valdés is the author of *Yocandra in the Paradise of Nada* and *Dear First Love,* among other novels. She has been named a chevalier dans l'Ordre des Arts et des Lettres by the French government. Born in Cuba, she has lived in Paris since 1995.

Véronique Vienne is the author of the best-selling *The Art of Doing Nothing* and of numerous articles, essays, and books on design, photography, and architecture. She now lives in Paris after having spent most of her adult life in New York.

Judith Warner is the author, most recently, of *We've Got Issues: Children and Parents in the Age of Medication,* as well as *Perfect Madness: Motherhood in the Age of Anxiety.* She is a frequent contributor to the opinion pages of the *New York Times.*

Caroline Weber teaches French and comparative literatures at Barnard College and Columbia University. Her most recent book is *Queen of Fashion: What Marie-Antoinette Wore to the Revolution.* She contributes to the *New York Times Book Review* and other publications.

Walter Wells worked at the *International Herald Tribune* for twenty-five years and retired as its executive editor in 2005. He was awarded the French Légion d'honneur the following year. His *We've Always Had Paris . . . and Provence,* written with his wife, the food writer Patricia Wells, was published in 2008.

Edmund White won the National Book Critics Circle Award for his biography of Jean Genet. He has also written eight novels, several memoirs, and short biographies of Proust and Rimbaud. He teaches writing at Princeton University.

C. K. Williams is the author of numerous books of poetry, including *The Singing,* which won the National Book Award in 2003, and a translator from both the French and ancient Greek. He teaches at Princeton and lives part of each year in France.